CHAPEL

The joyous days and prayerful nights
of the Nonconformists
in their heyday, circa 1850-1950

KENNETH YOUNG

So, while the light fails
On a winter's afternoon, in a secluded chapel
History is now and England.
With the drawing of this Love and the
voice of this Calling.

Four Quartets, 'Little Gidding' by T. S. Eliot

Eyre Methuen
LONDON

First published 1972
© *1972 Kenneth Young*
Printed in Great Britain
for Eyre Methuen Ltd
11 New Fetter Lane, London EC4P 4EE
by Ebenezer Baylis and Son Ltd
The Trinity Press, Worcester, and London

SBN 0413 27870 0

to my son
JULIAN

CONTENTS

ILLUSTRATIONS

PREFACE

I am not a Nonconformist though I was brought up as a Wesleyan. My mother was a Wesleyan, my father devout Church of Scotland. Finding himself having to live in England, he went to the Wesleyan Chapel because he could not abide the Romanising tendencies of the local vicar and bishop, with whom he engaged in an acrimonious correspondence in the local weekly paper. I am Church of England of, reflecting him, the 'low' variety, which is now rare to find in Anglican observances and so the more precious.

My interest thus declared, I should say that the book that follows is composed very largely from the memories of those many generous people who have spoken or written to me, as a result of my letters to those journals which have been kind enough to print them. A list of these correspondents is given at the back of this book. I have also read a great number of local chapel histories and related material.

The man to whom above all I owe gratitude in this, as in other projects, is my old friend and former colleague, W. T. Oliver, who helped me run the *Yorkshire Post* for five years. As a life-long Methodist and student of Nonconformity, he is the fount of all knowledge on this and other subjects.

Professor Asa Briggs, vice-chancellor of Sussex University, has read the text and corrected my more egregious historical errors, and I have had assistance from Dr Bryan Wilson of All Souls College, Oxford. Sir John Betjeman has been an inspiration for many aspects of the subject, as has Kenneth Lindley.

Miss Alison James has engaged on some research for the book and has typed the manuscript. To all of these – and to my wife as always – I am grateful.

35 Central Parade,   Kenneth Young
Herne Bay, Kent.
August 1972

CHAPEL

Introit

WHAT CHAPEL WAS

I remember a Sunday evening in January 1905, when I came with my sweetheart to this church which at that time met for worship in the small brick building on Ball Hill. It was all very strange to me: the old wooden pews, the platform with its pulpit desk, the American organ and the choir and most of all, perhaps, the small congregation which I felt were all looking at me, 'a stranger'. Soon, however, I found friendship and Christian fellowship, which has lasted through all the years since then.[1]

This book is about that Christian fellowship, where social and religious elements were inextricably intermingled, which gave Nonconformist chapel life its distinctive atmosphere. Strictly speaking Nonconformists were those who in 1662 left the Church of England rather than submit to the Act of Uniformity. In this book, however, the word is used to describe those who, since the establishment of Protestantism, have refused to conform to some of the doctrines and practices of the established Church of England, and have worshipped in their own fashion in their own buildings. There were, of course, Nonconformists in a broader sense in England from the times of Edward VI.

This book deals mainly with the last one hundred years of Nonconformity and is based on the memories of living people, not only on what they personally remember, but also on what they recall of what their parents, grandparents, and long-dead members of their communities passed on to them. Most of my correspondents are middle-aged; many are now in their nineties.

The heyday of 'Chapel' is a long time ago. Chapels and their congregations are today far fewer and their social fellowship has largely (though not entirely) been superseded. Writing in 1936,

[1] So wrote Mrs E. M. Summer in *The Witness*, Stoke Congregational church, Coventry, in April 1963.

almost forty years ago, in *As I Remember*, E. E. Kellett, born in 1864 and brought up as a Methodist, says of Chapel that 'It took, by itself, the place now hardly filled by theatre, concert-hall, cinema, ballroom and circulating library put together. Here were all things required for social intercourse: recitals, songs, lectures with or without the lantern, authorised games and talk. It was a liberal education. Politics were freely discussed, books criticised and lent, music, and that not merely sacred, appraised. It was, in fact, the nearest approach I can think of to the agora of ancient Athens, where Socrates posed his questions and the Acharnian charcoalburners compared the claims of war and peace. It may have been a small and narrow society, but it was one which pulsed with life.'

A forgivable exaggeration; one can think of nearer approaches to the free-and-easy, give-and-take of what Kellett refers to as 'the agora', not least in the salons of eighteenth-century England and France. Kellett in any case, educated at the Wesleyan public school, Kingswood, Bath, was writing about the upper reaches of Nonconformity. Yet it was true that, almost until the start of the Second World War, Chapel was the centre for many millions of ordinary English people of what leisure they had. It was just as in pre-Reformation times, when Church was where one went for everything – schooling, festivals and plays, games in the churchyard.

Nonconformity of one sort or another has existed in England since Henry VIII's Act of Supremacy in 1534, when he abolished the authority of the Roman Papacy by declaring himself to be the only supreme head on earth of the Church of England. The Puritans, as they were then called, were at first a party within the Church, affected to a greater or lesser degree by such continental reformers as Luther, Calvin and Zwingli. Under James I some broke away completely and, often in exile, joined the Anabaptists. John Smythe of Cambridge University founded the first English Baptist church in Amsterdam in 1609 and in London in 1611. Others, while professing themselves loyal to the Church of England, sometimes formed independent congregations (hence Congregationalism, founded by Robert Browne in Norwich).

It is, however, no part of my aim to write a history of Nonconformity, or Dissent as it was sometimes called. I am concerned mainly with the period from about 1850 to 1950, when most, though not in the early part of the period all, of the inhibitions on dissent from the Established Church had been lifted; and when, incidentally, a few people still living recalled Methodist preachers being stoned, even to death.

This period itself, however, was not all of a piece. In the early years of the period and probably until the First World War, leisure life for the working and lower-middle classes was either Chapel or pub, God or gin. One could go to the tavern and music-hall, or alternatively to the prayer meeting and Service of Song. It was not yet the era of hobbies; not yet was there sufficient money left over from the basic expenses of a very basic existence for fretwork or French knitting, although the poor man who had energy remaining after the gruelling day's work could cast a line into the canal or stream, grow a few cabbages in an allotment or even, if he were bold, poach. None of these pursuits was exactly 'social'. So that, as G. M. Trevelyan wrote in *British History in the Nineteenth Century*, 'Chapel occupied a central place in the affections of people who had little to do with anything else. The men and women who were drawn into the brisk, alert and ardent life of the new religion found plenty to occupy their minds and to stimulate faculties and interests that were otherwise left neglected.' In the 1920s and 1930s cinema and broadcasting developed; again these were scarcely social pursuits.

What then was 'Chapel'?[1] The largest groups – all with their own splits and sects – were the Congregationalists, the Baptists, the Unitarians, the Wesleyan Methodists, splitting into Primitive, United, Free, Independent, Bible Christians, and other permutations of Methodism, some of whom were reunited in 1932. In the nineteenth century emerged the Brethren (known as Plymouth Brethren, though they were founded in Dublin) and their stricter branch, the Exclusive Brethren; the Salvation Army which had 'citadels' and hostels but whose evangelism generally took place at street corners under the stars – or the snow. Smaller sects such as the Pentecostal, Christian Scientists and Jehovah's Witnesses, Mormons and other importations,

---

[1] It will be obvious that by this word I do not refer to chapels in cathedrals, chapels-of-ease or school chapels.

mainly from the United States, I have not sought to bring within the scope of this book.

Nor have I tackled that great homeland of Nonconformity, Wales, mainly because to do so would require Welsh which I do not possess. The Scottish Presbyterians, on the other hand, would scarcely relish description as 'Nonconformists', nor would they so rank since, among other reasons, some of their kings professed Presbyterianism; you can scarcely get more establishment than that and above all Nonconformists were never establishment. If I had followed my own circumscribed thesis I should have devoted much space to the Salvation Army for which, in war and in peace, I have the warmest regard and in which I have the greatest faith. But the Salvation Army, despite its firm nucleus of 'soldiers', has exercised its influence among those of many faiths and none; it has seldom had a large static following able to develop in such diverse fields as did the Methodists, Congregationalists and the other large groups.

The complicated doctrinal differences between, for example, the Unitarians (who claim that they are not Christians) and the Bible Christians are not relevant to my object – except where, as with the Exclusive Brethren, such differences are reflected in the socio-religious life of the particular community. The Society of Friends (Quakers), who date from the seventeenth century, agree with some other non-established churches in refusing to be called Nonconformists, Dissenters, or Free Churchmen; and partly because of their peculiarities of worship, partly because they have been much written about, play only a small part in the pages that follow. I have, however, in passing gathered material about such small English sects as the Peculiar People who flourished in Essex for just over a century from 1838.

Most of the first-hand material in the book comes from the big Nonconformist groups – the Congregationalists, Methodists, and the Baptists. The lives of their members were, indeed, 'ardent', as Trevelyan wrote, and what a full life it was! Some had been 'converted' with sweating, beating of the breast, deep sighs and night-long struggles with the Devil within before they came to the penitent form in front of the table at which, usually no more than once a month, was celebrated the Sacrament of the Lord's Supper. Many are the stories of great sinners, drunkards,

wife-beaters, loose-livers who were thus redeemed by the grace
of God and through the ministrations of preachers – Exhorters
the Primitive Methodists called them – cast in the mould of
John Wesley. Conversion is now an almost forgotten mode,
except during the missions of Dr Billy Graham.

Some, perhaps the majority of Nonconformists in the period
with which we are mainly concerned, were not 'convertees'.
They went to Chapel because their parents before them had done
so, much as other families went to the Church of England. They
were solid citizens – many of the large town chapels smelled of
prosperity and Mansion Polish, the pews had cushioned seats –
and they would not care to make themselves conspicuous. But
when the ardent fires glowed less brightly and congregations fell
away, Revivalist preachers – usually laymen – were called in
by some chapels (not Unitarian or most Congregationalist)
to fan the embers in a week of meetings in the open air, in
marquees and in chapels, with prayer meetings and conversions.

Always there was singing and how they sang! There was
nothing palely Anglican about the thunderous surge of sound in
Chapel. Nor were the hymns merely rousing or emotional.
Often they were soft, sad, contemplative. Many choirs had near-
professional standards; some organists and choirmasters were
in fact professionals.

Nor were all chapelgoers sober-sides, as is sometimes supposed. Though most chapels banned dancing and card-playing,
there were secular concerts in some Sunday Schools – the usual
venues for social activities – and recitations and humorous
sketches were performed. Pantomimes were put on at Christmas. There were also lantern lectures ('limelight views of
Morocco'), faith teas when everybody brought what they could
and put it into the general pool, ham and tongue or meat-and-
potato pie suppers. (Love Feasts, which had died out by the
1920s, were not in the same category; they were in essence
prayer meetings when people gave their 'testimonies', a mug of
water was passed round and sometimes dry bread or biscuits
were consumed.)

Until the middle of the nineteenth century Sunday School
pupils were provided with beer and other comestibles for their

outings by horse-drawn char-à-banc; the prohibition upon alcohol for chapelgoers was not yet the general order of the day, the Wesleyans for long holding out against teetotalism. These outings, whether with beer or tea, were looked forward to with mounting excitement. So, too, were the Sunday School Whitsuntide walks through towns and villages which usually ended in games (including sometimes kissing games) in a friendly farmer's field.

Chapel was fun. Even its services were fun. As well as the joyous rumbustious singing, there were comic preachers, some by design, some by nature. Some had real Thespian gifts. Many are the stories about preachers and their oddities. To sermons, always longer in chapel than in church, the Nonconformists were no less attentive than sixteenth- and seventeenth-century Englishmen who flocked to hear the words of divines such as Dr John Donne, Baxter and Calamy. In the 'great' era, Nonconformist ministers were often better educated than those in the Church of England; they had studied Hebrew, Greek and theology; they frequently were voracious readers with wide fields of interest. Above all they had the gift of translating their erudition into homely terms the ordinary chapelgoer could understand. They could wring the heart-strings, they could invest their sermons with drama and humour, they could fire their congregations with hope and determination. The great Baptist preacher, C. H. Spurgeon, put the aim succinctly and frankly: 'If a man is going to sleep in my congregation, don't wake him up; wake *me* up.'

Nor was it merely the celebrated few – Dinsdale Young, Cloudesley Shovel, Luke Wiseman, Samuel Chadwick, C. H. Spurgeon, Hugh Price Hughes, Leslie Newman – upon whose words congregations hung. Many laymen, who had passed the required examinations,[1] were often no less powerful preachers, though they spoke with the broadest of accents. While they knew nothing of Hebrew and Greek, they often had a burning faith, a gift for exposition, a true wisdom.

Chapel, however, was not all preaching, hymn-singing, extempore praying or even having fun. Chapels had to be lighted, heated, painted and kept in good repair. It was in this sphere

[1] These examinations were mainly confined to the Methodists.

that many men and women had opportunity to exercise gifts of organisation, leadership and fund-raising, that their often humble daily work denied them. They discovered aptitudes within themselves that they had scarcely believed themselves to possess. The proof of their abilities and skill lies in the fact that chapels, great and small, continued to exist through all the economic ills of the nineteenth century and early twentieth century and, such was the devotion of un-named millions – along with a few rich benefactors – that few were in debt for long.

Chapel, it is often said, was a classless society in which a herdsman could be a local preacher, a clerk a deacon or an Elder, and a miner the steward or trustee. This must be qualified. Counting heads doubtless would show that a majority of Nonconformists were of the working or lower-middle classes. As time went by, however, some of these prospered and were able to give more financial support to their chapels. Among Congregationalists, Methodists, Unitarians and in particular in the Society of Friends (Quakers) there were very rich men such as the Cadbury, Rowntree and Fry families (why Quakers should attract chocolate or chocolate Quakers might be a reasonable Ph.D. subject; so would the fact that the great Nonconformist eaters – and non-drinkers – were the Plymouth Brethren). Yet it remains broadly true that Nonconformity broke through the aristocrat-squirearchal-landowning hierarchy and gave the humbler ranks their opportunity; and it is significant that some Nonconformists in the big industrial areas preached Christian Socialism and became the kernel of the Labour movement, although the 'chapels' of trade unionism descend from the medieval guilds, not from the Nonconformists.

Nevertheless the essence of Chapel lay in the saving of souls ('You have nothing to do but save souls' said Wesley) and not in the amelioration of temporal conditions or the righting of social wrongs. 'Help for the helpless' – yes; and in this respect the Salvation Army with their hostels and their unostentatious aid were, and are, pre-eminent.

But what counted most was not political change but a change of heart. Today, although the change began in the nineteenth century, Nonconformist ministers sometimes appear to be welfare

workers or politicians in disguise, whereas in the past most
ministers were careful not to disclose any party-political sympathies for fear of alienating one or other section of their congregations, though this did not alter the fact that most ministers
supported social reform by whatever party it was brought about.
'Today, as in the Apostolic age, we suffer from a fifth column
within our ranks,' an elderly Methodist from Birmingham
writes to me and asks, at the end of a long letter of memories:

> Perhaps you would like to know what I think of the new
> set-up. There have been many innovations which in them-
> selves may be good. But where are the prayer meetings and
> the class meetings? The chapels are open for Divine Service
> only on Sundays. There are very few appeals from the pulpit
> to a man or woman who wants to change over and live a
> Christian life. Spiritual atmosphere is non-existent.
>
> We are told we must move with the times, but where are
> we moving to? Not enough interest in the Sunday School.
> Not enough teachers, so children are allowed to romp about
> and do as they like. Consequently children from good Chris-
> tian homes are kept away as the parents do not want their
> children to turn out to be rough and untidy. The missionary
> spirit is not there. We have let the fire go out through lack of
> initiative.
>
> But the church people themselves seem to be satisfied. They
> sit in their comfortable seats, hear a nice flowery sermon and,
> to my mind, are lulled into inertia.
>
> They can't be disturbed about evil as long as they feel good
> themselves. They have forgotten that Christ once said 'I am
> not come to bring the righteous but sinners to repentance.'
> This should be the first and last desire of all Christians.

What my correspondent suggests is that the fire – and the
fun – that was Nonconformity is all but out. The embers are so
low that they would require not merely a revivalist week to puff
them into flames but a national bellows. A life-long Methodist
told me that he doubted if such would happen in his time – or
ever. If this is true – though I do not fully believe it, as I have
explained at the end of this book – then the pages which follow
are a requiem for a way of life.

I do not for a moment suppose that the diversity of community life described below will recur since it was due to temporal circumstances and historical, unrepeatable situations. I do believe that somewhere, sometime, somehow, men and women will once again understand that in order to change life it is necessary first to change hearts. As W. H. Auden wrote:

> And all that we can always say
> Is: true democracy begins
> With free confession of our sins;
> And all true unity commences
> In consciousness of differences . . .

1

AT SUNDAY SCHOOL

When we mingle here no more, but have met on Jordan's shore,
We will talk of moments o'er, at the Sabbath School.

Anon.

The start of religious life for the Nonconformist was in the Sunday School. These schools were not, as is sometimes supposed, the invention of Robert Raikes, the eighteenth-century Gloucester printer and newspaper owner. They existed in all religions from ancient times. Raikes, however, gave them their educational slant – though not at the expense of the religious – at a time when, for the poor, tuition in reading, writing and arithmetic was not easily available. These subjects were still being taught at the beginning of the 1850s and ceased only after the Education Act of 1870 had been fully implemented, which took a good many years.

In the early days scholars were sometimes physically disciplined; *and* they drank beer and wine. At Paddington chapel, Marylebone Road, London, for example, when a scholar grossly misconducted himself, either in school or chapel during morning service, the bell was rung in the middle of the afternoon, the teaching was stopped and the offender was placed on a form. He received a reprimand from the Superintendent before the whole school, followed by a few sharp strokes on the hand by way of application; and in the case of an incorrigible offender, he was led to the door and publicly expelled by the Superintendent, for one, two or three months as the case might be.

The Child's Own Book for the year in 1832 gives a supposed conversation with three scholars in respect of the commemoration proceedings of the Jubilee of Sunday Schools. Apparently a combined meeting of various schools was held in Paddington chapel, and James, a scholar at Paddington, speaks as follows:

We went up to a chapel and also, I think, paid attention to the whole service. The singing pleased me: you know I am not old enough to sing much. After Chapel was over, we all (I mean our school) took a walk, two by two, the girls first, with a flag in the middle. I had a medal, and so had many of us. We went a long way, to a gentleman's house; he let us into his garden: I remembered having seen him often in our school; it was he that gave me 'Cottage Scenes' one Sunday. Most of the children sat down on some forms; but I had to stand. After we had sung an hymn, we had each a nice bun and a glass of wine; the gentleman paid for it all, and gave all our teachers some likewise. We sang again, and after making a bow, came away. We then called at another gentleman's house, and sang again. We all then came to our school, and had dinner – cold beef sandwiches, plum pudding, and some beer; but we did not stop very long; the teachers wished to go to a meeting of their own. I almost forgot to say I received a little book about Elizabeth Myers, and so did all who were present.

In those far-away days the scholars who attended the morning service in the Paddington chapel sat in the upper gallery (which was removed many years ago), and had to stand up for what was known as the 'long prayer', turn their backs to the minister and kneel on the seat. The 'long prayer' would last for some twenty minutes.

The rules were strict at most Sunday Schools and, for example, at the Zion Congregational chapel at Flockton, Yorkshire, the refractory boy had a rough time of it. There was a code of rules. Boys were forbidden to bring sweets on Sundays and girls to enter school in pattens. If boys misbehaved in the street the school served as a 'house of correction'. The rules were periodically proclaimed by the Superintendent, and for breaches of discipline boys were punished with a wooden clapper, the noise of which, however, was perhaps worse than the pain inflicted. Others were ordered to stand on a form, holding a Bible overhead, which, though a milder punishment, lasted considerably longer than the occasional clapper.

This account from a local paper continues:

Once a year, viz., in July, the scholars participated in a treat, which, however, at times was a toil of a pleasure, at all events to the younger portion. They were paraded in the neighbourhood until, at the finish, they were quite wearied. Then all were offered a bun each, and 'tots' of beer. Many could neither eat the dry bun nor face the drop of home-brewed. The 'old-stagers' believed in the good properties of this home-brewed, and the young element were desirous of effecting a change in favour of tea or milk.

Then ensued a battle royal. This was in the middle 1860s. The old people stood up stoutly for the continuance of the old custom, and would not compromise in favour of tea to those who desired it, and beer to the remainder. Meeting after meeting took place until the voting on beer versus tea resulted in a tie. At subsequent meetings each side tried to snatch the victory and it ultimately rested with the tea drinkers. Temperance reformers will be glad to know that from that time to the present 'Beer, glorious beer' – as the old song puts it – has not been served at the children's school feast.

Nor was the beer always taken in moderation, at least by the elders. The grandmother of a former Methodist, writes Peter Fletcher in *The Long Sunday* (London, 1958), recalled that at the quarterly meeting, when the elders of the chapel met to organise its affairs and audit its accounts, a barrel of beer was provided 'and the event was not regarded as a success unless most of the company finished the day under the table'.

It was in the Wesleyan Church that teetotalism grew slowest. In 1840, indeed, two candidates for the ministry who claimed teetotal principles were ordered to forsake their heretical doctrine or withdraw their candidature. The Rev. Jacob Stanley, a respected leader, went so far as to issue a pamphlet in favour of moderate drinking and denouncing teetotalism. Not until 1874 were Bands of Hope allowed on Methodist premises. All other Nonconformist Churches were well in advance of the Methodists in this matter.

Beer, however, went hand-in-hand with 'good' reading at Dogley Lane Congregational church near Huddersfield where a library was started for the use of the scholars and teachers.

The exact date it opened is not clear, but it was an established institution in 1842, and its nature can be gathered from such a resolution as the following:

> That the following works be purchased, and added to the library:
> 5 volumes of Ancient History (by Religious Tract Society).
> 2 volumes of Old Humphrey.
> 1 volume, Sober Mindedness recommended to the Young.[1]

At this chapel evening classes took place on week nights, when reading and writing were taught. The teachers were carefully chosen for their work, and had to satisfy the President and Committee of their fitness and capacity for service before being admitted. The annual meeting of the Sunday School was held on New Year's Day and as early as 1840 the custom of holding the Sunday School anniversary on the second Sunday in August was established. This was changed to the present date (second Sunday in May) only in 1904.

The greatest event in the Sunday School year for this chapel was the Trinity Monday festival. This was the direct ancestor of the Sunday School treat held on the last Saturday in June, but combined other features with that of feasting. The teachers and children were assembled for public examination, received an address and exhortation to diligence and 'some refreshment'. This was the arrangement for the festival of 1837:

> 1st. That Stephen Arlom shall act as president, and conductor of all business. The teachers and children to assemble at 12 o'clock, and be separated into their respective classes and commence by singing and praying.
>
> 2nd. The teachers to call over the names and collect 2d. from each scholar.
>
> 3rd. That Jas. Binns be appointed to receive all moneys in the Vestry.
>
> 4th. That David Hampshire be appointed to draw the beer, and Adam Boothroyd to convey it to the teachers; John Brook to take care of the bread, deliver it to David Fitton

[1] I have not been able to identify these works.

and Isaac Horsfall who will take it into the chapel for the children.

5th. The children to remain in the chapel and receive ¾lb. of bread and one tot of beer before the Service.

6th. The Service to commence at 2 o'clock and not to exceed one hour and a quarter.

7th. That immediately after the Service the children be dismissed in their respective classes, that names be called over, then each scholar to receive ½lb. of bread and 2 tots of beer and be dismissed by singing a hymn.

Sunday School examinations were often on a national basis and at Easter the results of the local and national scripture examinations were announced. Thus books might be collected by the diligent Sunday School scholar. At a chapel in north London, a correspondent writes:

Local Sunday School Unions arranged for examinations in Bible knowledge, graded for various ages, and special evening classes for these exams. There were prizes and certificates and a special evening service to distribute them. The zealous could collect quite a row of good books over the years. (By 'good' I don't mean 'pious'.)

I collected *Westward Ho, Hereward the Wake, The Last of the Barons, Ben Hur*, Scott's Poems and Josephus – all my own choosing. There was once an extra very Protestant class and examination on 'How we got our Bible', for which the prize was 'Historical Tales for Young Protestants'. I also got a copy of Foxe's *Book of Martyrs*, suitably abridged but useful later in historical studies. I suppose I got two prizes, because I remember only one such course at a time when feeling ran a bit high. The prize is dated 1911.

Nor later on in chapel life was good reading confined to works of piety. In Norfolk one lady recalls:

It was in the little schoolroom attached to that little chapel that a number of young people first heard the names of Paganini and Stradivari, of Plato's Republic and of Lord Shaftesbury and Robert Owen. There were readings from

Dickens and Bret Harte, from Wordsworth and the two Brownings and occasionally something from Mark Twain and the 'Ingoldsby Legends'.[1] Everyone was encouraged to read aloud, to memorise and recite and especially to sing.

In many places in the early days Sunday School developed into full-time day school. At Bury in Lancashire Brunswick[2] chapel had a day school for sixty-five years. In 1870 George Wensley became the first headmaster, and for fifteen years 'worthily discharged' his office. He was a local preacher, Sunday School teacher and enthusiast for Foreign Missions and local philanthropic work. He literally, we are told, 'spent himself for God and man'. The man with the longest service was Mr Isaac Ingham, who for thirty-four years 'gave his personality and abilities to the work of the Day School and to the culture of the young lives who came under his influence'.

This school continued until 1935 when, because of the demolition of house property in the neighbourhood and the reorganisation of schools whereby children over the age of eleven were removed to senior schools, the numbers in attendance had fallen to too low a level.

Important church people often gave special prizes for high marks:

One gentleman was informed when any boy formerly in the school reached twenty-one and the latter was presented with a book suitably inscribed as a guide to life. One we had was 'From Boyhood to Manhood' which in present conditions would be regarded as rather tame. Text cards were sometimes given to homes. Many will recall the 'unseen listener in the home' etc.

The preacher was not forgotten. Before children's addresses were the fashion in the chapel service, the children had little part. In our pulpit someone inserted a card of reminder just out of sight 'Please remember the children' and on the vestry

---

[1] *The Ingoldsby Legends, or Mirth and Marvels* by Thomas Ingoldsby Esquire, 1840. Ingoldsby was the Rev. R. H. Barham.

[2] Many Wesleyan chapels were named Brunswick or Hanover as a sign of loyalty to the Crown when, during the French Revolution, Methodists were suspected of being revolutionaries.

was a straight hint to all comers 'The work of the world is done by few. God asks that a part be done by you.'

And there were competitions:

At some of the tea parties in the earlier history of the present school at Millgate, it was a custom to hold a competition which took the form of the maximum number of verses from the Bible that could be repeated from memory. On 5 March 1895 such a competition was held and the winner, a lady, repeated four hundred and thirteen verses, commencing at the second chapter of St John's Gospel, for which she received Farrar's *Theological and Biblical Dictionary*.

There was a great sense of pride when Sunday Schools were enlarged. At Hollins Methodist Church and Sunday School, Millgate, on the occasion of the removal to Moss Grove, the following lines were composed and may well be reproduced to illustrate the feeling of advance and attainment:

> We had some men that did begin
> To try and stop our ways of sin,
> Our School began to multiply –
> Like sparks that from the fire do fly;
> When Copster School became too small,
> And then it would not hold us all –
> From there to here we did remove,
> That they might better us improve.

Pride there was – and immense faith in Sunday School, to the point of expecting to talk over memories of it in Heaven. As a Colchester correspondent puts it:

The first Superintendent I remember was Mr Charles Pannel and one hymn he was very fond of and often had it sung, has always been stored in my memory:

When the dewy light drives away the night
With the sun so bright and full
And it draws its line near the hour of nine
I'll away to the Sabbath School.
For 'tis there we all agree, all with happy hearts and free
And I love to be early, at the Sabbath School.

I'll away, I'll away, I'll away to the Sabbath School.

On the frosty dawn of a winter's morn
When the earth is wrapt in snow
Or the Summer breeze plays around the trees
To the Sabbath School I'll go.
When the holy day has come, and the Sabbath breakers roam
I delight to leave my home, for the Sabbath School.

In the class I meet with friends I greet
At the time of morning prayer,
And our hearts we raise in a hymn of praise
For 'tis always pleasant there.
In the book of holy truth, full of council and reproof,
We behold the guide of youth, at the Sabbath School.

May the dews of grace fill the hallow'd place
And the sunshine never fail,
While each blooming rose which in mem'ry grows
Shall a sweet perfume exhale.
When we mingle here no more, but have met on
Jordan's shore,
We will talk of moments o'er, at the Sabbath School.

Towards the end of the nineteenth century, one elderly gentleman from Rutland recalls:

We used to pride ourselves that our Sunday School was one of the best in the Circuit[1] and I believe it was. We went over to the graded system almost at its inception. I was placed in the primary department, much to my disgust. I felt that at seven years of age I ought to have had something much higher than this. The leader was a very sincere lady but who somehow seemed unable to place even seven-year-olds among those who knew anything. Thus, to take one matter only. The leader would announce a request for any child who had had a birthday that week to hold the collection box; a glass spherical article so made that we could see our pennies as they dropped in. The appropriate child having been selected, he (or she)

[1] Methodists were organised into geographical groups, based on population, headed by a Superintendent Minister. These groups were known as Circuits.

would then stand in the front whilst we all marched past as
the piano tinkled and our voices burst forth into:

> Hear the pennies dropping,
> Listen while they fall,
> Every one for Jesus,
> He has made them all.
> (Here follows the chorus.)

At seven years old, to tramp round the room to drop a
penny into the box was to me beneath my dignity.

After a year of this I was promoted first to the junior and
then the senior departments. The impression which lingers
with me from this period is of the teachers in these departments. One ought first perhaps to explain that most of the
scholars in that school came from homes which had no
contact whatever with any church or any sense of religion.
They were literally little demons; uncouth, ill-mannered
and not above hurling epithets far from the King's English
either at a teacher or anybody else if they felt like it. Why
they ever came at all has often been a mystery to me. But
even more remarkable was the continued devotion of the
teachers. I have often thought that nothing short of an army
of prize fighters was any use for keeping those gatherings in
order.

Two teachers linger in my mind. One was an ex-coal miner;
a good Methodist and a local preacher but a real rough-and-
ready type. The other, a retired man (though what he was
retired from I never knew); of little education but with a
passionate temper. Talk about rough handling; there was
certainly plenty of that. Whether there was ever any religious
instruction I have often wondered. It was uphill work but on
the whole I think it was worth it.

The greatest highlight was the Sunday School anniversary.
What a day this was! We all 'sat up' to use the colloquial
phrase. The church was packed till one just could not breathe
and we sang and sang until we were hoarse. Fathers,
mothers, brothers, sisters, uncles, aunts, grandmas, grandpas,
cousins, and goodness knows who else from miles round just
swarmed into the place; there is no other word.

The other highlight was the summer treat. This took various forms; from a barge trip along a canal to outings to a nearby farm. Being a time when neither cars nor coaches were as plentiful as now one could not go a great distance.

The little demons this writer mentioned certainly existed. At Zion Congregational, Flockton, Yorkshire, we learn that the old, narrow, high-backed pews in the area where the scholars formerly sat, the adult congregation being accommodated in the gallery, offered especial facilities to the youngsters to indulge in their pranks, when the eye of the teacher – who attended every third Sunday – was not upon them.

The preacher was elevated to a great height, occupying the second storey of the double pulpit; but the children could not possibly see him, so they amused themselves in so far as they dared, for it must be remembered that the rod which the teacher held was chiefly employed in keeping order. Some of the scholars came long distances and attended school at nine o'clock and one o'clock, and Divine Service in the sanctuary in the morning and afternoon, and they naturally indulged in little diversions to relieve the monotony; but ever and anon the sound of the rod in collision with some poor fellow's pate resounded through the building.

One Norfolk character, 'Frisky' Youngs, at the Primitive Methodist chapel in Hintringham, was renowned for his ebullience, whether playing, singing or composing doggerel verses such as these, written in a style not entirely according with modern taste. Headed 'The Removals from our School this Year are Nine', the composition began and ended lachrymosely and had an explanatory middle:

> Poor Mary Ann the Master called for,
>   And took her home to be at rest;
> Wrapt her up in His bright glory
>   Where she is for ever blest.

> The other eight removed far from us,
>   Gone to earn their daily bread;
> And I pray that God may bless them,
>   And to be their help in time of need.

Now Lord let Thy lasting blessing
  Rest on those that still remain;
We need Thy help, O come and help us,
  And revive Thy work again.

We are trying, dear friends help us,
  To distil into their minds
The principles of that religion
  Which no other can outshine.

Now, dear Teachers, you press forward,
  Do not loiter in the way;
Your reward is just before you,
  And will never decay.

A palm, a harp, a crown of glory,
  And a white robe you'll ever wear;
O press forward do not tarry,
  For I'm bound to meet you there.

Soon our work on earth will finish
  And we can here do no more good;
Then we shall hear the Master saying
  'They really have done what they could.'

O may all our kind supporters
  Gain with us the heavenly rest;
Meet with those just gone before us,
  Where we shall be ever blest.

In later days, when the three R's were taught elsewhere, the emphasis was on the religious side. At Underbank Wesleyan Sunday School, Holmfirth, Yorkshire, the great majority of the teachers and workers up to this period were ordinary people, working long hours. Their opportunities for reading and culture were very few. Some certainly had a moderate knowledge of the Methodist Hymn Book, and of Bible characters and stories. Their ignorance was not their own fault. They simply had a desire, having been saved, to show their love and gratitude.

To them being a teacher in a Sunday School was a serious business. To help them Underbank Wesleyans in 1871 formed a class specially to teach the teachers: 'The lessons given proved very helpful and the meetings were often a real means of grace.'

In this school, as in many others, much importance was attached to Catechism lessons. They were usually given from the desk by the Superintendent, who would distribute a few Wesleyan Catechism books among the best of the readers on the boys' side of the school. He would read questions from the book and the boys would read the answers. A few explanatory remarks followed.

Such a book is 'The Catechisms for the use of The People called Methodists, containing a summary of Christian doctrine and Bible History'. It was 'compiled by order of the Conference' and published by the Methodist Publishing House at 2 Castle Street, City Road, London. It runs to almost one hundred pages and contains such far from easy questions as 'What is meant by salvation?' 'Can we repent of ourselves?' and 'Who were the chief prophets raised up to testify in Judah?'

Small wonder perhaps that pupils and teachers sometimes slacked. From a brief history of Underbank Wesleyan Sunday School it is clear that a number of teachers became very careless and indifferent, lax and irregular and unpunctual in their attendance. They set a bad example to their scholars by leaving the school on Sunday afternoons before the service closed. After being irregular in their attendance for a while, they ceased coming altogether without giving any reason why. The reasons for such conduct, the history claims, was that some of the teachers had no personal experience of true religion.

There was, too, the problem of getting the scholars to come to school – especially the boys. From time to time there was a decrease of male scholars, and many of them, when they came, came late; and in the afternoon they caused annoyance by leaving the school before the service.

There were, however, devices to ensure regular attendance as a lady from Brondesbury Baptist church, London N.W.6, recalls:

At Sunday School each had a card stamped with a star.

Even away on holiday we were expected to go to Sunday School and our card would be stamped. My sister for several years always had prizes for regular attendance. Morning Sunday School at 10 a.m., then service in the chapel at 11 a.m., home for dinner at 1 p.m. and School again at 3 p.m., then to Evening Service. Four times every Sunday seven or eight of us i.e. mother (father died when I was four) brothers and sisters occupied one pew.

Another device, used at Eastbrook Hall mission, Bradford, was to catch a potential Sunday School scholar at birth:

The Cradle Roll was started in September, 1904, and since that time the name of every baby baptised in Eastbrook Hall has been recorded on the Roll, the child receiving a birthday card until he is three years old, and then invited to attend the school. During this period the home of the little one is regularly visited by the Cradle Roll Secretary.

Teachers *cared* for their pupils, as a former Sunday School teacher from Norwich writes:

If I had a child missing for more than two Sundays, I should go to their homes and find out the reason why. Some of my class became baptised later and I am still in touch with them today.

Yet even in the latter part of the nineteenth century there were children who had no knowledge of Christianity. In the Leeds Wesley Circuit:

About the early summer of 1885 my mother discovered a little boy (with nice parents and a good home). The child had *never heard of Jesus*! My mother felt so shocked, she began a Sunday class in our home at 2 p.m. in the afternoon, the only stipulation being that they attended no other Sunday School. Numbers increased, and the class was kept on for several years and several of us collected for Foreign Missions.

Sunday School had its less didactic aspects. A gentleman from Sheffield recalls that the local preachers generally had the local accent (Yorkshire) with frequent dropping and addition of

aspirates. The usual order of service was followed – hymn, Te
Deum or similar, prayer (extempore) – hymn – Bible reading –
children's hymn and address – hymn, during which the collection was taken and the children filed out, not being expected to
contribute – sermon and last hymn, during which two earnest
and important looking chapel leaders would disappear into the
vestry to count the takings.

The children were seated in the front three or four rows
and, having endured Sunday School before the chapel service,
were usually fidgetty and talkative which evoked 'psts!' from
the congregation and cuffs from the teachers. One local
preacher with a broad accent began his children's address:
'Now boys and girls I 'ave a special word for you this
morning, a very good word and one I want you to remember.
It is a five letter word and I wonder if any of you can guess wot
it is? No? Well, I will spell it out for you – Haitch – Haye – B –
Hi – T, 'Abit.'

My father being very keen and from very strong Methodist
families on both sides, it was compulsory for myself and my
elder sister to attend morning service and afternoon Sunday
school. It was explained to me after being led by the ear once
or twice that it was our 'duty' to God who, as a special
concession, did not require our presence at morning Sunday
school or evening service at this tender age.

The Sunday School Superintendent was a short plump man
with a fresh complexion, a high polished forehead with a
marvellous kiss-curl sticking up in the middle, like a cockatoo's
crest. He had a slight lisp and would punch the bell
ferociously for silence and address the mixed school like this:

'Now boyth and girlth – quiet pleathe! Ev'ry 'ed bowed
and ev'ry eye clothed!' And a drawn out extempore prayer
with lisps would ensue, part in James I language and the rest
in a Yorkshire dialect.

Later I was blackmailed into sharing a class with my
cousin, alternate Sundays, and very soon grew tired of the
printed curriculum supplied by the establishment as a guide
to teachers. The boys were also weary of it. 'We don't want
that, mester, we 'ave it at school all week.' 'Read us a story.'

And so to help put a stop to the pellet-flipping and interference with the next class I produced *Treasure Island* and *Just William* and mine was the quietest class in the school, with the extra help of a bag of sweets.

This went on for nearly a year until one afternoon I looked up and found the parson had crept alongside and was listening too. Result – resignation.

Star cards [marking individual attendance with a stick-on star] were marked with great assiduity and any blank square challenged by authority at once. Bird-nesting and similar Sunday afternoon recreations were made just not worth while in view of the terrible wrath invoked by father from above when he found out.

My father was christened Horace to his great regret and once showed me a Sunday school attendance prize given to him as a small boy. The gummed label stuck on the fly-leaf bore the message 'To Oris Wood for good attendance' which showed that they pronounced his name exactly as they thought it was spelt. He had a story of the good boy who went up on the platform to receive his good attendance prize. The title was 'The Cricket on the 'arth'. 'Eh, baa goom, there'll be some broken winders 'ere if they doan't watch out!'

Many Nonconformists have vivid memories of their teachers and of odd incidents in Sunday School:

As a child I attended the Primitive Methodist chapel at Mirfield. The Sunday School was underneath the chapel and was heated by a stove, which we fed with coke. This was in the year 1927 and I remember a local preacher, Mr Ernest Auty, who always brought a concertina. We had wooden dumb-bells which we moved to the tunes he played. One favourite was 'My drink is water bright, straight from the crystal stream'.

Our Superintendent was Mr William Armitage, one of the finest Christian gentlemen I have ever met. His portrait still hangs in the new Sunday School. His favourite hymn was 'The old rugged cross'. When we attended the Band of Hope he brought a box of sugared almonds. Every child was given a sweet and was good as gold. Our anniversary was outdoors on a raised platform with the local band playing. A Leeds gentleman, Mr Charlie Thornton, conducted and we sang joyously.

I remember once a few stout ladies sat on the same plank, and caused it to break. The band was playing 'Stand up, Stand up for Jesus', when all the ladies fell down.

I remember one local character who after a drink of beer at Sunday noon, came into the chapel and insisted on us all singing 'Throw out the lifeline across the dark waves, Throw out the lifeline another to save.'

The highlights of the Sunday School year were the treats, the Whitsuntide walks and the anniversary, which the smallest children, debarred by their tender ages, watched with longing. In Norfolk, 'they came at dark in farm wagons, singing hymns and every child had a lantern'.

In some places these were great, joint events:

The Piece Hall at Halifax is a square space of about 10,000 sq. yds. in area surrounded by stone walls on to which back 315 small rooms, some two and some three storeys high. The balconies of these rooms are reached by stone staircases. The Hall was built in 1779 to form a central place where cloth pieces could be brought for sale from the surrounding districts.

From 1831 to 1890, mostly at five-year intervals, assemblies took place in the Piece Hall of teachers and scholars from all the Sunday Schools in the district, there to join in singing specially prepared and practised hymns, the singing being led by a large band of instrumentalists. Each contingent marched from its school and was led by its own band of players.

On the first occasion when over 10,000 persons were present a gill[1] of beer and buns were served to the singers. On the last occasion in 1890 a crowd of 30,000 assembled including 500 instrument players and 600 vocalists. The manager of the town's Markets Department has a programme for the 1885 event which shows that ninety-six schools took part with 3,716 teachers and 24,714 children. The railway companies ran special trains for the convenience of the many visitors from other places.

[1] Yorkshire for half a pint.

I was born in 1891 so missed the first of these celebrations but I have often heard older people tell of scholars and teachers from our village school marching the three and a half miles to the Piece Hall. The banner used hung until recently in a frame in the Sunday School.

After the cessation of these efforts the Halifax Sunday School Union for a long number of years issued a booklet of about eight hymns with tunes every year in time for rehearsals to take place before Whit Monday when most local schools had their own march and sing around their district.

At the Whit Monday treat large currant buns were served along with coffee brewed in large earthenware bread crocks. Incidentally after games in a nearby field on these occasions 'kissing rings' were formed when such catches as 'The green leaves are falling', and 'Oats and Beans and Barley' were sung. At some appropriate point in the singing the odd person out of the ring chose a person of the opposite sex to kiss and exchange places with.

Two or three times a year an outing by horse-drawn wagonettes would be arranged. Scholars and teachers were conveyed to some place a few miles away where refreshments and games were available. Sunny Vale, Shipley Glen and Hardcastle Crags were often chosen. On one occasion the wagonette ordered by the Band of Hope for their journey failed to arrive so the Superintendent of the school who drove the wagon which delivered beer barrels for the local brewery secured that vehicle and the temperance body made its way to its destination with the words 'Aspinall's Fine Ales' prominently displayed on the means of transport.

Individual classes in the Sunday School usually had a private outing of their own with their two teachers. This usually was made on foot with the long walk involved playing a major part in providing pleasure. Choir outings were on a more ambitious scale, perhaps because a sum of money was annually given to the members by the trustees for their excursion. Seaside resorts or inland beauty spots were reached by train.

A lad Edgar in his late teens once volunteered to waken

those going by a very early train to Skegness on one such outing. He did his duty well and all were in good time for the train except Edgar who had fallen asleep in a chair at home after completing his task.

Much organisation was involved in some of the joint affairs in the cities – and the inner man was not neglected. Before the Whitsuntide 'Sings' in the parks, breakfasts were prepared by Sunday School teachers for all the scholars. The teachers would arrive as early as 6 a.m. to cut the bread (no sliced loaves then) and spread margarine on one slice of bread and potted meat on the other to make a sandwich. At Trinity Wesleyan chapel, Highfields, Sheffield, one correspondent remembers that breakfasts for over two hundred children were prepared. In those days a free breakfast was not to be turned down lightly. When sufficient sandwiches had been eaten cakes were handed round, but only one for each child.

At Eastbrook Mission Hall, Bradford, until 1934 the Whit Monday treat was held on the Pollard Lane Cricket Field. Wagon loads of children preceded by the Sunday School banner made their way to the 'bun field' while the junior and senior scholars climbed the steep slope to the Pollard Lane Field, to enjoy the Whitsuntide buns, tea from the milk churns, and the scramble for nuts.

But later, after the field became a building site, the treat went further afield. In 1938 and 1939 there were outings by train to Southport. Inevitably the war years brought the treat nearer home again, and buses were hired to convey young and old to Cottingley or Woodhouse Grove. Since 1949 there have been coach rides to Filey and St Annes-on-Sea.

At Tingley in West Yorkshire in the later nineteenth century, school feasts were held on the Monday nearest to the longest day. Breakfast was provided at the Sunday School and at nine o'clock the teachers and scholars, headed by the musicians and banners, set out to sing all round the village. They halted only for midday dinner and tea and generally arrived back at the Sunday School about nine at night, footsore and hoarse, but nevertheless having thoroughly enjoyed themselves. Sometimes they returned even later and sang by lantern light.

A minute in the Tingley records for 4 June 1877 provides 'that twelve stones of flour be made for the scholars cakes' and 'that two stones plain cakes for teachers' tea' and 'that seven pounds of ham and bread be provided at Hill Top for musicians and singers'. The musicians and leading singers were paid and there is a record that 'ten shillings be allowed for beer for the musicians'. By 1897 these school feasts were curtailed. They started out at one o'clock on the school feast Monday and so continued until 1915 when the day was changed to Saturday.

The choosing of the musicians for the school feast 'sing' and anniversary was a serious business. Many hours were spent in solemn conclave before such far-reaching decisions were passed as shown in the Tingley minutes of 23 March 1897: 'That Herbert Longden be the conductor of scholars, and that Sam Walker, Aaron Earnshaw and Tom H. Gibson be asked to come as first violinists, and that Joe Gambles, Ben W. Bedford, Willie Leach and Thomas Walker be asked as second violinists, that we get the man from Morley who has played for us previously for the double bass, Wm. Scott as single bass, Wm. Westmoreland to play the euphonium and that Ben Brook of Tingley, be asked to play the piccolo.'

Alas, some children were barred from the joys. At Bedford on anniversary Sunday when, as elsewhere, special hymns practised for weeks were sung and the chapel was crowded, sometimes with chairs down the aisle, most children had a new 'rig out' and felt very smart and happy, but:

> Some children had poor homes and no Sunday clothes. This made them feel out of chapel pleasures and they went bird-nesting or wandered by the river, consequently they missed the training of Chapel and Sunday School. Beer was only twopence per pint – and some 'Dads' drank too much – and home life was spoiled.

To many Sunday School pupils, the 'best of all pleasures' was the Sunday School outing in summer holidays. 'Sometimes,' this Bedford correspondent recalls, 'we were taken in two horse brakes into some kind farmer's field where we had picnic tea and games. "Mrs Farmer" would boil water for tea. The Sunday School crockery was carted to the field, also the prepared food.

Each child and person had a paper bag – containing slices of bread and butter in big slabs – it was lovely. The little ones could not eat it all at once; usually a big sister or mum – or teacher – would be prepared to take care of the food bag – for eating later. Nearly always it was beautiful summer weather – oh what happy days they were!'

Songs were sung en route in Cambridgeshire – and collections made:

The Sunday School anniversary was something to look forward to and the services were taken by a special preacher. On the Monday we hired three brakes which were drawn by two horses each. We left the chapel at 9 a.m. in the morning and took provisions with us and sang our songs as we passed through the villages and I used to play an accordion to help them. We would stay in some nice spot and have dinner and be home at the chapel for tea and sports afterwards; of course there were collections for chapel funds all the way.

The Denby Dale brass band led the procession at Underbank, Holmfirth, where it was noted that scholars' attendance increased considerably a few Sundays before the great day.

After singing in front of the school, they made a practice for some years of joining the mother school in Victoria Street, where they sang together. After leaving the street they sang at Bank End, Well Hill, and other places, then returned to the school where the younger scholars received a large currant bun and tea. This part of the proceedings was always very much enjoyed by them; they also received a school cake to take home. The scholars in the Bible classes had their teas along with the teachers in the schoolroom. There was a gala field provided, in which all who wished might go and enjoy themselves in various ways and manners. Selections of music were discoursed by the band to the delight and pleasure of many. No dancing was ever allowed.

A curious custom happened at least at one Sunday School, that of the Wesleyan Methodist church in Batley Carr, Yorkshire. The scholars followed a banner proclaiming who they were; they were all dressed in the previous year's Whitsuntide dresses; they wore white pumps – and they carried a cane, bought for one penny at the corner shop. The cane was a 'must'. Behind them, a lorry carried the harmonium and the choir master. At selected halts they sang the Whit hymns from a printed sheet.

The last stop was always at the house of the local mill-owner who had not only lent the lorry, but also the field to which the children repaired for the 'treat'. Tea was in individual bags – one potted meat sandwich, one long bun and a piece of seed cake. Games were played till dusk, three-legged races, egg and spoon and so on. When wet, the 'treat' took place in the Sunday School, with round games such as 'King William was King David's son' – a well-loved kissing game.

The Whit Monday was no less, and perhaps more, important than the Sunday, at any rate in the Leeds area before the First World War:

We sang the hymns on Whit Sunday but this was only a dress rehearsal for the Monday. After an early dinner we assembled at the chapel and formed a procession. If money was available we hired a milk float, horse-drawn of course, and the men lifted the harmonium out of the chapel on to the float. But this was a rare enrichment; usually we sang unaccompanied. The procession made its way round the village, singing at the houses of the more prominent chapel members, the sick or the very old.

There were five chapels and one church in Kirkstall, all playing the same game and some manoeuvring was necessary to avoid clashes. The church always hired the boys' band from what was then the Adel Reformatory. We thought this conceited and consoled ourselves with the knowledge that the band consisted of naughty boys, who had been found out. But the noise of the band put out of effective action any other procession which came anywhere near it. There was some rivalry between the chapels as to the length of procession. We were happy to equal the Primitives or the Congregationalists; the others were outside our reach. The walk round always ended at our house. If the weather were fine, my invalid brother would have been lifted outside in his long wheeled invalid carriage, the front room windows were opened wide, I went inside and played as loudly as I could and we made our biggest noise of the day. And here was a tub of oranges, one for each child, provided out of our scanty 25/– a week by my mother and father.

We then moved, in relative disorder, to one of Bailey's fields where there were races which I was never able to win and, again if the weather were fine, an open-air tea. If the weather were not fine – and I hated the races so much that I often hoped that it would not be – we had tea and games in the chapel. But my most vivid memories of the day are set in an ambience of blazing heat.

And Whitsuntide was the time for the new suit – the only time. What had been my Sunday suit became week-day and the new suit was never worn except on Sundays. 'Sunday' clothes meant something in those days.

In some parts of Yorkshire the Sunday School anniversary was known as 'the sermons'. To some this seemed a misnomer since the preacher was given little time to preach because there was so much singing. This festival often lasted the whole weekend. There were services on the Saturday and Monday evenings – three on Sunday. To draw the crowds a 'popular' preacher was invited to be in the pulpit.

The children of the Sunday School would sit on raised platform in the chancel of the chapel. The girls would be dressed in white with their hair in curls. These children would have been attending rehearsals for some six or seven weeks before the great day. Hymns with choruses were the most popular.

The chapels were packed for people would do the rounds, attending all the Sunday School anniversaries in their locality. On that one day the usually empty galleries were full half an hour before the service began.

Later in the year, normally in October, came 'Children's Day', when Sunday School teachers talked to the older scholars about Christian Commitment. Each child was handed a card in case he/she wished to make a written promise of his/her commitment to Christ. The Sunday School kept the cards.

A variety of games were played at Sunday School anniversaries in Colchester; there even adults joined in the 'kiss-in-the-ring':

Sunday School anniversary services were held every year on Whit Sunday and Monday. Three services on Sunday, and how we all looked forward to the Monday, as for several years we had a hot dinner! Hot joint and vegetables – Yorkshire pudding – and plum pudding. The friends had been busy during the morning preparing the dinner. While a public tea was held in the chapel we had games on the Malting Green near by. Scrambles for nuts and pennies and there were two or three stalls on the green with all kinds of sweets and ginger pop etc., where we spent our pennies and had change back – perhaps we would have a farthing's worth at a time to make our money hold out.

Then our evening service for a short time, when the best items were picked out from the recitations and dialogues which we had had on Sunday were recited and that finished our anniversary, except that we went on the green and had games again. The adults as well all joined in the kiss-in-the-ring, etc., and how we enjoyed it; no thought whatever about going to the seaside – that took place later on and is still carried out.

For those special occasions the chapel was full of people, even to the pulpit with the preacher and some standing at the open windows to hear the items and the singing.

Sunday School anniversaries were the most popular event in the Chapel year – for some they were the only one they regularly supported. At one June anniversary in Lancashire, a retired minister recalls, the preacher bluntly observed: 'Lots of you have not been in this church since last anniversary day and you will probably not be here again until our next anniversary. So let me take this opportunity of wishing you a very happy Christmas.'

Special tiered platforms were erected for such anniversaries at chapels in Lancashire:

In the recesses on either side would be a four-tiered wooden platform, erected by the men of the church and draped in snowy white calico – gift of the local mill-owner. The church would be packed, often people seated in the aisles. At precisely 2.20 the Sunday School Superintendent would appear at the door leading by the hand the smallest little girl and followed by the members of the Sunday School classes all in their best dresses and suits. These would be helped up the steps of the platforms on either side, the lower level being reserved for the Sunday School teachers.

A Wakefield Nonconformist writes with real nostalgia:

I always looked forward to Whit Sunday when we all had our new clothes on. How proud we were walking in after having our star card marked! We all had star cards in those days – I often had the 104 marks for the year.

Whit Tuesday was our school feast. My little friend and I were often first behind the band all dressed in our new white hats and dresses, going to several houses in the village singing the hymns. Then there was tea in the school room for grown-ups and tea for the scholars was on the grass, behind the school. Tea was brought in large cans and clothes-baskets full of home-made long buns, cut up and buttered.

After tea we all went into the adjoining field where the band played. Our mothers and grandmothers sat under the trees whilst we played 'pice' ball[1] and cricket.

In some places in the south, Cranbrook (Kent) Congregational chapel, for example, the Sunday School anniversary included an afternoon Flower Service where children's gifts of flowers were arranged on the chapel platform. The flowers were afterwards sent to a hospital or to the Ragged School Union.

Not everyone took Sunday School special events entirely seriously. A Sheffield gentleman writes:

The signal to go was the distant sound of the Loxley brass band, marching past our house, followed by a long column of straggling children, letting fly at Colonel Bogey or a Sousa march. The Sunday School children had been fortified with the official 'bun and coffee' breakfast to sustain them over the two-mile walk.

The boys produced peas and pea-shooters and all passers-by received a broadside as the column moved past. The girls in their new Whitsuntide dresses brought 'Kali suckers', com-

[1] Pice in Yorkshire means to throw. Pice ball was similar to rounders, the ball being hit with the hand.

prising a triangular paper bag containing sherbet, with a short length of liquorice tube sticking out through which the contents could be sucked; or liquorice telephone wires, yards of it; also there were the inevitable Whitsuntide squeakers – a sausage-shaped balloon was inflated and on release the back pressure produced a foul wailing noise.

There were also Sunday School Union services when a number of chapels of various denominations were addressed by a delegate from the National Sunday School Union, an appointed Visitor reported on the work of the schools, and a discussion followed. At the Beult Sunday School Union in mid-Kent this was followed by a 'cold collation', after which toasts were drunk (not in alcoholic liquor), beginning with the Loyal Toast. Individual members of the host chapel would have prepared the cold meat for the feast. All chapels by this time (early twentieth century) supported the temperance cause and Sunday School pupils were required to join the Band of Hope:

Once we had a week of 'Gospel Temperance' when the school room was hung with diagrams of human organs before and after maltreatment by alcohol.

Not all children enjoyed Sunday School. Apart from the runaways mentioned earlier, there were those who found the atmosphere stultifying and dull. Quite how awful to the sensitive child were the extreme forms of Nonconformity may be gathered from Edmund Gosse's *Father and Son* (1907), but less well-known sons could be just as alienated:

I must confess [writes an elderly Cranbrook Congregationalist] that in my early days I did not like Chapel or Sunday School and only attended under compulsion. Our Minister then was an elderly and scholarly man, who was reputed to be a good expository preacher. I am afraid his discourses made little impression on me; but I do remember him describing how Jeremiah was let down into an old cistern, and I pricked up my ears on one occasion when he referred to the theory that life might have been brought to this earth 'on the moss-grown fragment of another world'. He was against the theory, of course.

4

Much depended on the locality and the ministers and teachers who ran the Sunday Schools. Certainly many children of no mean intelligence found stimulus in the teaching at Sunday School. Most pupils enjoyed its social side and some remained practising Christians to the end of their days. Had it not been for Sunday School – particularly in earlier times before day schools were made available to all – they would have remained illiterate and innumerate and they would have lacked that good fellowship which, apart from the religious aspect, Sunday School uniquely offered in industrial suburbs, tiny hamlets and villages, spreading towns and cities in the days when there was little mobility for the vast majority and few interests outside the home.

In the words of the verse appended to the announcement of a General Sunday School sermon at a Baptist meeting house in December 1814:

> Delightful task! to rear the tender thought
> To teach the young Idea how to shoot,
> To pour the fresh instruction on the Mind
> To breathe the enlivening Spirit, and to fix
> The generous Purpose to the glowing breast.

Not everywhere, at all times, with every child was this objective achieved but generally it was.

2

CONVERSIONS, BACKSLIDING
AND REVIVALS

My heart is fixed, eternal God,
  Fixed on Thee:
And my immortal choice is made:
  Christ for me.

F. R. Havergal.

Death of mercy! can there be
Mercy still reserved for me?
Can my God his wrath forbear?
Me, the chief of sinners, spare?

John and Charles Wesley.

Conversion is as old as Christ, indeed very much older since a kind of conversion took place within the Greek mystery religions. Conversion may come after much thought and inquiry or on a sudden with apparently little predisposition. But in either case it is felt as a striking change, 'a new birth' in Bunyan's words, or in George Fox's: 'Then, O! then I heard a voice which said "There is one, even Christ Jesus, that can speak to my condition," and when I heard it my heart did leap for joy.'

Personal conversions have occurred in most Christian denominations but in the last two centuries it was mainly the Nonconformist who positively went out to convert and bring souls to the knowledge of God. More particularly it has been the Methodists, the followers of John Wesley who 'felt his heart strangely warmed' in an Aldersgate Street meeting in 1738. For them, until recent times, conversion has been the *sine qua non* of religion.[1]

[1] It is a fact, however, as E. E. Kellett records in *As I Remember* (1936), that the Roman Catholic, Father Ignatius, in the latter years of the nineteenth century conducted revivals, 'outwardly indistinguishable from those of Primitive Methodists, and V. S. S. Coles, vice-principal of Pusey House, did the same'.

The nature of conversion has been admirably – and sympathetically – described by Sydney G. Dimond in *The Psychology of the Methodist Revival* (London, 1926). He sees it as 'the development of an emotional revival as a result of the conviction that flashed upon the active mind of John Wesley at his conversion; the stimulation of dormant instincts occasionally to the point of violence; the power of religion to break the bonds of a narrow rationalism and to kindle in a neglected and debased population a new moral enthusiasm. . . . Conversion opened the way to new intellectual insight, finely directed activity and deeper emotional life within the circle of the movement, a new social order emerged which created its own philosophy, interpreting religious experience in vital and imaginative form.'[1]

The poet, John Masefield, in *The Everlasting Mercy*, describes well the sensation the converted had of being 'in a new world' (Wesley's own phrase):

> I did not think, I did not strive,
> The deep peace burnt my me alive;
> The bolted door had broken in,
> I knew that I had done with sin.
> I knew that Christ had given me birth
> To brother all the souls on earth,
> And every bird and every beast
> Should share the crumb broke at the feast.
>
> O story of the lighted mind!
> How dead I'd been, how dumb, how blind.
> The station brook, to my new eyes
> Was babbling out to Paradise;
> The waters rushing from the rain
> Were singing Christ has risen again.
> I thought all earthly creatures knelt
> From rapture of the joy I felt.

It is true that some found embarrassing and psychologically suspicious the tears, the beating of the breast, convulsive tearings, groaning, trembling and shouting that occurred in some conversions. Yet it is also true that conversion often preceded

[1] Dimond, p. 246.

the creation of a new emotional and moral stability, personal
efficiency, kindness and goodness, and that in many cases these
lasted throughout life.

Some of the more dramatic occasions are recalled by elderly
correspondents, one from Essex:

> I well remember how there were revival meetings and the
> tears that were shed with the adults crying to the Lord to save
> their souls and one dear man came out and said to his young
> sister: 'Come on, Nellie and help me sing, I'm on my way to
> glory where pleasures never die.' It made us young ones feel
> we wanted Jesus, and I praise Him for the happy day when
> He washed my sins away.

The Rev. J. Baker Norton's notes[1] of his early days – around
the 1850s – in the Ministry:

> We had been praying for an outpouring of the Spirit and it
> came with a rush. One Sunday evening the congregation
> seemed completely awed, and men and women were so
> pricked of the Word that they fell in their pews and cried
> aloud for mercy. It *was* a time! Some obtained liberty, and at
> once began to rejoice, while others continued in perfect
> agony.
>
> What with the praises of pardoned sinners and the groans
> of burdened sinners we were almost bewildered. About ten
> o'clock we made an effort to dismiss the people, but many
> refused to go, and some remained nearly all night. For weeks
> after, the chapel was always open, and there was a well-
> attended service each evening.
>
> The news of this astonishing outbreak flew like wildfire, and
> the chapel became an attraction to the whole parish and to
> many outside. Our hands were full. We were sent for to pray
> with persons in their homes and to make known to them the
> way of salvation, which we were only too glad to do. The
> revival was the talk of everybody, and there were very few
> who did not come under its influence.
>
> Men could not settle to work and it was no unusual thing
> for the miners, in the bowels of the earth, to lay aside their

[1] From *The Methodist Magazine*, Winter 1899.

tools in order that they might hold prayer meetings. I conducted some of them. Those underground services were memorable. Down in the gloom, heaven's light shone in upon penitent hearts and they became new creatures, as their lives ever since have testified. You know Edward ——, Henry ——, James ——, and Robert ——; they were brought in at that time, and noble fellows they have made, and others have gone home [i.e. died]. They were converted just in time.

Of course there were those who resisted the Spirit of God. One of them, I, the writer, visited a few weeks before his death. He had been a fine young fellow; 'from his shoulders and upward he was higher than any of the people'. With his companions he attended the services. They yielded to their convictions, but he held out until he became so miserable that he resolved, by some means, to stifle his feelings.

In order to do so he took a train to Plymouth and went to the theatre. When he left the building it was raining heavily and, having no overcoat or umbrella, he got wet through. On reaching home about midnight he was exhausted and trembling from head to foot. He had taken a chill which became a serious illness. This was the beginning of the end. He lingered for many months and when I, the writer, saw him towards the end, sitting propped up with pillows, in an armchair by the fireside, he said:

'What a fool I was. I ran away from the Spirit of God, and now I am paying the penalty. God has had mercy upon my soul, but my body is only a shadow of what it was, and that will soon be lying in the churchyard. Tell the young men whom you meet of my case, and let it be a warning to them not to fight against God.'

I have made reference to Captain Kent's power in prayer, and there was no mistake about it, as the whole neighbourhood knew. Hence, in the greatest difficulties, his services were invited and freely given.

The following was related to me by one who was present: a hard drinker was suffering from a terrible attack of delirium tremens. He was most violent and demonlike; it required six men to hold him in bed, and there were times when even their combined strength was taxed to the utmost.

Being at their wits' end the Captain was sent for, and he came. Quietly entering the room, with all possible calmness he said to the six: 'Take your hands off that man and leave him to me.' 'We dare not' was the reply. 'He will be out of bed in an instant and kill somebody or jump out of the window as he has tried to do before.'

'You do as I tell you,' cried the Captain, 'and be quick about it.'

Immediately, but fearing what might happen, they obeyed, and to their surprise the object of their alarm did not stir.

The Captain fixed his eyes upon him for a few seconds then fell upon his knees and began to pray. At first the man raved and made use of awful language, especially when the name of Jesus was mentioned; but subsequently his blasphemies were exchanged for moans, followed by earnest and pathetic cries for mercy, which was offered to him on the condition of true repentance and simple faith in Jesus Christ. He accepted the offer, and was freed not only from the yoke and condemnation of sin, but also from the craving for strong drink.

It is difficult not to conclude that Captain Kent and many others like him had gifts that the best psychoanalysts have possessed; these religious 'converters', however, had something positive to offer in place of despair; they were not merely re-equipping a man to face the world from which he had sought escape but changing his view of the world.

Some workers in the conversion field were almost embarrassed by their success:

Almost every night the two classrooms upstairs [at Underbank Sunday School, near Holmfirth] were full of earnest inquirers. Some remarkable conversions took place. Strong men trembled, and many, both men and women, were melted into tears. Sometimes the rooms were so crowded with those who were distressed on account of their guilt and sin that the workers were embarrassed, and scarcely knew what course to take. The services could not be given up at the time but had to be continued on certain nights for about a month. Some objected, but it was done night after night, and often a crowd would follow and enter the chapel, where many were brought to their knees. The whole of the neighbourhood was influenced by these simple efforts. In many of the houses and mills the hymns heard in the services were sung daily.

Some of the workers at the school were diffident about the whole affair, but they were convinced afterwards, when, in the open school, a large number of young people got up and bore testimony to what the Lord had done for their souls.

Many individual conversions long ago are recalled:

There were many whose lives were completely changed and I think of one – a nail-maker, Jim Melling, who had been converted standing on a chair in his home and declaring that he was the 'son of a King', to whom his mother said, 'have you gone out of your mind?' 'No' was the reply, 'I'm coming back to my mind.' W. H. Lax, who lived at Hindley in those days frequently preached at Bispham [near Blackpool]. I know of one occasion when he was entertained by Mr Henry Laithwaite, farmer (another Bispham pioneer). He must have done well, for young Lax received the blessing of his host, who putting his hand upon his head said, 'Someday, you will become a great man.' Mr Laithwaite must have known because Lax of Hindley and Bispham became 'Lax of Poplar'.

The devotion of laymen to the task of converting sinners is striking:

When I was in my teens the Methodists of Bowes, [north Yorkshire] always arranged to have a special mission every two years. These services made a great impression on my life, and eventually led me to accept Jesus Christ as my Saviour and a few years after I became a preacher.

The mission at Bowes that I remember best was conducted by a man who lived at Kirkby Stephen called Mr James Mason. He was a local preacher and a grocer by trade. He came on the six o'clock train each night a distance of nearly twenty miles and went back to his shop each week day on the eight o'clock train every morning.

The mission lasted three weeks. Mr Mason preached about twenty-three sermons in twenty-one days, preaching twice on a Sunday and sang a solo nearly every night. He was a lovely singer and a grand preacher. There would be nearly forty converts during those services. I remember one Sunday night there were thirteen young people kneeling at the old-fashioned penitent form. The mission I have just mentioned and other missions were all preceded by many weeks of prayer meetings. I can remember my father and other farmers walking over a mile night after night to pray.

I can remember some wonderful cases of people being converted. There was one man who was a slave to drink; he was ruining his life and his home and never attended a place of worship. But during one mission conducted by a minister, he came into a service and went forward to the penitent form; he went home and burnt his pipe, and never drank again and became a real Christian gentleman and served the Methodist Church faithfully, as steward, preacher etc.

Another young man whom I knew caused a disturbance outside one chapel and when the Society steward asked him to be quiet, he used very filthy language. But he went to another Dale and was converted and came back and preached two sermons one Sunday in the same chapel in which he had sworn at the stewards.

Some evangelists, for instance Jim Beesley, from the Methodist training school, Cliff College, who visited Halifax when 'the Minister's vestry in the chapel became holy ground' had an extraordinary effect:

> Every night during the crusade that tiny room became alive with the Power of God, as Jim Beesley stormed the gates of heaven in prayer. On his knees, perspiration mingled with his tears as night after night he communed with God – a living God. No wonder he entered the pulpit with a radiance around him that amazed us all.

There is something here reminiscent of the accounts of the spiritual strivings of the mystics such as St John of the Cross and St Teresa.

The methods of conversion were sometimes drastic – at least in earlier times. In the 1830s a strong Methodist was unequally yoked with an unbelieving wife, whose insults and sneering at his piety were incessant. After enduring the torment for years he finally said, 'Well you've nagged at my Methodism long enough; I'll give it up.' He left the house, called on the minister and surrendered his ticket of membership. Thus restored to heathenism, he was free from the obligation to turn the other cheek. On the way home he cut a stout sapling with which he administered to his wife so sound a thrashing that, seeing what his Methodism had saved her from, she begged him to rejoin the brethren. Next day he went back to the minister and asked for two tickets, one for himself and one for his wife. 'I was assured that the treatment produced a permanent cure; the lady became a life-long, excellent church-member!'

Strange stories are told of conversions, rather resembling that of St Paul, on roads and elsewhere. In *The Methodist Magazine* of Winter 1899 we read:

> Prominent among the Methodist laymen of Horbury [West Riding] is John Turton, who lived to the age of ninety-seven. Apprenticed to a worsted weaver in Dirtcar he became fond of music. A fiddle which he bought and learned to play bewitched and threatened to destroy him. When convinced of sin this 'snare of the devil' came in between him and salvation. One night, however, on the road between Horbury and Dirtcar the struggle culminated. The question agitating his mind was: Shall it be the fiddle, the public house and the devil; or Christ, the chapel and salvation?
>
> While pondering it, a sudden flash of light surprised him in the darkness. Looking in the direction whence it came, he saw a 'wick' fire in a field, and, as though by inspiration, jumped the hedge, made for the fire, and thrust the fiddle into it – thus breaking the bridge that linked him to the old sinful past. Converted, he began to preach, 'and was greatly owned of God'.

Among the converted themselves there were a number of miraculous physical cures:[1]

> An evangelist, named Albert Shakesby from Tiley was staying with us and he was a very good preacher and rather

[1] See below, Chapter 7, for the cures carried out by the Peculiar People.

excitable. He made many converts because during one service he prayed very hard for help and a cure – he being on crutches at the time. After this particular service he threw away his crutches and with tears streaming down his cheeks cried out that he was healed.

It made a big impression on the crowd and my grandfather told me when I grew older that the cure had been maintained as he afterwards wrote to grandfather and we also read of his revival meetings all over the country.

Nor was conversion confined to adults. A Norfolk correspondent writes:

I am eighty-six years of age, came on full plan[1] as a local preacher in 1904. In the village which I lived at the little Wesleyan chapel a mission was being held. Four lads were converted, including myself. It consisted of three members, no leadership. It had a good Sunday School, so I went to the Superintendent begging for a class as I said there is work to be done I must start at once.

The new-found joy, the good news of the Gospel, Salvation, oh the joyful sound! With that start we also commenced a prayer meeting weekly, a class meeting Sunday mornings. Both these meetings have wonderful memories for me, wonderful answers to prayer and often in the class meetings two getting up at once to tell their experiences.

God was blessing our service, everything, revival, souls being saved in the prayer meetings. Outstanding in my memory was the middle life and old people who came and made decision for Christ. To get to the chapel many had to cross the village green. It was called Long Green. No torches in those days but the old-fashioned lanterns with candle inside for light. In the schoolroom I have seen a row of them the length of the room.

The greatest venture to embark on for lads with the love of God in their hearts, led only by the Holy Spirit filled with a joy that was unspeakable. We became very concerned about

[1] Local preachers had a trial period after which, when they were accepted by the Superintendent Minister, they were assigned to preach on the plan (usually a three-monthly period) of the Circuit.

those outside. We wanted them to come and be sharers with us.

After much prayer, the Holy Spirit used boys with no Church guidance to hold open-air service with no adult help. The village postman with his accordion, small and feeble, was the beginning, but the results were wonderful. This led to visitation to follow up the work. One of our appointed local preachers was so surprised at the packed chapel, he came and asked me to take the service. Why I have been prompted to write this, when I opened the paper there recorded was the death of one of those lads aged eighty-two. The last time I saw him his last words to me were, 'Albert, I am still holding to the Faith.'

Conversion had curious effects on the cynical, as a Leeds correspondent makes clear:

I myself had been converted at an evangelical mission as a boy. The chapel had been well-filled and we had all been worked up into a fine religious frenzy. We sat, heads bowed, while the evangelist urged us to put up our hands when we felt we had been saved. I had shared in the communal passion and, not without embarrassment, I at last raised my hand. Someone called out 'Hallelujah!' and I burst into tears. I was taken on to the knee of the one woman of the ordinary chapel members whom I most disliked and she pressed me closely to her loathsome bosom. . . . The conversion made no difference to my way of life. I bragged about it the next day to my friends, but they were unimpressed.

Some chapelgoers shrank from the fervours involved in some such services; and the Congregationalists never indulged in them:

Some of the local preachers were good and worth listening to; they could illustrate their sermons from shop floor experience. But occasionally we would get one of the evangelist type who would embarrass the congregation at the end of his sermon by asking all those who felt they had been saved that morning or evening to step forward to the pulpit rail. I never saw anyone go, not even father who felt this was carrying emotionalism to extremes especially if it followed a very ordinary sermon.

There were other difficulties, such as over-evangelisation referred to in *The Methodist Magazine* of 1899. The passage also suggests some sort of competition for the gleaning of souls:

Sunday and weekday alike the work went on. Converts were added at the rate of hundreds per year. Because of these traditions and ideas, Revivalists could always draw a crowd in this town [Congleton, Cheshire], and number up a long list of 'penitents'. Clowns, sweeps, threshers, clerics of all grades and hues, if only they were enthusiastic and rampant, were sure of a large audience.

In short, the place had been over-evangelised. That is always the danger where the work has been notably successful in past years. We must beware of the spasmodic!

Nearly every man skilled in the promotion of revivals will assert that it is best to allow a considerable time to elapse between one special effort and another. My personal opinion would state it at six or eight years, unless the toil and growth have been quite extraordinary; and, whenever such effort is made, it should be scientifically, enthusiastically, thoroughly entered into.

Congleton contained some hearty souls, and these hailed my advent with delight. But O what a heavy lift that was! There were local circumstances which conspired against success. After the first Sunday – when the signs were propitious – there was a sudden stoppage. Evening after evening proved blank, and only at the end of a fortnight was there anything to repay for all the labour expended.

Associated with this are certain entries in my private book: 'Neither congregations nor converts increase as I expected.' 'O this dearth upon our churches!' and so forth. The nervous force ran down; there were broken and fretful nights; but the teeth were set and the battle was joined afresh. Then the entries continue – 'Ten services, and only at the final one have we won.' 'Some capital cases; encouraged at last!'

Twice only were the meetings given up before the time announced; once because the preacher had heard the chiming of every hour during the night previous; but the second occasion always furnishes matter for self-reproach. There had been little or no preparation: the gatherings were of the thinnest; and so the concluding service was thrown up – a cowardly policy that, and one that has since been sufficiently repented of. A leader suggested that the members should be invited to the communion rail, ostensibly with the view of seeking for a special baptism of the Holy Spirit, but really with the idea of beguiling some of the unconverted into coming forward – an artifice from which my mind revolted. It is best to be quite straightforward. Better defeat than the loss of self-respect.

Music was almost always an aid to conversion:

This mission band (a brass one) was conducted by a Brother named Jacobs who once played in the Salvation Army Household Band. It also paid visits to other churches in the neighbourhood and was the means of bringing many to Jesus. We believed in those days that people needed to come to Him.

When numbers were getting low and love [of God] getting cold we used to have a mission most often conducted by James Dykes. It never failed: people were converted – scores of them, and also in other churches in the area. We never talked of shutting up, but rather filling up.

I remember too how we used to have an Exhorter I think he was called; his job was to keep us up to scratch. The one that I remember was named Hogben.

I don't seem to remember much else only that preaching was different, God seemed real, the Devil we tried to flee and we preached for results and got them.

The Salvation Army, needless to say, was often in the forefront, as a correspondent from Melton Mowbray recalls:

About 1880 or 1881 two Salvation Army girls came and conducted services at our chapel and in the homes and a great revival was the result, not such a one since. Richard M. Seager came and quite a few converts. I kept in touch with nine as long as they lived: that would be about 1898. Geo Wilkinson came for a ten days mission about 1904 when twelve joined us.

When the Salvation Army came a lot of young folk wanted
to have a Sunday morning meeting. There was only one place
– a little bit of ground at the back. They asked the first steward
(my father) if they could build a vestry. He agreed. They
begged the material and built one. When the minister came
there was trouble, he had not been told, the chapel committee had not been asked. The steward replied, 'If you want
to make a weld, you must strike while the iron is hot,' and
added, 'If I've done wrong, elect another steward.' The vestry
was built then and soon in use.

When the Salvation Army girls were here they taught 'pop'
songs with 'gingle' instruments and sang: 'We'll roll the old
chariot along, and don't lag on behind,' 'We are marching to
Zion,' and others that have left a lingering memory in my
mind. I was too young to realise what was being done but
many were saved and went into the world to show the way of
salvation; a few stayed in our little village.

Revivalist meetings were sometimes begun for polemical
reasons:

Revivalist meetings were arranged possibly for one or two
weeks. One point which struck me was that laymen (at one
session women) were the missioners and not a minister.

One such campaign followed a visit by an atheist doctor
who held meetings in the local market square, making light of
Christianity and attracting large crowds. To counteract this,
the local preachers brought down from London a prominent
speaker from the Christian Evidence Society to speak at a
series of meetings in the borough hall and redress the
balance.

In my youthful innocence I was surprised to learn that the
speaker charged a fee of five guineas for the week.

We tend to think – and so do many of those who have given
their memories to me – that the great days of chapelgoing were
between 1850 and 1914. Perhaps in one sense they were, yet
already by 1851 the Methodists were bewailing the drift from
the chapels. They ascribed it to the constant drift from the villages into the towns and cities, particularly where new industries
were centred. Thus uprooted, some former chapelgoers found

new distractions on Sunday. Methodist documents[1] speak of 324,000 embarking and landing one Sunday in 1852 at the piers between Chelsea and London Bridge, while only just over 20,000 attended the sixty-seven Wesleyan chapels in the metropolis. Meanwhile 'destitution, vice and crime' grew in the great centres.

It was, therefore, decided to build Central Mission Halls in towns and cities where the population had grown inordinately and there were few chapels. The idea was to make Chapel less formal, less middle class and more welcoming to the passerby. In some places theatres were hired for Sunday services but special halls to seat about 2,000 people were thought better. They were built or adapted to look as much like a public hall or theatre as possible:

> If we invite, we must welcome. [So wrote the Superintendent of the Leeds mission in 1902.] We set ourselves to welcome everybody, make them feel at home, and secure their interest from the start. Fifty workers distribute hymn sheets, conduct people to seats, smile and shake hands. There is not a dull moment from start to finish. Before a man knows it, he is caught in the swing of things and forgets he is a stranger.

Part of the welcome at every mission, writes the Rev. George Sails, was the assurance of a free seat:

> Today an occasional complaint is heard about a worshipper being asked to move from a certain pew and to sit elsewhere, but these instances are happily rare, and many people in consequence may find it difficult fully to appreciate the tremendous importance to the non-churchgoer of the nineteenth century of being offered a free seat. To quote again the words of Samuel Chadwick, referring to the churches of that time, 'pews were rented, privileged and unsociable'.

At the central halls gimmickry was eschewed:

> Our services [wrote the Superintendent of Oxford Place chapel, Leeds] are very plain, even old-fashioned, but very hearty and distinctively Methodist. We have tunes that every-

---

[1] *At the Centre: the Story of Methodism's Central Missions,* by George Sails (London, 1970).

1 SPURGEON: One of the most celebrated Nonconformist preachers.

2.1 SPREADING THE GOSPEL: Handcarts or 'chariots' such as that shown above, were often used by revivalists and missioners to carry leaflets or hymn-sheets and as open-air platforms.

2.2 BROTHERHOOD: A Sunday afternoon meeting for men only which flourished a the large mission and central halls of Methodism. Men came in their thousands befor and after the First World War and at Bradford, for example (above), were addressed b such celebrities as Sir Oliver Lodge, Sir Arthur Conan Doyle, C. T. Studd (th cricketer evangelist), and Rev. G. A. Studdert Kennedy ('Woodbine Willie').

body can sing and the whole of the service is so arranged that the interest never flags.

The Hull mission reported in 1895: 'We use no means but what we are sure God will approve. Our aim is to preach Jesus Christ simply, earnestly and lovingly, and we find that to working people the old story has lost none of its interest and power.'

The missioners did not discuss theories of God and religion. They spoke simply of the fact that they had 'actually and gloriously got Christ'. But they did preach 'for a decision'. Conversions were the rule rather than the exception. 'A Sunday with no conversions would be mourned as a calamity.' Many of the converts were from 'public houses, singing saloons, houses of ill-fame and from prisons,' but while there was this heartening response from the hitherto unchurched masses it should be noted, continues the Rev. George Sails, that just as the mission services drew from all classes of people, so the response to the appeal of the Gospel came from all sections of the community. 'Our converts have come from all ranks, from respectable commercial men to the drunken, ragged scamp who is the despair of civilisation.' 'Our converts include tradesmen and tramps, professional men to the poorest of the poor.'

In some chapels, too, before membership was allowed, *public* conversion was required, after which the converted were entered on the Disciples' Roll and given membership cards.

A retired Methodist minister, the Rev. H. R. Hindley, writes:[1]

I remember one such ten-days' mission of an unusual character at Chasetown, Staffordshire, conducted by Cissie Roberts, a young girl of fifteen, who is now a minister's wife. She seemed to me to be a kind of spiritual Joan of Arc; and her ninety converts, of all ages, became Christian stalwarts on Cannock Chase for the next thirty years.

Five miles away, at my home-town of Hednesford, a similar mission sparked off a revival which produced many Sunday School teachers, local preachers, and town councillors. It

[1] In *The Record*, the monthly magazine of the Mutley Methodist church, Plymouth, March, 1968.

5

also included scenes of spiritual ecstasy like those described in the Acts of the Apostles; Bunyan's *Grace Abounding*; and Wesley's Journal. 'My God, I am Thine' was our marching-song back to Chapel from the open-air. At about the same time, three hundred miles away in Cornwall, a girl about my own age, who was destined to become my wife, gave *her* heart to God in similar circumstances.

It seems strange to us that such facts, fully examined in Dr George Jackson's *The Fact of Conversion* and William James's *Varieties of Religious Experience*, should now be questioned in Methodist circles. Some people who lived at that time seem to have forgotten the evangelistic warmth of that halcyon half-century, which began with the Methodist Forward Movement in 1885, led by Hugh Price Hughes, Charles Garrett, and Samuel Collier. It included the second Moody-Sankey mission to Cambridge, in which seven undergraduates ('The Cambridge Seven') surrendered to Christ, and went as missionaries to China.

Seven years later came the conversion of Grenfell of Labrador under Moody, in 1892, gratefully recorded in Grenfell's *What Christ Means to Me*. Devoted evangelistic work was also done by such musical converts as Jenny Lind (the 'Swedish Nightingale'), Jessie Strathearn, and the organist, W. H. Jude (in five continents, as recorded in his *Music and the Higher Life*).

Our finest convert in the Manchester mission was a rich young American, an inveterate gambler from California. Being unlucky nearly every time, he brought disgrace on the family by gradually squandering his share of the inheritance, and fled to England.

Standing on the edge of the crowd one Sunday evening he came into the late Gospel service at the Central Hall, and was soundly converted. Well-educated, and possessed of a rare literary gift, he became editor of the mission magazine. His name was George Rogers.

In 1904, we had the Welsh Revival; then, at short intervals, in 1905 and 1908, the Torrey-Alexander and Chapman-Alexander missions from America, like Billy Graham's, in all our large cities.

Mr Hindley speaks of his own experience in his home town of Hednesford, Staffordshire, in October 1902:

Every time I go home, I go into the chapel and kneel at the rail where, at the early age of nine, I first sang, 'O happy day that fixed my choice on Thee, my Saviour, and my God!' The following week I joined an adult society class of twenty to twenty-five regular members, made up of local tradesmen, coal-miners and their wives, many of whom had been converted that week or in similar previous missions. I was struck by the intense reality of their testimonies, given after a short Bible address by our leader, G. M. Goscomb. Like many church prayers, these testimonies were oft-repeated, the speakers being illiterate; but they were all genuine and garnished with phrases from the Bible and hymnbook. Like the market-woman at Bedford, who helped forward John Bunyan's conversation, 'They spake as if joy did make them speak; and as though they had entered into a new world' (as, indeed, they had, like John Wesley at Aldersgate Street!)

The meeting was radiant with their faith. Every now and then, moved by the Spirit, a man or woman would burst forth with a well-known chorus, in which all would join. I sometimes smile now, as, on the wings of memory, I hear myself singing at the age of ten:

> Thank God for what He's done for me,
>   Once I was blind, but now I see;
> I on the brink of ruin fell,
>   Glory to God, I'm out of hell!
> (Chorus)   And above the rest, *this* note shall swell
>   My Jesus has done all things well!

At that early age, they made me their precentor at the regular Sunday open-air meeting at 5.00 p.m. This would mean an early tea, especially if there had been a teachers' meeting after Sunday School. We used to form a ring in the middle of the street, like the Salvation Army, and were seldom disturbed; for traffic was rare, and sometimes nil. An occasional cyclist would pass by, and we could easily stand aside for the doctor's horse-and-trap! Sunday teatime was very peaceful in the average provincial town, and only two Hednesford men owned a motor car!

The final speaker usually concluded his address with the words of Moses, 'Come thou with us, and we will do thee good', and a few listeners on the pavement would follow us down the street, and into chapel during the first hymn.

There were a few notorious characters in my home town, former scholars who knew that we were praying for them, sometimes by name. These men would be challenged by their mates in the street, 'Are you coming to the mission, Bill? 'Twill be the best day's work you've ever done!' One or two would come in on the last night, and go forward to the communion-rail, in response to the evangelist's appeal.

One could see them writhing under conviction of sin, and struggling for release, like some of those mentioned in Wesley's Journal, until at last they 'came through', moved to lurch forward by the singing of such a verse as,

> Nay, but I yield, I yield;
> I can hold out no more;
> I sink, by dying love compelled,
> And own Thee conqueror.

The following night, on his way to class, a member would call for a backslider (and friend of his youth); and the man would give his testimony, in broad Staffordshire dialect. 'Well friends, some of you know what a bad lad Ah've bin. But it's like old times to be back in this classroom, for I was brought up in this Sunday "skewl". I only wish me owd mother could see me *now*! 'Er used to mek' me put me pipe on the mantelshelf the night afore I went back to my job in Birmingham; and I know'd 'er would throw it on the back o'th fire after I'd gone! But the next time I com' whum [came home] I'd allus bought another! If it'd only bin smokin', it wouldn't ha' mattered. But I thank God for what I done last night; and with His help I mean to go straight, Amen.' He, or the friend who had brought him, would then start up a chorus with memories of their boyhood, in which all present would join:

> I do believe, I will believe,
>   That Jesus died for me;
> That on the Cross He shed His blood
>   From sin to set me free.

As may have been guessed from some of the foregoing, conversion and revivalism became the work of professionals – often their only work. Like fund-raisers or marketing campaign organisers today, they carefully surveyed the field and provided detailed, private instructions to the chapel leaders beforehand. For example, the revivalist would advise that the inquiry rooms (where the newly-converted could be 'consolidated' in private) be as near as possible to the penitent form and where necessary signposted. Attendants in the inquiry rooms were forewarned of the kind of question likely to be asked and how they should be answered. Precise instructions were given about a period of hymn-singing before the service started, the hymns to be exuberant and joyful during this 'warming up'. After the evangelist had made his final appeal for 'decisions' the congregation was to bow in prayers for two minutes after which, *pianissimo*, the choir and organist were to render one only of certain hymns, among them 'Throw out the lifeline across the dark wave' or 'Jesus is tenderly calling thee home'.

The whole arrangement, writes Peter Fletcher in *The Long Sunday* (1958), was like an order of battle, and he describes how in silence the evangelist 'entered the pulpit, bowed for a moment in private prayer, then stood and slowly, deliberately, swept the congregation with his eyes until they were held in complete stillness ... The device is known to every practised public speaker.'

3

SINGING, SACRED AND SECULAR

O for a thousand tongues to sing
My great Redeemer's praise!

Charles Wesley.

In the New Testament Christ and the apostles sang a hymn (ὑμνήσαςτεν ἐξῆλθον)[1] after the first Lord's supper; and Christians have sung, some sects less, some more, ever since. But the Church of England had no official hymn book of its own until 1736 and its singing was largely confined to the psalms metrically rendered by Sternhold and Hopkins or Tate and Brady. Anglicans also knew George Withers's 'Hymns and Songs of the Church' and Samuel Bury's 'Collection of Psalms, Hymns and Spiritual Songs' containing the best of the Stuart hymnists, but all these were intended for private, not public devotional use, as were those of George Herbert ('King of Glory, King of peace').

It was the eighteenth century that saw the first great flowering of hymns as we understand them; of the 1,410 authors of original English hymns, catalogued in 1863, no less than 1,213 are of later date than 1707. The Independents (later Congregationalists) started the flowering with the hymns of Dr Isaac Watts and Philip Doddridge; and then came Charles Wesley, said to have written some 6,500 hymns. Among the Calvinistic branch of Methodists, the Olney hymns of Cowper and the Rev. John Newton (both in fact Evangelical C. of E.) are pre-eminent. Toplady's 'Rock of Ages' belongs to this school.

Although hymns gradually became popular in the Church of England, it was the Nonconformists – Methodists and Congregationalists in particular – who made them an essential part of their worship. Hymns had a powerful suggestion and auto-

---

[1] St Matthew, 26, and St Mark, 14: 'And when they had sung a hymn they went out into the mount of Olives.'

suggestion, they were educational in religious teaching and, combined with music, they imprinted unforgettably ideas and impulses of the religious life. To the Methodist the hymn-book was both creed and catechism, whether sung to old English church tunes of the sixteenth and seventeenth centuries, to German chorales, or even to song tunes of the day. Charles Wesley wrote words to the music-hall tune of 'Nancy Dawson', popular with sailors.

Hymn-singing caught on. The American Unitarian, Dr Samuel Johnson, wrote hymns including the magnificent 'City of God, how broad and far, Outspread thy walls sublime'; and in the nineteenth century many of the best hymn-writers were such Anglicans as A. C. Benson, Anne Brontë, John Keble, J. M. Neale and J. H. Newman (later a Roman Catholic Cardinal).

By the latter half of the nineteenth century, hymn-singing had become an English national pastime. W. T. Stead (1849–1912), the famous journalist who edited a collection called *Hymns that have helped*,[1] wrote in its foreword and without exaggeration:

> The songs of the English-speaking people are for the most part hymns. For the immense majority of our people today the only minstrelsy is that of the hymn-book. And this is as true of our race beyond the sea as it is of our race at home.

> At this moment on the slope of the Rockies, or in the sweltering heat of the jungles of India, in crowded Australian city or secluded English hamlet, the sound of some simple hymn tune will, as by mere magic spell, call from the silent grave the shadowy forms of the unforgotten dead, and transport the listener, involuntarily, over land and sea, to the scene of his childhood's years, to the village school, to the parish church. In our pilgrimage through life we discover the hymns which help. We come out of trials and temptations with hymns clinging to our memory like burrs.

Stead assembled his collection after personal inquiry of the famous. To each he wrote:

> What hymns have helped you? And if they have helped you how can you better repay the debt you owe to your helper than

[1] Published in London, n.d., but around 1896–1900.

by setting forth, stamped with the tribute of your gratitude, to help other mortals in like straits to yourself? All of us have our moments when we are near to the mood of the hero and the saint, and it is something to know what hymns help most to take us there, and keep us at that higher pitch.

Stead sometimes got rather dusty answers. Lord Rosebery, the Liberal leader, for instance, declined 'confession in general' to the public on the subject. The Archbishop of Canterbury referred Stead to a hymnal he himself had compiled many years ago! The Prince of Wales indicated his preference for Mrs Adam's well-known hymn (presumably 'Nearer My God to Thee'). The Dean of St Paul's disapproved of the principle of the hymn-book and wrote:

I imagine that hymns are one of the best instruments for implanting religious ideas in the minds of children and as I cannot think of any religion that can have the desired influence from which the essential doctrines of Christianity are excluded, I must decline to accept your courteous invitation to take part in compiling an unsectarian hymn-book.

As if, Stead observed, the 'essential doctrines' must be excluded because the hymnal was unsectarian!

Mrs Humphrey Ward was little help. She replied that the question she was asked was one which should not be answered, if one set any value upon religious feeling and religious life. 'This,' comments Stead, 'is rather a hard saying, coming as it does from the author of *Robert Elsmere*, which is a more or less successful attempt to unveil the hidden movements of religious thought and religious life in the soul of her hero before the eyes of the million.'

Sometimes he got the tart answers he might well have expected:

Dear Sir, – I fear I shall be unable to aid you in the under-taking described in your letter of the 11th. My own experience furnishes no examples of the kind you wish. If parents had more sense than is commonly found among them they would never dream of setting their children to learn hymns as tasks. With me the effect was not to generate any liking for this or that hymn but to generate a dislike for hymns at large. The process of learning was a penalty and the feeling associated with that penalty became a feeling associated with hymns in general. Hence it results that I cannot name any hymn that has helped me. – Faithfully yours, HERBERT SPENCER.

There was one aspect of hymns and other church music of which Stead did not approve:

If the Te Deum has been used to express the gratitude of man for crowning mercies, it has often been used as a kind of Christian war whoop over fallen foes. If our forefathers sang it with full hearts when England was delivered from the fell attack of the Armada, it was also chanted at Rome in honour of the massacre of St Bartholomew. If, as an ancient heathen poet declared:

> Unholy is the sound
> Of loud thanksgiving over slaughtered men,

impious indeed must have been the exultant strains that have gone up on high over the hecatombs of the battlefield.

Stead, the son of a Congregational minister, was a radical and discovered a hymn which was, he thought, the 'democratic anthem of the masses in vogue in Labour churches, Pleasant Sunday Afternoon meetings, and Congregational churches of the more advanced type'. The hymn was written by Ebenezer Elliot, the Sheffield Corn Law Rhymer, 'a sturdy uncompromising democrat, with a heart embittered against the landed classes, whose chief aim in making laws in those days seemed to him to be keeping up the price of bread, regardless of the needs of the hungry poor'.

> When wilt Thou save the people?
>> O God of mercy when?
> Not Kings alone, but nations?
>> Not thrones and crowns but men?
> Flowers of Thy heart, O God, are they:
>> Let them not pass, like weeds away –
> Their heritage a sunless day.
>> God save the people!

Shall crime bring crime for ever,
  Strength aiding still the strong?
Is it Thy will, O Father,
  That man shall toil for wrong?
'NO' say Thy mountains; 'No' Thy skies;
  Man's clouded sun shall brightly rise,
And songs ascend instead of sighs:
  God save the people!

When wilt Thou save the people?
  O God of mercy, when?
The people, Lord, the people,
  Not thrones and crowns, but men?
God save the people, Thine they are,
  Thy children, as Thine angels fair;
From vice, oppression, and despair,
  God save the people!

It is, Stead wrote, the 'nearest approach to an English *Marseillaise* that a sense of social injustice has wrung from the heart of the oppressed'.

Being a journalist Stead could not forego a good 'story':

Among the multitudinous testimonies which poured in upon me from those who had been helped by hymns, none touched me more than the story told by a poor Lancashire lass who, under the stress of passionate temptation, had forgotten the responsibilities of her position as Sunday School teacher and the obligations of her maidenhood. She married her lover before the child was born, but the sense of her sin burnt like vitriol into her life.

She wrote: 'It seemed to me no soul in hell could be blacker than mine. To feel that I had disgraced the Master's service and dishonoured His Holy name, was the bitterest drop in my cup. Never shall I forget those awful months of my torture. If any soul doubts the reality of a hell let him live through what I lived then. I have been there and know it exists.

'My girls brought me out and begged me to go back to teach. Good God! a thing like me to go back to teach those poor innocent creatures! I shrunk away, feeling I could never desecrate the threshold of God's house by my presence. They came again; it was Christmas Eve. They sang the carols at our door and then came in, kissing and making much of me.

'Presently my husband began to play on the piano the dear old hymn, "Begone, unbelief", the girls all joining in with lips untouched by care. I had to leave the room. All the pent-up agony of months were in the strain since I was not even fit to it, and then kneeling at my bedside in the darkness there came to me two lines of the hymn they had been singing:

How bitter that cup no heart can conceive
Which He drank quite up that SINNERS might live.

'Bitterer than even mine I thought, and He drank it for *me*. That was the miracle for me, and I knew myself forgiven, knew that Christ was looking at me, not with angry, but pitying eyes. Ah, the blessedness of it. But do you suppose I could ever forgive myself more than ever I blamed and hated myself.'

A Scot wrote about Dr George Matheson's moving hymn, which begins 'O Love that wilt not let me go':

At a time of great spiritual darkness, when God, Christ and Heaven seemed to have gone out of my Life, and neither sun nor stars in many days appeared, after months of hopeless misery of mind, I heard this hymn sung in a little country chapel. The first two lines haunted me for weeks, and at last brought light and comfort to my dark soul.

There were two other Victorians, not mentioned by Stead, who expressed their hymn preferences. One was the poet and critic Matthew Arnold. To him the finest hymn in the language was Isaac Watts's 'When I survey the wond'rous cross'. For that other great Victorian, Dr David Livingstone, it was Doddridge's 'O God of Bethel' that was pre-eminent: it was sung at Livingstone's funeral in Westminster Abbey.

Hymns, unlike the services of which they were an integral part, have never lost their popularity. They are the thread – almost the only one – connecting the present thin chapel life with the great days, now almost forgotten, when religion, whether devotional or social, was the centre of life for many millions.

The continuing popularity of hymns is attested by programmes put out by the B.B.C. on Sunday nights. What now are the popular hymns? Dr Cecil Northcott, a correspondent of the *Daily Telegraph*, wrote on 22 May 1970 that he had recently conducted a private poll in this country and in Canada and Australia as to which hymns on radio and television are most in demand, 'come wind come weather'. These were 'the old war horses of hymnology which have conquered the English speaking world':

Abide with me (*Lyte*)

All hail the power of Jesu's name (*Perronet*)

Breathe on me, breath of God (*Hatch*)

Crown him with many crowns (*Bridges*)

Dear Lord and Father of mankind (*Whittier*)

For all the saints (*How*)

Glorious things of thee are spoken (*Newton*)

Guide me O Thou great Jehovah (*Williams*)

Jesu Lover of my soul (*Wesley*)

Jesus calls us (*Alexander*)

Jesus shall reign (*Watts*)

Lead kindly light (*Newman*)

O sacred head sore wounded (*Gerhardt*)

Praise my soul (*Lyte*)

Praise to the holiest (*Newman*)

Rejoice the Lord is king (*Wesley*)

Rise up O men of God (*Merrill*)

The day thou gavest (*Ellerton*)

The Lord's my shepherd (*Psalm 23*)

There is a green hill (*Alexander*)

In the United States, Dr Northcott reported, they wanted to

add 'The Old Rugged Cross', 'In the Garden', 'I need Thee every hour', 'Rock of Ages', 'Now the day is over', 'What a friend we have in Jesus', and 'Nearer my God to Thee'. When it came to choosing the topmost hymn of all it was a tie between Charles Wesley's 'Jesu Lover' and Henry Lyte's 'Abide with me' with the United States weighing in strongly to put Wesley in the lead.

As with dress, flowers and dogs, fashion plays a part in the popularity of hymns. A correspondent born in 1902 writes that he enjoyed playing the three-manual organ, he cherished his singing and was in the Burnley Municipal Choir and the Burnley male voice choir, where he was always learning new music and enjoying the old:

> Choir weekends were special occasions for well-known hymns – and we almost always had 'Jesus shall reign' to the tune of 'Rimington' composed by Francis Duckworth and I have a copy of a splendid tune called 'Old Earth', and sung to 'All praise to thee my God this night'. I have not seen it in any tune books.[1] One I loved more than all and still do is 'I'll praise my maker' to 'Monmouth'.
>
> Another hymn we enjoyed hugely was 'These things shall be a loftier race', to 'Simeon', but one of our more modern ministers told me he didn't agree with the idealism of John Addington Symonds (1840–1893); on this score I cannot agree.
>
> Evening hymns were used a lot in those days, but seemingly they are not fashionable now – witness the dropping of the very popular 'Day is dying in the west'[2] (by

[1] Hymn tunes, of which there is no authoritative study as far as those used in chapels is concerned, were often as important as the words. Many could hum tunes though ignorant of the words. The provenance of the tunes ranged from medieval chants to adaptations of music hall or folk ditties.

[2] Day is dying in the west,
  Heaven is touching earth with rest;
  Wait and worship while the night
  Sets her evening lamps alight
    Through all the sky . . .

For not obvious reasons this hymn is now regarded in some quarters as vulgar claptrap.

the American, Mary Ann Lathbury). And a Sunday wasn't complete without 'Saviour, again to Thy dear name we raise' or 'The day Thou gavest' and 'Glory to Thee my God this night'.

It is not clear why Symonds's impeccably 'progressive' hymn – 'Nation with nation, land with land, Inarmed shall live as comrades free' – should have earned the disapproval of this correspondent's 'modern' minister: what could be more vaguely aspiring and unrealistically optimistic than a 'loftier race' rising 'with flame of freedom in their souls, And light of knowledge in their eyes'?

No mystery, however, attaches to the disappearance of certain hymns; some of these, if still sung today, would attract the attention of the racialists and their official boards. Yet it was true that in the wilds of Africa and the pestilential, inhuman slums of south-east Asia:

> Souls in heathen darkness lying,
>   Where no light has broken through,
> Souls that Jesus bought by dying,
>   Whom His soul in travail knew;
> Thousand voices, Thousand voices,
>   Call us o'er the water blue.

Some white men knew from first-hand experience that:

> A cry, as of pain,
> Again and again,
> Is borne o'er the deserts and widespreading main;
> A cry from the lands that in darkness are lying,
> A cry from the hearts that in sorrow are sighing;
>   It comes unto me;
>   It comes unto thee;
> Oh what – oh what shall the answer be? (composer and author: Sarah Geraldina Stock).

And to their eternal renown, unnamed thousands went into the steamy forests and up the crocodile-ridden rivers in order – to the best of their ability – to solace those crying hearts and lift them out of their primeval misery.

Less suspect were the hymns, recalled by one correspondent, that were in the Sunday School Hymnary by Carey Bonner in the late 1890s. Among them were:

'Yield not to Temptation – for yielding is sin'.

'Around the throne of God in Heaven thousands of children stand'.

'When Mothers of Salem their children brought to Jesus'.

'O, happy band of pilgrims'.

'Hushed was the Evening hymn, The Temple Courts were dark'.

On the other hand, contemplative hymns – whose sentiments were not dissimilar from those of many great English poets – would now be regarded as doleful and depressing:

> Days and moments quickly flying
> Blend the living with the dead
> Soon will you and I be lying
> Each within his narrow bed.

> Go bury thy sorrow, the world hath its share
> Go bury it deeply – go hide it with care.

One need not draw comparisons with A. E. Housman alone; there are parallels in Shakespeare, Donne, Shirley and a score of others.

It is, however, typical of the sometimes gay morbidity of Nonconformists that the same correspondent should recall another rendering of this verse by 'naughty boys':

> Here we suffer grief and pain –
> Over the road they're doing the same,
> Next door they're suffering more
> Oh, won't it be joyful when we part
> to meet no more.

Recalled, almost in the same breath, is a 'lovely hymn we sang for closing afternoon Sunday School':

> God our Father we would praise Thee
> For Thy loving smile today;

> In Thy mercy wilt Thou guide us
> As we go our homeward way?
> *Refrain*   – Hallowed be Thy name for ever
>   May Thy glorious kingdom come,
>   As in Heaven Thy saints adore Thee
>   So on Earth Thy will be done.

Hymns – though not the best of them – might carry somewhat pedestrian, not to say minatory, messages. At Bethesda Baptist chapel, Ipswich, in 1897, the hymn-book in use was Steven's Selection. One page was headed: 'Hints on an early attendance on Public Worship.' Here are some of the verses:

> Can those who once have tasted Jesus' Grace,
> Choose to be absent when He shows His face?
> Shall a few drops of rain, or a dusty road,
> Prevent their public intercourse with God?
>
> Bear with me when I say the crime is great
> Of those who practise coming late;
> As if God's services were far too long,
> So they omit the opening prayer or song.
>
> A little less indulgence in the bed –
> A little more contrivance in the head –
> A little more devotion in the mind –
> Would quite prevent your being so behind.

And for bathos (or comedy) this, used at Ferme Park, Hornsey, London, Congregational chapel in the nineteenth century would be hard to beat (I omit most of the banalities):

> Mariners we
> Sailing life's sea . . .
>
> Boats for the Kingdom
> Set sail every hour.

Nonconformists were always readier to adopt new hymns than were Anglicans. As a history teacher, W. M. Wigfield of Ilminster, remembers:

DICK'S FAIRY.

A Service of Sacred Song

Compiled by I. A. EDGAR,

FROM THE POPULAR STORY BY

Rev. SILAS K. HOCKING, F.R.H.S.

Author of "POOR MIKE," "HER BENNY," &c.

LONDON :

S. W. PARTRIDGE & CO., 9, PATERNOSTER ROW.

MANCHESTER :

"ONWARD" PUBLISHING OFFICE, 207, DEANSGATE & 13, BOOTLE ST.

PRICE FOURPENCE. 3s. 4d. per Dozen, post free.

AN OLD NOTATION EDITION AT THE SAME PRICE.

50 Copies at Half-price, post free 8s. 4d.

3 SERVICE OF SONG: These, once popular in Methodist chapels, included readings from an edifying story–such as that by the Rev. Silas K. Hocking, shown above—interspersed with more or less appropriate hymns and solos.

4.1 CHOIR TRIP by wagonette in the Midlands pre-1914.

4.2 CONGREGATIONAL CHAPEL: A typical interior. (Warwick Road, Birmingham

Baptists and Congregationalists were singing Whittier's[1] hymns ('Dear Lord and Father of Mankind', 'O Lord and Master of us all', and 'Immortal Love, for ever full') for twenty years before the Church of England became aware of them. Bunyan's Pilgrim Hymn, 'Who would true valour see ... His first avowed intent, To be a pilgrim', first became current near the end of the 1914–18 war, as a Sunday School Anniversary hymn. There were chapels that sang Moody and Sankey (American Evangelists of the 1870s) but they were definitely a minority. The Congregationalists sang Stopford A. Brooke's[2] lovely hymn:

> When the Lord of love was here,
> Happy hearts to him were dear,
> Though his heart was sad
> Worn and lonely for our sake,
> Yet he turned aside to make
> All the weary glad.

It was not in the other books at that time.

Sankey's general emotional and intellectual level can be judged from some of his words:

> 'I would like to die,' said Willie, 'if my papa could die too.
> But he says he isn't ready, 'cos he's got so much to do;
> And my little sister Nellie says that I must surely die,
> And that she and mamma' – then she stopped because it made her cry.

> 'There will be none but the holy – I shall know no more of sin;
> There I'll see mamma and Nellie, for I know he'll let them in;
> But I'll have to tell the angel, when I meet him at the door,
> That he must excuse my papa, 'cos he couldn't leave the store.'

Still lower in the religious scale, a Leeds correspondent thinks, were most of the hymns and songs of the evangelists,

---

[1] John Greenleaf Whittier, 1807–1892, was an American Quaker poet – author of 'The Snow-Bound' and 'The Tent on the Beach' – as well as a great hymn-writer.

[2] Man of letters and Anglican parson who seceded in 1880.

6

Torrey and Alexander. Here Jesus bade us shine with a clear, pure light, like a little candle gleaming in the night and wanted us to be sunbeams to shine for him each day. But the lowest – and the most popular – of all the hymn-books was a collection by someone called Hoyle. These were only sung at such almost irreligious meetings as the Band of Hope. They had most un-hymnlike tunes and the marked rhythms and easy flow of popular songs. One concerned Merry Dick.

> Merry Dick you soon would know
> If you lived in Jackson's Row;
> Each day with a smiling face
> He is ready at his place.
> Should you ever with him meet
> In the shop or in the street,
> You will find him blithe and gay,
> Singing out this merry lay:
>
> My drink is water bright, water bright, water bright;
> My drink is water bright
> From the crystal spring.

The other is a tragic ballad of a small boy sent to fetch his father from the public house:

> Father, dear father, come home with me now,
> The clock in the steeple strikes one;
> You promised, dear father, that you would come home
> As soon as your day's work was done.
> Our fire has gone out, the house is so dark,
> And mother's been watching since tea,
> With poor brother Benny so sick in her arms
> And no one to help her but me.
> Come ho-o-ome, come ho-o-m-e,
> O father, dear father, come home.

Most chapels and churches today have an organ to accompany the singing, but it was not always so. Thomas Hardy's mid-nineteenth-century Dorset church was far from unique in having instrumental ensembles. Indeed at Holmer Green Baptist chapel in Buckinghamshire until 1939 instrumentalists were to be seen taking part, with the harmonium, in ordinary church worship, varying from a single violin or 'cello or flute to a quartet or more. At one point in the 1870s, soon after the chapel had been built, a newspaper even went so far as to make use of Italian jargon to describe the players, and we read of 'W. James (violin primo), T. James (violin secondo), C. Winter (tenore) and D. Dean (violoncello)', the report adding that 'the assistance of the above gentlemen has been one cause of the pleasing fact that this little sanctuary is being attended by friends of all denominations'.

Writing more than sixty years after the event, a stranger from Norwich who had taken part in one of the evening services at Holmer Green about that time recalled that upon the announcement of the first hymn 'a really fine string band, situated in the gallery across the back of the chapel, struck up the tune, and as a musical man I can truthfully say that their playing was an inspiration. I have never forgotten it – it was one of the most helpful services I was ever at, and I have often spoken of it since. The singing I remember was wholehearted and tuneful.'

At Tavistock, Devon, Congregational church, in the mid-nineteenth century there was no organ – but there were three flutes, a violin, a 'cello and a double bass. Hymn-books were dear and in every congregation there were many persons who could not read – so two lines only of each verse were read at a time, then sung.

The inability to read certainly slowed things down. A correspondent writes:

I am now seventy-two and as a boy I lived in a small town in Lincolnshire and was taken (very unwillingly I'm afraid) to a strict Baptist chapel on Sunday afternoons. There was no organ or other musical instrument and each hymn was started by the precentor or clerk, as he was called, striking a tuning fork after reading the first verse of the hymn. This was then sung and the second verse read and sung and so on till the hymn was finally finished. A hymn-book known as Gadsby's was used.

Again, at Bispham, near Blackpool, the singing of the early

Methodists was often led by a 'fiddlers pew', but sometimes, when musicians were not available, by an appointed 'Leader'. Later their worship was led and aided by an American Organ which sufficed until the year 1923, when a pipe organ was installed by the members and congregation.

The band was sometimes a little uncoordinated. As E. E. Kellett writes:

> The band was not always of the highest order, and a musical doctor, called out to a case just before its performance of Jackson's Te Deum, remarked that he was taken away from the evil to come. Some of the hymn tunes, also, were of a peculiar kind, with endless repetitions – it was almost a rule that the last line of every verse should be sung at least twice – nor did the enthusiasm of the congregation invariably make up for the cacophony or for the ridiculous collocations which sometimes occurred.
>
> Old people still recall such grotesqueries as 'And take a pill, and take a pill, and take a pilgrim to the skies', or 'Come down Sal, come down Sal, come down salvation from above'. That such things should have survived a single performance is one of the anomalies which no mass psychology seems able to explain.

Some tunes really played havoc with the words, says the historian of Bethesda Baptist chapel at Ipswich:

> 'My poor pol, my poor pol, my poor polluted soul'
> and 'Stir up my stu, stir up my stu, stir up my stupid soul'
> and best of all,
> 'Oh for a man, oh for a man, oh for a mansion in the sky'.

Chapel bands persisted generally until the early years of the twentieth century. At the Little Mission chapel, Birmingham, from 1896, a correspondent recalls:

> I bought an organ, at least Mr Pritchard helped me in the purchase of it. Eventually he had it in mind to form a string band. We had a violinist when Mr Pritchard was on the clarinet. He found another good violinist. I bought an

old cracked violin from a pawn shop which had been made playable with the application of a little cobbler's wax. Well, I was only a young chap with little pocket money. But I got a good tune out of it. We had some good times together with yours truly playing seconds. The band eventually grew. We now had three violins, a clarinet, piccolo and a double bass.

We had a glorious day at our Sunday School anniversary when the band sat in front of the raised platform of children. The church was packed, even the vestry was packed, and we nearly raised the roof of the little mission. There was no need to make a special appeal for funds; we nearly doubled the collection that year, and we played and sang the hymns twice over.

Instrumentalists were, however, far from universally popular. At the Providence Place Congregational chapel, Cleckheaton, Yorkshire, where in the early nineteenth century services of five or more hours were common, Mr Kidd permitted one Henry Birkley to bring his single bass into the singing pew, but when he proceeded to tune it up, one Joseph Dean, a deacon, rose up in sore bewilderment at the shriek of the unholy fiddle, and crying out in a loud voice, 'If Dagon has come, it is time for me to go,' then walked out of the chapel shaking the dust off his feet, and, putting on another man's hat in his confusion, incontinently departed.

Many players were determined, above all, to make themselves heard. At Wirksworth in Derbyshire there was a certain John Oxspring, the double bass player. Of him it was told that when about to begin that section of 'Messiah' 'Who is the King of Glory?' he remarked 'Hand me the resin to rub my bow and we shall see who is the King of Glory!'

Much talent, nevertheless, lay among the simple chapel musicians. At Talbot Street Independent Congregational chapel, Oldbury, Worcs., around 1914

was a smith working on an anvil as edge tool forger for Brades, famous garden tool experts. His name was Mr Arthur Stringer. Fifty I should think at the time. He was musically-minded and first formed a young people's choir.

At that time you could buy simple four-sheet anthems at about 3d. per copy and we had a number of these.

In addition to this, he was interested in making violins and had actually made and sold several to our young friends, violins and violas. We expanded to a sizeable string band, possibly twelve instruments. I myself played the cornet a little, having had a little training in the Salvation Army as a boy.

The chapel band was the cynosure of many young eyes:

My early years (and until the age of approximately thirty) were spent at Thornton Heath, Surrey (when it really *was* a Heath!). There were two Mission Halls run under a Superintendent – the large one I attended for Sunday School and the secondary one for morning service, where well over 120 children gathered with a few adults.

The music was led by a piano and 'orchestra' of three violins. It was my great delight each Sunday to observe the angles at which the hatpins of the violinists were put, which overlapped the crown of the hat by at least three inches front and three inches back! They always took their places with great dignity and solemnity, followed by the one male violinist, most immaculate in dress!

At the then remote little Primitive chapel at Thornhill Edge, near Dewsbury, Yorkshire, the Ramsden family played violins 'without fee or earthly reward'. Along with Brother John Cave and his 'cello, they formed the first combination of musical instruments to play within this chapel. The brief history of the chapel adds that at a later date it was decided to purchase a 'Seraphine', advertised for sale at Heckmondwike, for the sum of thirteen pounds. This was an instrument with a very small keyboard and could be played only with one hand. Brother Edwin Lodge, son of George Lodge, was the only one who could play this instrument so he became the chapel's first organist:

This innovation started a new era in the history of our Chapel. It was found essential to increase the church's seating capacity and a gallery was erected at a cost of twenty pounds. Later the 'Seraphine' went into retirement and a small pipe organ was purchased from the aforesaid George Lodge for the sum of thirty-two pounds, quite a large sum of money but proved itself worthy of the cost. 'Progress' has become the watchword and talk is rife with the demand for a new and larger church.

At the same small chapel such was the musical enthusiasm that a brass band was started which had its origin in the church.

How long it had been in existence I cannot say, but this I know, those who were associated with it were no mean players. By 1900–1904, the brass band went out of existence – to be replaced by an orchestra known as the 'Christian Brethren Brass and Reed Band', having Messrs Ezra Lodge and John William Summerscales as joint conductors, the number of players being thirty-six, all instrumentalists of no mean order.

Please do not think that those who were in authority had more thought for music than the saving of souls, this not being the case.

The progression from band to organ could be expensive. At Zion Congregational, Flockton, Yorkshire:

In days when organs were not so common nor so magnificent in places of worship as now [about 1900], the singing was accompanied by string and wind instruments. Towards the close of the old dispensation at Flockton these instrumentalists were a diminishing quantity and the consideration of procuring an organ forced itself upon the members of the church.

It was rather an interesting negotiation, and we have the story from the mouth of one who actually participated in the affair. Several gentlemen were despatched to Sheffield to see one that had been taken out of a chapel there and placed in a warehouse. It looked a rum affair, but it was probably as good as they might expect for the sum they were prepared to give.

When it came to the question of bidding for it, the senior members of the deputation were afraid to hazard a sum, but the youngest member was bold enough to say £15. Fancy £15 for a chapel organ! His companions were well-nigh disgusted with what they considered almost a mean offer. Even the parson at a meeting subsequently, sarcastically remarked, and in a deep voice, 'the idea; bidding £15 for an organ!'

No wonder they failed to get the instrument there and then, but eventually the owners accepted the price, and the organ was duly installed in a loft specially provided for it. Of course it required considerable repairs, but it served the church for many years.

The musical personalities of chapel – and their eccentricities – were closely observed and remembered. At Hampstead for example the choral portion of the services was directed by a gentleman who sat in the large table pew under the pulpit and who gave the keynote upon a little flageolet which he appeared to blow surreptitiously under cover of the table. The honour of conductorship was conferred upon him in consequence of his musical reputation, he being a very fair performer upon various instruments and tutor to many young Hampsteadians:

To us juveniles, however, these accomplishments were quite eclipsed by his capacity for the vast quantity of snuff he consumed during the service. Previous to this latter musical arrangement, however, I remember that, quite early in the 1840s, some ancient musicians sat in the west gallery and played upon weird old-world instruments under the leadership of Mr C. The introduction of a harmonium in the late 1850s was looked upon as a not altogether desirable innovation by many of the older members.

There was no mistake as to the heartiness of the singing of the congregation. This, however, was characterised more by its enthusiasm than by its correctness for time and harmony. One lady, indeed, a fair *blanchisseuse* (washerwoman) of the town who possessed a very powerful and very high soprano voice, excelled, and in her zeal outsang everybody. Especially was this the case in her favourite hymn, where the refrain 'Crown Him',[1] occurred with frequent repetition, and the way she mounted to and sustained the upper C was marvellous.

The idiosyncrasies of organ players – and of the censors of the hymns – is brought out by a correspondent now (1971) well over ninety years of age. He was born in the village of Messingham, Lincolnshire, a pillar of the Wesleyan Methodist chapel. ('It was not called a church in my early days.') When he was twenty, i.e. in 1900, he went to live at Tuxford, Notts:

There was a very musical family there and on the very second Sunday I was at Chapel and they had me in the choir. There was a fine pipe organ and a very capable player. He was only about twenty years of age, and he would have amused you with the theatrical ways he attacked some of the hymn tunes. I especially remember two. Dr Isaac Watts's[2] hymn 'Sweet is the work, my God, my King' contained this verse: 'Fools never raise their thoughts so high, Like brutes they live, like brutes they die, Like grass they flourish till thy breath, Blasts them in everlasting death.' (This verse is regrettably omitted from hymn-books published in the twentieth century. The sentiment is, perhaps, too harsh for modern stomachs.) Well, Richard would start off this very loud, then gradually reduce his stops and volume of tone until he reached the last verse: 'Blasts them' and ceased playing, leaving choir and congregation to sing unaccompanied. He then came in full blast for the next verse.
　Another hymn by Dr Watts, 'God is the refuge of his saints, when storms of sharp distress invade', has a verse thus: 'Let mountains from their seats be hurled, Down to the deep and buried there – Convulsions shake the solid world, Our faith shall never yield to fear.'
　When this hymn came along, Richard would have made you jump, if you had been there. He would put his both

---

[1] The hymn was 'All hail the power of Jesu's name' by Edward Perronet (1726–92).
[2] Isaac Watts (1674–1748), a Congregationalist pastor in London, wrote beautiful and popular hymns, such as 'O God, our help in ages past', 'When I survey the wondrous cross', and 'Jesus shall reign where'er the sun'.

hands flat on the keyboard, also both feet across as many pedals as possible until the organ gave out an awful noise as the mountains were hurled down and the 'convulsions shook the world'.

As I have gone about, I have met with various types of organists in village chapels, one of whom was 'as deaf as a post' as the saying goes.

Organists were an eccentric breed. At Billinge, Lancashire, Teddy Webster was the first organist who used his own harmonium. To prevent anyone else using it, he used to stuff it with newspapers, so that no one other than himself could play it. The harmonium was carried around when members went carol-singing.

At a Sheffield chapel when a regular organist could not turn up through illness or other reason, the deputy took over. He was a very small man in every way and he had a tendency to play hymns either too fast or too slow:

On one Sabbath morn the hymn chosen was 'Now thank we all our God' and the organist set about it like a Sousa march. My father gave a very loud 'Ahem' to attract his brother's attention in the pew across, extra loud to indicate his intention of slowing down the tempo. Both had strident tenor voices which they let loose now at maximum volume at *half* the organist's tempo.

As children witnessing this exhibition we were not a little embarrassed at the resulting commotion when the organist turned round to see what was going on and nearly fell off his stool in the effort! From the looks of the congregation anybody might think we kids had made off with the Sacrament wine! Incidentally, the organist resumed at his old pace.

No less autocratic was the organist at the Mint Methodist church, Exeter. Mr John Callaway Guest was, in April 1843, asked 'to preside at the organ for the next three months' but remained (unpaid) organist for fifty years. He must have been difficult to deal with at times for his son wrote: 'Between the lessons, announced or not, the choir and organ started off whatever they intended to perform and the parson had to give in.'

Organs in those distant days were not blown by electricity. Someone had to pump a handle. The oddities of organ-blowing and blowers are described by a Leeds correspondent, himself an organist:

> Percy blew the organ by pumping a long handle up and down and the amount of air at the player's disposal was indicated by a small lead weight suspended at the end of a tatty piece of string which rose and fell as the air reservoir emptied and filled. He was a good deal older than I was and, in spite of his sacred function, was generally regarded as a good-natured bad lot. He walked as if he were always sore; he never seemed quite thoroughly washed; he was dark-complexioned and his features, in some vague way which I'd never defined to myself, seemed misdirected and ugly. He had badly spaced, black teeth and carried round with him a faint and unpleasant smell. Among my age group he had the reputation of being and the status which belonged to a persistent fornicator.

At Mount Tabor Wesleyan church, Halifax:

> A minor part in the music matters was played by the organ blower. There was considerable competition for this job among the older boys of the school, possibly because of the slight remuneration which it carried with it. Some of them made their mark at their work, as initials carved in the woodwork bear witness. The post became a memory in 1932 when electric lighting was introduced and an electric blower installed.

Electrical blowers had their disadvantages at least to certain young people in a Sheffield chapel:

> The arrival of an electric pressure-blower for the organ broke up a regular Sunday evening pontoon school in the organ loft. Four young men from the Young Men's Class were 'volunteered' to blow the organ in the evening service because 'Blow Wild', the statutory blower, had succumbed.

Blow Wild was what we should call today a grown-up backward boy and he knew all about keeping the bellows full and in fact knew the job. The four young men (I was one on two occasions) played good pontoon (if there is such a thing) between hymns taking turns about for each hymn. Between, the cards were out and a natty gambling game proceeded.

Suddenly the organist would give a loud kick on the boards for wind for the next hymn. Whoever's turn it was would leap up from the card table, knocking all the cards and winnings flying in his anxiety to get to the bellows and the other three would pick up his cards and pocket his winnings and willingly start the hand again.

At many chapels it was regarded as a great honour to become a member of the choir — and some of the rules were strict in Victorian times. This is a typical example:

CHOIR RULES

That we have a Choir Committee which shall consist of the Choir-master, Secretary, Treasurer, Organist, and one representative of each voice.

That each member of the choir shall pay 2d. per month for membership.

That we have a rehearsal every Thursday evening unless notice is given to the contrary.

That rehearsals begin at 7.30 p.m. and members' names be called over and attendances marked.

Any member who cannot attend rehearsal or services through illness must acquaint the Choir-master or Organist to obtain their mark.

All fine money to go towards Annual Trip.

Any members absenting themselves from rehearsals or coming more than fifteen minutes late shall be fined one penny, unless they can give a valid excuse.

Any members absenting themselves three consecutive Sundays are expected to send an excuse to the Choir-master, failing which they shall no longer be considered members of the choir.

No person shall be allowed to become a member of the choir until his voice has been tested.

Any members absenting themselves on any special occasion to be fined 6d. unless they have a valid excuse.

The Choir-master and Organist to select all music.[1]

The choir itself, in which so many could take part – even if their voices and musical knowledge were mediocre – was a great object of admiration. A Halifax correspondent writes:

My chief interest has always been in the choir. As a small boy I admired James Gardiner above all, and longed to sing like him; wear a wing collar, and have eyeglasses. I had just been accepted for the choir when we moved to Sowerby and I came the seven or eight miles each Sunday to take my place beside the man I admired. Later I was to take his place both there and as a paid singer at Northgate End.

Hymn-singing was not purely an inside-chapel activity. There was carolling at Christmas and, as a former deaconess recalls from about 1914, when their Dorking, Surrey, minister, the Rev. J. H. Hopkins, came to conduct a mission, on the Saturday evening the congregation went round the town singing – stopping at each public house for a talk. They gained a following and ended at church for a service at midnight.

The singing and playing in chapels was not confined to hymns nor even to purely religious music. Quite small chapels such as the Congregational at Elland in Yorkshire produced Handel's 'Samson' and 'Judas Maccabaeus', and Mendelssohn's 'St Paul' in the 1920s. Burlington Baptists at Ipswich gave Elgar's 'For the Fallen' in 1916. At Barrow-in-Furness Methodist New Connexion chapel:

In 1917 when I was fifteen I became a member of the choir for which there was a long waiting list, but I was learning the piano and church organ with the organist and I still remember the first work I practised in (as tenor): this was Arthur Sullivan's 'Festival Te Deum'. One anthem I

[1] This rule sometimes, as was hinted above, caused clashes with the minister or local preacher.

recollect from that period, and a great favourite of mine was 'A Day in Thy Courts'.

Early in 1923 we moved to Burnley in East Lancashire. The chapel I joined wasn't large but we had a big choir and our organist-cum-choir-master was William Smith, a splendid bass who often sang on the wireless from Manchester. Here I got a real education in oratorio and cantata.

All the local churches vied with one another in having the most famous singers for our oratorios – invariably given at our festivals and annual choir weekends. We sometimes had outside soloists for a Saturday night concert, but generally managed this ourselves. A performance with Isobel Baillie, Gladys Ripley or Kathleen Ferrier, Muriel Brunskill or Frank Mullings, Edward Lloyd or Robert Radford or Norman Allin was something to remember.

Here I participated in oratorios such as Handel's 'Alexander's Feast', 'Israel in Egypt', 'Judas Maccabaeus' (a great favourite), 'Samson' and our almost invariable yearly performance of 'Messiah'. We often joined a local Church of England in a yearly Easter performance of John Stainer's 'Crucifixion'.

Other cantatas were 'Ruth' (A. R. Gaul), 'Holy City' (Gaul), 'Olivet to Calvary' (J. H. Maunder) and the beautiful cantata 'Bethlehem' (J. H. Maunder), 'A Song of Thanksgiving' (J. H. Maunder), 'Daughter of Jairus' (John Stainer), 'Golden Legend' (A. S. Sullivan).[1]

One mustn't forget the great 'Elijah' (Mendelssohn) and 'The Creation' (J. Haydn). Another well-loved cantata was 'The New Jerusalem' (T. Mee Pattison).

There were other variations on 'making a joyful noise unto the Lord':

I commenced playing at Sunday School and for Divine service at the age of eleven. In this village of Hasland, near Chesterfield, two Methodist chapels sprang up in the 1890s (one, so my mother says, for the 'pit officials' and the other for

---

[1] Other such were 'The Day of Rest' (John S. Witty), 'The Home at Bethany' (Arthur Berridge), and 'The Prince of Peace' (Arthur J. Jamouneau).

the railway families who had moved from Gloucester and Northamptonshire in the agricultural depression and found work on the newly-expanding railways). These were Primitive and Wesleyan respectively.[1]

Our village also had a prize silver band and this was linked in a way with 'our' Wesleyan chapel, owing to the fact that the Primitives had 'a pipe organ and proper pews' and the Wesleyans had a harmonium. On the occasion of the Sunday School anniversary, members of the band would be invited to 'help with the music' and any local violinist, 'cellist, clarinettist etc. would also come along.

Action songs, in which the singers moved with their hands and arms in time to, and as approximate illustration of, the words, were popular. So were cantatas such as 'King of Glory' by Fred W. Peace – a composer well known in his native Yorkshire – 'Olivet to Calvary' by Maunder, Stainer's 'Crucifixion' and Gaul's 'Ruth'.

The great singing event in almost every chapel was 'Messiah', given before Christmas. One correspondent writing about her chapel life fifty or sixty years ago:

I was brought up in the Wesleyan faith at a Pennine village near Rochdale in Lancashire. My father was the choir-master and sometimes the organist as well. There were several special services in the year beginning with an anthem for Easter, Chapel anniversary, Sunday School anniversary, choir sermons, harvest festival and lastly Christmas. In between were often rallies with other churches, special services for missions, home and abroad, and revival campaigns – these latter noted for the hearty singing of Moody and Sankey hymns.

At Christmas would be performances of the whole, or part of the 'Messiah' when choir members would assist each other at local churches to augment the usual choir. I've sung in as many as seven 'Messiahs' on consecutive Sundays in Wesleyan Methodist, Primitives and Baptist churches, where we would be entertained to tea at members' houses, returning this hospitality at our own performance.

[1] This was unusual: Wesleyans were normally top Nonconformist dogs.

There were comic aspects of these performances, as noted by a Sheffield correspondent:

At Christmas time 'Messiah' would be performed in one or other of the chapels in the district and voices would be summoned from all around to make up the chorus. Mostly the principals would be locals and splendid voices some of them had too.

On one occasion I was prevailed upon to join the basses and, as the trumpeter rose to his feet for 'The trumpet shall sound', emptied the 'gravy' from the tap on his instrument, and with relish rubbed the mouthpiece round his lips, a contralto below me was heard to say: 'By gum, look at 'im – I bet 'e can kiss!'

When the 'Amen' chorus came and all stood up, the bass next to me carefully removed his top denture with his handkerchief and pocketed it, explaining that he had on a previous occasion lost it among the contraltos below when singing 'A – ah – ah – men' too loud and too long!

From time to time there would be singings of solos and anthems during the service. For a number of years my sister and myself suffered to hear the leading soprano letting go at anything her husband, the organist, put in front of her. There are those who know they can't sing, those that can sing and won't, and those that don't know they can't sing but WILL. She was one.

After a collection one Sunday the preacher announced that Mr B – (one of the basses) would sing a solo from 'Judas Maccabaeus', 'Arm, arm ye brave'. His trouble was that he couldn't pitch a note himself. In this aria the organ plays a couple of staves of introduction and the soloist is left to pitch the first 'Arm, arm ye brave' by himself. The introduction was played and there followed a long embarrassing silence when the soloist whispered loudly 'Gie us t'nooat, 'Arry, gie us t'nooat!'

But, even in early days, some of the choral events were quite magnificent. At Lumb chapel, near Rossendale, Lancs. in mid-century the Sunday School 'Charity' took place on the second Sunday in June:

Months of preparation were necessary; the choir must learn new anthems, each more intricate than the last; the players must spend hours rehearsing their accompaniments; the scholars must be taught their special hymns, a duty generally undertaken by one of the 'Layrocks'. When the long-awaited day arrived the girls from the Sunday School, arrayed in their best frocks, were arranged on a special platform, rising tier upon tier, from the singing pew almost to the top of the pulpit, and any of the boys who were considered specially proficient were pushed into the singing pew, along with the choir and the players. Thomas Newbigging in his *History of Rossendale* has a vivid description of Lumb 'Charity'. 'The impression produced upon my mind by a visit paid some years ago, in the month of June, to Lumb chapel, on the occasion of the anniversary services there, will not be easily effaced from my memory. It was quite a field day among the "Deghyn Layrocks" and they mustered in strength as though bent on maintaining the reputation they had acquired for their musical display.'

The singers' gallery was thronged to excess. In the forefront was a dazzling row of buxom girls with ruddy faces and sparkling eyes, the picture of that rosy health which the fresh and bracing air of the hillside alone imparts, and were all decked out in bonnets newly trimmed with artificial flowers and ribbons of the brightest hue, in every variety of colour and arrangement. Neither in their other apparel was there any lack of neatness. Many of the girls displayed superior taste, and of dressing in a manner approaching to elegance.

Behind the girls were the males of every age – from the youthful tyro to the hoary and spectacled patriarchs of the valley; and in the rear with scarcely room to exert their powers were the instrumentalists, amongst whom the fiddlers, large and small, predominated. The mellow flute and the clarinet had their representatives, and dotted here and there might be seen a brass instrument, reflecting the bright sunshine that gleamed through the windows of the humble edifice.

It may indicate a want of taste on my part, but I confess to having experienced a pang of regret that the old-fashioned instruments at Lumb chapel have been supplanted by the

7

more fashionable, but also more formal organ: 'Old times are changed, old manners gone!'

I entered just as the musicians were completing the tuning of their instruments, and found the chapel crowded in every part. Soon the minister ascended the pulpit, and opened the service by giving out the noble hymn of Dr Watts: 'Come let us join our cheerful songs.'

The tune selected by the choir was 'Nativity' and with a precision which long practice had rendered easy, and which Charles Hallé himself would have admired had he been there to listen, the whole body of singers and instrumentalists struck briskly off into the fine old lilting measure, the deep bass and manly voices alternating with the treble and alto of the lesser instruments, and the sweet clear silver tones of the females in the frequent repetition of the lines.

With reverent voice the minister then perused the 'Sacred Volume', his lucid comments enforcing the truth of 'Holy Writ', and with marvellous power bringing home the Bible narrative experience of our common humanity. Not less impressive and effective was the earnest prayer spoken in that homely vigorous Saxon, which needed no interpreter, and which is powerful to touch the heart. The hymn which followed the prayer was one familiar to many of my readers.

> God of the seas, Thy thundering voice
> Makes all the roaring seas rejoice,
> And one soft word of Thy command
> Can sink them silent on the sand.

This was sung to 'Glad Tidings' (composed by one of the first members, Robert Ashworth).

But the great treat of the afternoon was when, the sermon being concluded, the 'Hallelujah Chorus' was given by the choir. The fervent, enthusiastic countenances of the men, many of whom were awkward and even clownish in their dress and appearance, contrasted finely with the less serious, but not less earnest and expressive faces of the female portion of the rural choir as the grand anthem 'within no walls confined' rose heavenwards to the Great Eternal, who is the subject of its strain. Nor was the singing limited to the choir; the majority of the congregation were familiar with the song, and loud hallelujahs filled the House of the Lord, lifting them upwards in thought and feelings.

The choir itself was not numerically large, but it compensated for smallness of numbers in eagerness, richness of tone and general musical ability. The leader from the formation of the church, until his death in 1860, was James Ashworth of Spring Gardens, Dean, one of the 'Deghyn Layrocks' known as James o' Roberts, and he was succeeded by John Hargreaves of Water.

The most prominent amongst the sopranos was Susie Ashworth, the daughter of James Ashworth, known best as 'Susie o' owd James', who set the tunes at the prayer meetings, helped to train the children, and, as one old scholar remarked, 'sang her way through life to glory'. Another of the singers was Jenny Haworth of Clough, who led the contralto part for a long number of years. Amongst the men were John Ashworth and Lawrence Lord, both of whom helped in the bass pew.

But the most outstanding figure was Henry Whittle, one of the members transferred from Goodshaw in 1828. He belonged to a musical family well known in the Cliviger district, and was said by some to be the sweetest tenor ever heard. On one occasion he walked all the way to Manchester, just to 'have a look at "Samson"' and on his death in 1886 he was carried shoulder high over the hills to be buried at his old church at Goodshaw.

Midway between sacred and secular came the 'Service of Song'. This involved the reading of a story of an edifying though not necessarily religious flavour, with breaks for choir or soloist to sing more or less appropriate anthems or hymns. They were usually performed on Sunday afternoons in a period *c.* 1870 to 1930. One correspondent remembers reading the stories and 'very often they would make me cry as they were always so sad. The choir would sing the appropriate music and the story would be read by a good elocutionist. If you had a good weep I suppose it would be considered to be a good service and enjoyed by all.'

The words were not always very distinguished – indeed they

have mainly vanished. A Cranbrook, Kent, correspondent writes:

I have found the titles of some services of song which were performed at the chapel during the 1880s: 'Babes in the Basket', 'Pilgrim's Progress', 'Little Dot', 'Jessica's First Prayer', 'Given in charge'. The service of song went out of fashion. The last on my list, and the only one of which I have memory, is 'Little Abe' of which one number was: 'She sleeps in the valley so sweet', referring no doubt to Little Abe's mother.

One such service of song story was 'Dick's Fairy': A Service of Sacred Song, compiled by I. A. Edgar, from the popular story by Rev. Silas K. Hocking, F.R.H.S. (Price 4d., 3s. 4d. per dozen, post free.)

The story concerns a runaway child, Fairy, who was 'apprenticed' to Mrs Limber, in the fairground business. Dick finds her and takes her to good horny-handed son of toil, Luther, who has lost his faith. Luther pretends to be a private detective and visits Mrs Limber.

Dick makes and sells 'church weather glasses'. Fairy turns out to be his sister but vanishes again. Dick seeks her out. At the circus again, she has an accident. He ends up in a Birmingham hospital after a cab accident. She is blind.

They return to Luther's. Her sight returns. Though she had remained cheerful, only now does she sing again: 'an old hymn she had learned at the ragged school' ('Away my needless fears').

Luther recovers his faith: 'My heart's near bustin' up for very thankfulness . . . I thank thee for her blindness now. It's been a blessing to us all, but chiefly to me.' Before returning that night they had what Luther called a 'tyro' (trio) – 'Hark the glad sound.'

Four years pass. Fairy goes to school. Dick patents new toys and makes money. They move with a failing Luther into the country, near Manchester. Luther asks her to sing 'The Better Land' (Mrs Hemans, music by Frederick Cowen). He dies.

And Fairy and Dick live happily ever after: 'He thinks she grows more beautiful every day; while Fairy thinks there is no man in the world to be compared to her brother, and so is quite happy in his love. What the future may bring, we cannot tell; that we must leave.'

And so to 'Hark! The Vesper hymn is stealing.'

Secular concerts with solos – vocal and instrumental, recitations – comic or pathetic, and playlets, often in dialect, were given by some but not all chapels. At Redditch, Worcestershire Methodist chapel a playlet called 'A Village Wedding' (no author named) had the following characters:

'Bridesmaids Miss Sally Squirt and Rosy Budd. Best Man, Mr I. B. Windy. Parson, Rev. Sam Skippet. Squire, B. E. Barmy. Oldest inhabitant, Grandpa Willi Snuffit. Aunts, Annie Underdone and Matilda Mildew. Schoolmarm, Miss G. Ography. Grandma Gertcha. Postmistress, Miss Lilian Lickem. At the piano, Professor Rattle. In charge of refreshments, Madam Tuck, Mrs D. O. Nutt, Miss Sal Tarna.'

During the interval wedding cake was sold for chapel funds.

Whether the congregation of Bates Hill Methodist chapel at Redditch found the names entirely tasteful is not recorded.

Some chapels formed concert parties in the early years of the nineteenth century. The Hollins (Millgate) Methodist concert party was intended to provide an interesting outlet for the activities of the younger members of the church and, at the same time, to yield some financial benefit to the Church funds. After the production by the young ladies of the operetta 'Princess Chrysanthemum', the young men were invited to join them in their efforts, and the first performance, which was of a miscellaneous character, proved a success. Subsequently numerous other successful concerts were given in the schoolroom, and as a result the party was invited to appear at various Sunday Schools in the district. For these visits the party made a small charge which covered expenditure and made possible donations to the Church funds.

Dancing, however, was barred. Evangelicals generally were opposed to it as dangerous to morality. John Wesley allowed some exceptions: he had no objection to dancing provided it was of men with men, women with women, by daylight and out of doors. In 1917, a correspondent recalls:

In those days, of course, dancing was not allowed in the Wesleyan chapel nor any make-up for the concerts, and I well remember during one Sunday School concert, although we were allowed to 'dress-up' we had to depict tableaux but were not allowed to move because of our costumes.

The question of dancing was hotly debated at Lumb chapel, Rossendale, as its history recalls:

There was no definite church rule which could be enforced, and for six months the question continued to be discussed at the monthly church meetings. In September 1890 the Church proclaimed its attitude in the following terms, 'Knowing that practice of dancing in vogue among us tends to feed and develop our baser passions, which we are expressly commanded to crucify, and that dancing is therefore inimical to the growth of our spiritual life and the teaching and spirit of the gospel; we as a Church pledge ourselves prayerfully and in the spirit of Christ to warn our young members of this evil, and to seek to win them from it, and the evils of dancing are of such a nature that in the spiritual interests of the Church we resolve that those who persistently adhere to this evil practice be excluded from our fellowship.' In consequence of this resolution it was subsequently decided to forbid dancing in the British school.

Lumb was rather severe. In March 1885 some members roundly condemned cricket and football clubs. Then another vexing problem arose:

In the summer of 1892 the Rawtenstall Corporation were making arrangements for the lease of a piece of land in the centre of the town for the building of a theatre. There was more agreement amongst the members on this question with the result that a protest was sent to the Corporation asking for the withdrawal of the proposal for this lease, because 'it was against the spirit of Sunday School and religious work, and therefore could not have that elevating influence which the borough ought ever to seek'.

Also barred was card-playing. As E. E. Kellett[1] remembered, however, there were some evasions:

[1] *As I Remember*, p. 119.

It was rarely that parents thrashed their children; prayer was more efficacious than the rod recommended by Solomon; but card-playing was regarded as one of the cases in which the *ultima ratio* was fully justified.

There were, however, means of evading the prohibition. I knew an Evangelical minister, no mean artist, who adorned a pack of cards with really beautiful pictures of flowers, in four colours. The rose was the Queen, the tulip the King. So long as this pack was exclusively used, whist was permitted in his house.

I seem to remember, however, that 'diamonds' and 'hearts' were words never heard; and that 'trump' was carefully avoided – possibly on the ground suggested by J. K. Stephen, that the note of the last trump is presumably 'D' natural.

Such subterfuges were, however, rare. I knew a man who was a passionate devotee both of whist and of chess. He became a leader of a class of young men, and – after a painful struggle – gave up both games as an example to his lads; for though he felt they were harmless to him, he feared they might prove snares to them. St Paul's remark about the weak brother weighed strongly with him. The same feeling prevailed about billiards – for which indeed there was little opportunity except in public-houses.

Yet despite such inhibitions – and, *pace* the shade of Kellett, I doubt whether chess was generally forbidden – the Nonconformists, or most of them were far from taking the pleasures open to them at all sadly. There were and are long, unsmiling faces in all religions; it is unlikely that, for instance, the Exclusive Brethren formed concert parties or put on dialect playlets. But for most Nonconformists life was full of fun. Sustained by a simple faith, happy in the friendship of Chapel, they entered with gusto into a far from narrow social life.

And always they sang, in and out of Chapel, at home, in fields and on hillsides. One fine, calm Wednesday, 23 June 1858, aboard the 'New Powerful, Fast sailing and commodious Steamboat "Robert Airey",' the members and friends of the Salem chapel, Jarrow, were on their annual excursion to the fine beaches and ruined castle of Warkworth. ('N.B. No intoxicating drinks allowed on board.')

With them went a choir and a band who performed selections from 'Handel, Mozart, Kidd, Fawcett, Beethoven, etc.' The sea was tranquil, the music's tones were sweet and, though the party started out at 5 a.m., 'everyone appeared to enjoy' the outing.

What could be more delectable than to sit on deck on a fine June morning watching the incomparable coastline of Northumberland slowly passing by while the choir sang the 'Hallelujah Chorus' and the band played the overture to 'Figaro'? *Douceur de vivre* indeed – and 'Fare there and back, one shilling'.

LOVE FEASTS, FESTIVALS, MAGIC LANTERNS

Take my life and let it be
Consecrated, Lord, to Thee . . .
Take my lips, and let them be
Filled with messages from Thee . . .
Take my silver and my gold;
Not a mite would I withhold,
Take my intellect, and use
Every power as Thou shalt choose.

F. R. Havergal (1836–79).

The Nonconformists as a whole – there were exceptions – were prolific in activities, religious, semi-religious and social, outside Divine Service which took place at least twice a day on Sunday (and sometimes, as at Paddington chapel, Divine Service on a week-night too). There were prayer meetings, love feasts, class meetings (among the Methodists), Pleasant Saturday Nights, Pleasant Sunday Afternoons, 'Men's Own', Christian Endeavours, Wesley Guild, Bright Hours, anniversaries, jubilees, Young Men's Mutual Improvement Societies, Mothers' Meetings, Infants' Friend Societies, Dorcas Societies,[1] Girls' Sunbeam Societies, Bands of Hope, lectures and lantern lectures, Flower Girls' missions, and bazaars.

In fact, for the chapelgoer the hours of leisure were fully booked as this programme for a typical week in June 1913 at the Paddington chapel shows:

Sunday: Divine Service at 11 a.m. and Young People's service – First Sunday evening of each month followed by the social hour. Sunday School at 10 a.m. and 3 p.m. Bible classes at 3.15 p.m. *Monday:* Mothers' meeting 2.30 p.m. Girls' Guild

[1] Object: 'providing of clothing to assist the deserving poor.' Dorcas, Acts ix, 36: 'this woman was full of good works and alms deeds which she did.' She was revived from the dead by St Peter.

8 p.m. *Wednesday:* Divine Service at 8 p.m. Women's Prayer
Meeting, 7.15 p.m., Band of Hope, 6.30 p.m., Branch Work at
Portman Hall, 53 & 55 Carlisle Street; Mission Hall, 111 &
113 Earl Street; and the L.C.C. school, Capland street.
Thursday: Boys' Brigade. *Friday:* Christian Endeavour
Society. Junior 6.54 p.m. Senior 8.15 p.m. Young Men's
Own 8 p.m.[1]

Such events required considerable organisation and chapels
had, in some cases, the panoply of officers we now associate with
large companies. In 1906, the Islington Central Wesleyan
mission in Liverpool Road had a President (the minister),
Vice-president and a general secretary. Other secretaries dealt
with the Roll, the magazine 'Look Out', Devotional, Literary,
Christian service, Social and Musical, Refreshment and Decorative, Lanternist, Photographer and Foreign Missions – all with
committees. 'Literary' incidentally presented in that year 'An
evening with Longfellow'. There was a lecture on the Sandwich
Islands; A Continental Tour (with lantern); Dante; a lecture by
a Pastor of the Flower Girls' Mission—and a note 'Punctuality
is the soul of business'. Meetings were at 8.15 (most people in
those days did not finish work until 7 or 7.30 p.m.).

Some of this socio-religious activity was intended to deal with
a problem. We read in the history of Lumb-with-Rossendale
chapel:

> In the last decade of the nineteenth century another prob-
> lem began to harass the Church – the problem as to how far it
> was to control the outside interests of its members. This
> question was largely the result of the improvement in the
> social conditions of the factory workers who formed the bulk
> of the population of Lumb. The Factory Acts had gradually
> lessened the risks of factory life and shortened the hours of
> labour; the Public Health Acts aided by local municipal
> enterprise had improved conditions of life and given more
> opportunities for the enjoyment of the added hours of freedom.
> The higher standard of living and the increased leisure of the
> people led to a demand for the provision of amusements.
> Public parks and athletic grounds were laid out; theatres,

[1] From *Paddington Monthly*, June 1913.

music halls and dancing rooms were built, and with them came a host of new difficulties to be dealt with. In a small village like Lumb, still cut off to a large extent from the world outside and communicating with neighbouring towns only by horse-drawn buses, at long intervals, where a visit to the theatre meant a walk of five miles, these problems did not assume such vital importance as in the more populous centres.

The object was to provide under the aegis of the chapel alternative leisure activities. Not all even of the most innocent-seeming secular pastimes met with approval from all chapels:

As early as March 1885 the influence of cricket and football had been discussed at length, and clubs of this kind had been condemned in strong terms by some of the members.

How far, indeed, was Chapel 'to attempt to control the outside interests of its members'? If, for example, you joined the Islington Wesleyan Mission chapel in 1906–7, and became an active member you were required to pledge that:

I will earnestly endeavour, in the strength of Christ, to live a truly Christian life, to read the Holy Scriptures, and attend to the duty of private prayer. I will attend my class with regularity, and fulfil to the best of my ability my duties as a Member of the Christian Church. Whenever possible, I will be present at the Devotional Meeting of the Guild, and take an active part in the proceedings, if desired.

You could become a companion member, in which case the pledge was somewhat attenuated, at least in length:

I will try to avoid in my daily life anything that would bring discredit upon myself or upon the Church of Christ, and will do my best to maintain the friendly spirit of the Guild.

While as a mere associate member, all you pledged was:

Forgetting the things which are behind and stretching forward to the things which are before, I press on towards the goal unto the prize of the high calling of God in Jesus Christ [Phil. iii. 13–14].

The manual for Paddington chapel 1911, shows that the members' attendance was closely watched:

> All church members are supplied with tickets, to be put into the plate when the collection is made at the communion service. By this means a careful record is preserved of the attendance of each member. If by some means the right ticket is lost, please put a card or slip of paper, with the name of the communicant written upon it. This is very important.

One of the most ancient observances among the Methodists was the love feast, possibly of Moravian origin, which the two Wesleys and George Whitefield partook of in Fetter Lane, London, as early as 1739. The love feast was, in fact, a surrogate Last Supper and has been traced beyond Christ himself to totemism. There may have been much love but there was very little feasting. To eat was 'specially made bread' (possibly, as with the Jews, unleavened bread) and for drink, cold water or tea. This antique rite – it vanished from Methodism in the early decades of the twentieth century – was essentially an occasion for extempore prayer and 'witness', i.e. how the individual had been 'brought over', 'saved for the Lord' or otherwise converted.

The history of Mount Tabor Methodist chapel at Halifax, 1820–1920, records:

> The love feasts at which members of the congregation gave their testimony to the power of God in their lives were also times of great blessing. An unusual feature of these meetings was the partaking of refreshment. Two large cups of water and baskets containing buns were passed round. At one time admittance was obtained only by the production of the ticket of church membership. So popular were these services that the chapel gallery where they were held was usually crowded to overflowing. Collections were made for the poor of the district.

G. Sutcliffe, who belonged to this same chapel from 1891 onwards, writes that love feasts were in those days held on the first Sunday of the month in place of the normal evening service. No preacher in charge. Class[1] leaders responsible.

[1] See below, page 114 f.

Hymns and choruses often struck up by some person in the pews – popular ones included 'There are angels hovering round' with reference to Mary and Martha having just gone along. Testimonies and prayers were made as those participating felt led.

During the meeting two large porcelain drinking cups inscribed with the words 'Love Feast' were passed from pew to pew each person present drinking from them of the water they contained. A shallow basket of buns was also passed round.

Water was mandatory, buns were not. At the chapel at Mytholmroyd, Yorkshire, after the opening by hymn and prayer and lessons, the stewards went down the aisles handing out Ratifa[1] biscuits which were in baskets and following would come the cup of water. The cups had two handles, some had three, and had 'Love Feast' on them.

An elderly Methodist from Sheffield writes of the pleasure, followed by disappointment, he found in this now forgotten chapel activity:

> I remember the joy I felt when the plan announced love feast instead of the usual evening service. After the opening, the meeting was thrown open for any member of the congregation to stand up, give his or her experience; start a favourite hymn in which we all joined; read or quote a passage of scripture; or 'offer a few words in prayer'. There was no difficulty in hearing what was said except for the loud cries of 'Hallelujah', 'Glory be to God' etc., during which it was sometimes hard to hear anything. But our joy reached its pinnacle when two elderly people rose at the same time, probably rather deaf and short-sighted, and we had the dialogue continued for several minutes.
>
> But the feast was a flop. It gave us no pleasure to eat a morsel of dry bread and drink cold water.

There were other objections. A Wirksworth Nonconformist, after noting that love feasts were symbolic of the Last Supper, cubes of bread being distributed, with drinks of water from a

---

[1] Perhaps this was the small macaroon called ratafia.

mug, asks 'Not very hygienic, was it?' Almost certainly *not* hygienic in days when typhoid, cholera, and tuberculosis were still rife. Yet chapels – and churches – long continued to take communion wine from one vessel the rim of which in some cases was perfunctorily wiped by the minister as it passed from one communicant to the next. Many churches still do. Others later on substituted individual tiny glasses, inserted into holes in a tray.

Love feasts were a sort of surrogate communion or sacrament, in the sense that they were celebrated in water rather than wine. The use of wine increasingly agitated chapels in the late nineteenth century after the preaching of total abstinence and the formation of Bands of Hope – to which in early days there was opposition, even to the point where hooligans broke up the meetings. But at a meeting of the Mursley Baptist church, Bletchley, on 10 November 1880 it was agreed by all present that in future the wishes of those members who objected to drinking fermented wine at the Lord's Supper, should be met by the introduction of unfermented wine which would be handed round in a cup which had been provided by those members at their own expense. The pastor said that, although there was this difference of opinion and taste among the members, 'we must by all means make up our minds to agree to differ and under the circumstances maintain the spirit of true Christian union and love'. All the members seemed pleased with the arrangement. One wonders whether those members who stuck to fermented wine, with its antiseptic properties, suffered less, or more, from contagious diseases, than their unfermented friends.

As mentioned above, the love feast differed little – apart from the bread and water – from the prayer meeting which, in its turn, has largely disappeared from Nonconformist practice, though it was fundamental to the Methodists. Prayer meetings took place at all times of any day of the week and in an earlier period sometimes at dawn. More commonly, in living memory, they followed the evening service.

Some prayer meetings went beyond personal testifying and had a touch of converting about them; indeed some chapels became known as 'converting furnaces'. A correspondent of over ninety years of age recalls from his Lincolnshire boyhood at a Wesleyan chapel:

After evening service at 6 p.m. (this would last about one and a half hours), the preacher came down out of the pulpit and led a prayer meeting at which he exhorted the unconverted to join the ones who were already on the Lord's side. That was the way most of the members had been brought in, as it was called; that is, they had come forward and knelt at the communion rail which went across a space in front of the communion table, and which was only uncovered when the minister held the sacrament service which would only occur about once every quarter.

Sometimes, as at a Wesleyan Methodist church in Batley Carr, Yorkshire:

Everyone would sit in silence until moved to utter an extempore prayer, or sing a hymn, or merely quote from well-known biblical passages.

More often, however, there was no lack of vocal praying:

I well remember the prayer meetings [in Sheffield about 1910] on a week night or after the evening service when some dear brother who prayed for what seemed to us hours on end, and when he prayed for something which another brother thought rather noteworthy the other brother would say very loudly 'Amen! Amen!' At these meetings, too, some of the members would stand up and give their testimony often telling how at one time, they spent most of their time in the public house and led a very sinful life but now they were reformed – at this point everybody would say 'Hallelujah! Hallelujah!' Quite often, tears would roll down the face of the person giving his testimony.

Thank goodness no one ever asked me to say a prayer! The twelve or eighteen regular prayer meeting attenders had it all their own way, resenting intruders. This number included an elderly gentleman with a bald crown and a great flowing beard who, I felt sure at one time, must be God Himself. After a few minutes silence one of the regulars would get up and address the Almighty in a sort of jocose Thee and Thou formula, with widespread misinterpretations of the English of the James I Bible language. 'O Lord Thou knows (not knowest) wot a wickid lot of sinners we are – do Thou forgive them turning to the ways of the Lord' etc. etc.

Comedy, or perhaps farce, could not always be excluded from such occasions:

I was at a prayer meeting in the mission. The vestry was rather full; we had to wait our time to offer our prayer as sometimes there were two at a time praying. A dear old lady and a good Christian was praying and she said: 'Lord, I am climbing Zion's Hill.' The class leader said: 'Stick your toes in Jane, wench.' Another occasion then in the Salvation Army ring a good Salvationist, a woman, offered her prayer, and her husband, also in the ring, but not such a good Christian, said: 'Lord, make me as good a man as my old woman.' He may not have been as good a Christian as his wife but I think God rewards us according to our desires if we try to be good.

At a prayer meeting at Moorends Wesleyan chapel (between Doncaster and Barnsley) a member who had already taken part was listening to his friend making a particular request and interjected: 'Aye, do Lord, I forgot to axe Thi that.'

To many children prayer meeting fervour was certainly rather a joke:

The prayer meetings, which were very frequent and at which we juveniles were expected to be present, were times of much trial and tribulation to our unregenerate minds. We therefore naturally found more interest in the personal idiosyncrasies of those who were called upon to 'address the throne' than in the devotional element itself. One kindly Christian man suffered from a nervous affliction which took the form of a succession of gasps, which he seemed quite unable to control during his supplications. Another devout member accentuated his fervid words with constant head-shakes, so frequent and vehement that one expected him to be suffering from a violent form of palsy; while yet another worthy man, through some peculiar dental disarrangement, every now and then emitted a shrill whistling sound during his devotions.

E. E. Kellett underlines the curiosities of these 'extempore effusions' in *As I Remember*:

Gravelled for lack of matter, one worshipper suddenly electrified his hearers by saying, 'Now, Lord, I will tell thee an anecdote': and I have heard a whole parable, somewhat damaged in the repetition, declaimed as an episode in a prayer long enough without it. A sarcastic youth, after listening to one of these performances, remarked, 'I understand now that verse in the hymn, "Satan trembles when he sees the weakest saint upon his knees." If he has any literary taste he may well tremble.'

There were preachers who were too dramatic and realistic. 'Look at him,' cried a theatrical pulpiteer, pointing straight at a well-known and harmless gentleman in his audience, 'look at him, steeped in every vice, plunged in debauchery soused in sin.' To the gentleman's obvious embarrassment the audience did look at him.

The prayers occasionally smacked of contemporaneity, as one correspondent remembers:

During the 1914–1918 war I used to visit, in the eastern counties, my aunts, who were Wesleyans, in a small town near Ely. On two occasions I attended midweek, *united*, wartime prayer meetings, at which a layman, who was always aware of his own importance, was the leading light. At a time when there was a supposed threat of invasion on the east coast, he used the phrase in his prayer – 'Tip up their ships, Lord, tip up their ships.' On another occasion he described the position of our troops – based on newspaper information and finished 'and now Lord, we only need Thy power' . . . etc.

An attitude of cynicism towards prayer meetings was evident as long as sixty years ago at least in one industrial town at a Methodist chapel:

My brother and I, much to the horror of my mother, while not exactly betting but trying something akin to it, would guess who would be the first to pray. Inevitably we would guess right. Then we would guess exactly what he (or she) would say and when he (or she) would sit down. The same process was undertaken regarding the second one to get up and the third and so on until, when Mr X got up, we knew the end was approaching. When finally he besought the Almighty, by requesting, 'Oh Lord, what we have failed in asking be Thou gracious in giving', we knew it was time to put on our hats and coats and go home. We were generally right.

The leaders of these meetings (generally the preacher who had conducted the evening service) also interested us. They were in the main men of modest means and limited education. They did not lack emotion however. The constant appeals to come forward and find salvation were quite a feature. Furthermore, couldn't they talk! How many really did find this salvation I never knew. I am afraid that the spiritual gain to my brother and myself was nil.

As a footnote to prayer meetings, Douglas Jackman relates in '300 Years of Baptist Witness in Dorchester 1645–1945':

Bastow (a well-known Baptist) had great influence with Thomas Hardy who was in the same architect's office. He persuaded Hardy, who had been brought up a very strict Church of England man, to attend a prayer meeting at Durnford. At the same time that the prayer meeting was to be held, Cook's famous circus entered the town and the two young men, Perkins and Bastow, apparently watched the procession while Thomas Hardy waited in the old, dark vestry. Three-quarters of an hour after the meeting was supposed to start they burst in on him. From that time Hardy seemed to have little interest in the Baptists.

While public extempore prayer has now almost vanished, there are signs that regular private prayer, whether at home or in churches and chapels, has increased. Prayer is no passing phenomenon, though where it takes place is subject to fashion.

Almost all Nonconformist churches had some kind of no-nonsense organisation aimed at keeping their members together and incidentally raising money. Most typical of these was the 'class meeting' instituted by the Wesleys themselves. The word

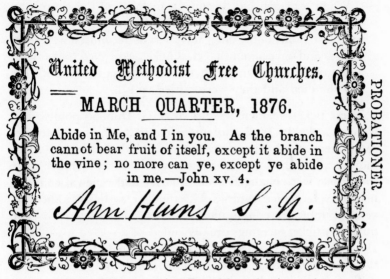

United Methodist Free Churches.

MARCH QUARTER, 1876.

Abide in Me, and I in you. As the branch cannot bear fruit of itself, except it abide in the vine; no more can ye, except ye abide in me.—John xv. 4.

Ann Huins S. H.

PROBATIONER

CLASS TICKET: These were in effect tickets showing active membership of a chapel and were usually issued quarterly. They were highly prized, some Wesleyans insisting that their tickets should be buried with them.

'class' had no scholastic meaning: it came from the Latin *classis*, meaning a 'summoning', and hence a group of the summoned. Each class had a leader who watched over the moral and religious life of his class, visiting each regularly in their homes and calling meetings in the vestry.

For example some seventy years ago in Halifax:

Class meetings met every week. Class leaders were worthy examples of what Wesley intended them to be – they led disciplined lives and held up their charges to high endeavour inspiring them to a sense of stewardship.

Members were expected to give some account of their religious experiences, an effort for some which led to set phrases being repeated by them on each occasion when called upon to speak. Regular visitation of members by the leader was made. Class money was paid by each member.

The class meetings were regarded very seriously by earlier generations. In Sheffield:

When a person had become a member of the church by openly declaring his faith in Christ they were then attached to a class. Some of the older members of the church were class leaders and once a month a class ticket was issued to you with a text on it. My grandmother kept all these tickets until the day she died and they were buried with her.

These tickets of membership, as S. G. Dimond points out[1], were regarded by Wesley as equivalent to the Pauline 'letters of recommendation'. They were at once a kind of passport and an inoffensive method of removing any disorderly member since the tickets were changed every quarter and renewal could, if necessary, be denied. A series of Methodist class tickets indicating years of unbroken communion were very highly regarded. The quarterly ticket meetings usually ended, as a retired Missionary Deaconess, Sister Chislett, recalls, with the singing of: ' 'Tis done, the great transactions done, I am my Lord's and he is mine'.

The classes in a big chapel were divided into small groups according to age and sex (some classes were mixed). Each group had a class leader who would meet his members every week for Bible study and discussion:

> The leader had to be a man of exemplary character. He was expected to take a personal interest in the individuals who made up his class. He visited them when they were sick or in any kind of trouble. Originally every member gave a penny to his class leader who entered it into his class leader's book. Once a quarter the minister visited each class for the handing out of class tickets on which was a printed text from scripture and the minister's signature. The minister himself would usually have one class or more; he would usually meet the older members of the congregation in afternoon classes.

Class leaders were, as might be expected, deeply involved in other chapel activities and sometimes class meetings shaded off into, for example, a weeknight preaching service.

> The interesting feature, which I still recollect, was of a dear soul who led the class of which my father was at one time a

[1] *The Psychology of the Methodist Revival*, pp. 220-1.

member. His leadership, devout though it was, had its humorous side. They were small meetings and more often than not the singing was unaccompanied. The leader of this class had no musical idea at all. All his hymns were sung to the only tune he knew and could start; viz. – 'Spohr'. I have heard my father say that at one meeting they sang 'Spohr' four times. He was, however, a very devout leader.

The history of Mount Tabor chapel, Halifax, 1820–1970, after describing how class meeting members met week by week under their leader and each was encouraged to speak freely of his or her difficulties, failings or triumphs, when the leader could discipline or encourage, claims that such meetings disappeared in the 1920s. This is not so elsewhere. The history is more generally accurate when it refers to the meetings held after every Sunday evening service which did cease about that time. Upon such meetings the history comments that 'the petitions to the Almighty at times tended to reflect the opinions of the petitioner on his fellow-worshippers but, nevertheless, these meetings usually created an atmosphere in which the Divine presence was very real.'

The Mount Tabor history, written in 1970, notes that what it calls 'Clerking' by members of the congregation has long gone:

One wonders what the loud ejaculations of 'Hallelujah' or 'Praise the Lord' shouted from the pews in pre-centenary days would have on a service today. They certainly used to keep the hearers awake, and often inspired the preacher to make emotional appeals for converts to come and kneel in penitence at the communion rail. Was the more sedate atmosphere of later years perhaps responsible for diminishing numbers of attenders? Perhaps the chief reason was that the introduction of better transport to town meant that the Church ceased to be the focal point of village life. A changed approach to religion induced by the war years, also meant a decreased interest in Church affairs. The records show that in the 1920s it was necessary to provide 400 hymn-sheets for the Sunday School anniversary service in the afternoon and 600 at night. Forms had to be brought into the aisles to accommodate all the congregation, whilst a large number of visitors had tea in the school between services.

Former generations, well within the lifetime of most of those now living, did not take so resigned an attitude to the secular vicissitudes which threatened their religious life. Did, as the history of Lumb-with-Rossendale chapel claims, a higher standard of living in the 1890s lead to a demand for the provision of amusements? Then Chapel would provide them. Was pub beer more enticing than Chapel tea, pub choruses than Watts's hymns, pub chatter than prayer meetings? Then the devil must be deprived of all the best tunes, Chapel must vie with pub in entertainment.

Consider this account – by a correspondent who attended a Methodist chapel in a small Midlands industrial town sixty years ago – of that much misunderstood phenomenon, the Band of Hope, the temperance movement which sought to lure young people into signing the teetotal pledge:

The age of my childhood was the one in which the temperance movement was to the fore. Most Methodist churches had a Band of Hope. This was a riotous assembly. As in the case of the Sunday School, most of those who came had no connection whatever with the church and, furthermore, being held on a week night it always seemed to me that further unruly licence was claimed. Still, they were interesting meetings. The great achievement was to recite. I well remember my first effort in this direction. It opened as follows:

> I'm only a little boy
> As everyone can see,
> But still I'm old enough to know
> That drink's not good for me.

The hymns at these meetings were of a real rousing type. We would raise the roof with:

> Standing by a purpose true
> Heeding God's command,
> Honour then the faithful few
> And join in Daniel's band.

    Chorus: Dare to be a Daniel,
             Dare to stand alone,
             Dare to have a purpose true
             And dare to make it known!

We must have been heard at least three streets away.

The Band of Hope had its highlights. The first was always held, at least in the Midlands, the first weekend in May and was known as 'The May Festival'.

The public hall of the town was packed to the doors for three nights, while the May Queen was crowned and enthroned, the maypole was braided and skipping undertaken. The whole was followed by an operetta which brought the evening to a triumphant close. The only temperance element as far as I could see was that it was organised by the local Band of Hope Union.

The second was the Whit Tuesday walk. Here the whole town was a seething mass of excitement. Brass bands from far and near came to take their place in the procession, which was made up of all the Free Church Sunday Schools; the May Queen and her retinue; elderly ladies and representatives of other temperance bodies. Each Sunday School entered a competition for a prize offered for a device which generally consisted of a decorated vehicle carrying a temperance motto. In addition individual prizes were offered to children for devices constructed and trimmed by themselves but again with a temperance motto.

After the procession each school adjourned to its own premises for a tea such as only the free churches seemed to know how to put on and the evening was spent on a local recreation ground enjoying entertainers, games and other pastimes. This was always a great day, except when it rained.

Again, however, there was a touch of humour. The brass band members were not by any means all temperance advocates. While therefore, the procession was forming in the market place, many of them would 'pop in' to the 'Green Man' or 'The Bull' or any other near-by hostelry. When all was ready to move off they would take their places at the head of the

procession which was broadly and in no doubtful voice declaring the evils of strong drink.

These jovial occasions are far from the usual mental pictures
most people have today of the anti-drink movement in
Nonconformity.

On the other hand some rather scarifying propaganda was
used against the demon drink. At Cranbrook, Kent, Congregational:

My own family had much to do with the Band of Hope,
which gathered the children once a week into the school room.
It had originally been founded by my grandfather, who had
become a pledged abstainer as far back as 1853. Once we had
a week of 'Gospel Temperance', when the school room was
hung with diagrams of human organs before and after maltreatment by alcohol. The Band of Hope was the first chapel
organisation to arrange summer excursions in a field at
Tunbridge Wells or the seaside, with a marquee, tea, games
and swings. The scholars had also a winter teaparty and
prizegiving.

The Band of Hope made a vivid impression on one small boy
in Leeds:

It attracted a lot of youngsters who never came to anything
else and they would sometimes so exaggerate the pathos of
'Father, dear Father' as to reduce the meeting to chaos. And
there was always the possibility of an outside speaker. One
would illustrate his talk with the display of what he said was
a human liver pickled hard in alcohol as a warning of what
would happen to our livers if we started drinking. Another
would show lantern slides illustrating the reading of a pathetic
story of the consequences of intemperance. If the story was too
short to fill the evening, there might be slides of a more general
character. I recall one example of an early moving picture.
It showed the head of a man sleeping with his mouth open.
The operator turned a little handle and we watched, fas-
cinated, a never ending series of mice – or rats – going down
his throat.

Another less rowdy alternative to the allure of the pub was the Pleasant Saturday Night, common to many chapels of which Newtown, St Helens, was one. There, a correspondent writes, the Pleasant Saturday Night provided a counter-attraction to the public house in the winter months. As John Burns, M.P.,[1] said, 'Anything that will give working people more pleasure will help in the way of temperance. Let those who want to give working people more pleasure, provide games and opportunities for social enjoyment and they will not seek the public house.' Newtown did this through Knowsley Road Social Football Club; Knowsley Road Social Cricket Club; and the Pleasant Saturday Night, etc., etc.

And at, for instance, Abeny Congregational church, Stoke Newington, London, there was a variant on the style of later working men's clubs – a Pleasant Sunday Afternoon for men which was very popular with its string band and a good vocalist.

Not necessarily to counteract drink and pubs were other satisfying ways of keeping out of mischief. Such was the Wesley Guild as we read in the history of the Hollins, Millgate, Methodist chapel:

> The scope of the Wesley Guild is infinitely wide and its interests so very comprehensive that every particular branch of youthful activity finds itself at home within it. Yet, though the constitution of the society approaches the ideal, its success or failure depends not so much on this as upon the efforts of those who are entrusted with its working.
>
> The earliest records the secretary can trace begin 26 September 1910 though it is certain that records were kept long before that date. Many and varied are the interests which have occupied the attention of the Guilders since then – from Christmas fancy dress carnivals to summertime trips to Windermere; from carol singing to open-air preaching services.
>
> February 1916 saw the first contribution to Overseas Medical Missions. The annual 'Tea to the Ladies' Sewing Committee' began in 1915 and the 'Supper to the Young

[1] M.P. for Battersea, 1892–1918. President of the Local Government Board, 1905–14. Trade Unionist who became a Liberal Minister. Died 1943.

Ladies' in 1921. Carol singing was revived in 1927 after a lapse of many years and probably between £90 and £100 has been raised for various objects by this means since that time.

For the war period the minutes are extremely interesting. Items such as the following speak for themselves:

28 Sept. 1914 'This meeting was called hurriedly to decide how the Wesley Guild could show its appreciation of the response made by two of its members to the country's call to arms.'

11 Jan. 1915 'That the Wesley Guild present Khaki Bibles to all Sunday School scholars who join the forces,' while American Teas, Jumble Sales, and so on, raised large amounts for Red Cross and Relief Funds.

These items and others like them, though indicating to some extent the outward activity, really give but slight indication of the real worth of the fellowship of the Society. Through the kindly encouragement given in the happy meetings and discussions, many young people have received training which has later proved invaluable both to themselves and to the Church. Through the comradeship of other young people with high objectives, many have learned the meaning of true life. In the spiritual tone of the meetings, everyone experiences the joy of fellowship with each other, and with the unseen Common Brother. Here is the very foundation of Wesley Guildry – its meetings must be essentially spiritual, and its activities must have their inspiration from the highest Source. And herein is the secret of success.

There is another point about the Wesley Guild emphasised by a Birmingham lady: 'Many a M.P., Councillor and local preacher learned to express himself in these Guild meetings. They took the form of lectures, discussions and social evenings. The talks were not necessarily religious.'

Whether organised by the Guild or not, the purely social side of Chapel life was strong:

We used to hold what was then called a social evening once a week; we all played 'Musical chairs', 'Spin the plate' and various guessing games, and a few songs round the piano. Our parents used to make sandwiches and cakes for us to give for refreshments for which a very small charge was made – I think the most was 3d.

Our parents used to attend social evenings and meat-and-potato pie suppers; all food would be given and a little charge was made. Everybody, as I can remember, used to have a very happy evening. The women used to have what they called a 'Faith Tea' – everyone who came was expected to bring some kind of food and place it on the prepared long table and then all would have and enjoy their tea, not knowing just what they were having. Going to chapel was a thing one looked forward to with pleasure.

Nor were such affairs without opportunity for what Wordsworth called 'glances of young love-liking'. In Sheffield:

Young men's and women's classes and the Sunday School would organise socials and concerts, usually held in the old Sunday school which was a 'woodin 'ut' with corrugated iron cladding. Here, after potted meat sandwiches, Co-op cake and tea drawn from shining copper urns, with plenty of bicarbonate added to make it look stronger, the business of the evening would usually commence with an extended session of 'King William was King David's son, all the royal races run' in the course of which the young men chose their favourite young ladies turns about, with intervals for kissing at the end of each stanza. Or 'spinning the trencher', with suitable forfeits. 'Serious' couples would disappear into the cellar where the warmth of the central heating plant encouraged a little necking.

Undoubtedly the great occasions were anniversaries where festivity combined with religion. Early this century in the wilds of Dorset at least one chapel in the first week of June all the children assembled in the middle of the village. A band arrived and all marched two by two to every outlying farm and hamlet perhaps six or seven miles returning to a field for tea and games. This was the temperance fête. Then came harvest festival with trays of apple dumplings, cakes and bars of chocolate which

were sold with the other offerings in aid of Chapel funds. 'Most
of the food was left inside the younger generation.' Then the
anniversary tea which was also held in the chapel, with seed
cake and brown bread cooked in an oven where wood had been
burning to heat it, then scraped out again!

During this time we said our bits of poetry or sang something. In the winter there were magic lantern slides usually on
the drink situation. I remember one was called 'What the fly
saw'. Then we did a small feature called 'Little Dot' – very
sad as all things were in those days. Although it is so long ago
I still remember one song:

> Close the door lightly,
> Holding the breath
> Our little earth angel
> Has spoken to death.
>
> Gently he wooed her,
> She wished not to stay
> His arms were about her
> He bore her away.
>
> Music comes floating
> Down from above
> Angels are chanting
> Sweet messages of love.
>
> Come stricken weeper
> And stand by the bed,
> Come gaze on the sleeper,
> Our darling is dead.

That chapel has influenced my life as nothing else has done.
I have travelled far since then and once was married to a very
high churchman who loathed Methodists. He has been dead
for years and although I have been to all the great and
wonderful Church services, I shall never forget the nodding
bonnets and real hearty praising of God such as my simple and
good parents did.

A Worcestershire lady writes:

My memories are of summer days, anniversaries, choir outings and suppers, choir practices, sometimes chaotic. Our voices (the girls) were drowned by one Lizzie who outsang the organ; at that time the wind was supplied manually by a strong lad! It was the wrong place to sing as we were too near the roof and I remember the battle the choir-master (a headmaster) had with the oldies, to get us moved downstairs.

At anniversaries we were asked to be 'half crown collectors'. This was quite a sum thirty years ago and none of us was well off. What an atmosphere there was at anniversaries and the poorest always managed a new outfit for the event! I remember one of mine made by my mother – a deep voile with little pink flowers (very maxi!) a large blue hat, fawn strapped shoes and a tallish umbrella, in case. I thought I was the last word. (We looked an odd lot on a snap produced some years later as our faces could not be seen for hats – today it is hair.) We usually wore buttonholes – Lilies-of-the-valley were in bloom at anniversary time.

Oh, the host of happy memories and what simple and quiet lives we led – what changes since the war! Concerts, weekday meetings in the form of a guild at which we got very good speakers, bazaars, school treats and the smell of cucumber sandwiches on hot summer afternoons, choir suppers and the tame games at which the young people of today would jeer perhaps; memories of nearly always being sick on the coach trips. I shall never forget my first trip to Church Stretton (Shropshire) on a choir trip – we arrived in the evening. It was so beautiful I thought Heaven could not be better. It has never seemed so exquisite since. Another time the unholiest of us imbibed in the cellars at Worcester's Dirty Dick's and felt quite devilish.

School treats were joyous events. At Holmer Green Baptist church, near High Wycombe, this was, one correspondent recalls:

a riotous affair with new bread and butter and cake, and tea in quaint mid-Victorian mugs bought, no doubt, for a few pence a dozen and now worth half-a-guinea a piece as antiques. After tea more uproarious delights on the Common and – thrilling climax – the dignified arrival of the slightly self-conscious Superintendent, never more greatly respected than at this moment, bearing huge tins of sweets to be scattered over the ground and scrambled for by the eagerly-waiting throng.

A parallel description, in a report of 1876, puts it in this way:

After tea the children retired to the common to enjoy the ordinary innocent pastimes so common to villagers, to wit, drop glove and pat ball . . ., but it is hard to believe that they were really so much more demure in those earlier days!

Then the return journey just as before, and at last, after another four-hour drive, the triumphal entry into Holmer Green, just before or just after the Wesleyans who had been doing precisely the same thing in precisely the same way, and a rending of the night air with singing and jubilation.

It is reported that on one occasion the chapel was 'most tastefully decorated with corn and fruit, noticeable being two large turnips, hollowed out to allow a candle to burn inside, showing through letters cut in the bark to form the words "One and all" and "Be thankful". These were placed on either side of the rostrum upon a pole and gave a most pleasing effect.'

'There will be a tea and meeting' was a frequent announcement at Mount Tabor chapel, Halifax, as elsewhere:

Bodily fortification was needed to face the issues to be considered afterwards. The annual Sunday School tea and meeting was an outstanding affair necessitating two 'sittings-down' for tea, long speeches from the elders, a lengthy secretary's report and items by the children at the evening meeting.

Before the First World War the charge for the tea was – adults 6d., children 3d. The fare included home-made bread, cakes, buns, fatty cakes and pastries with cream for the tea in lavish quantities, and its quality earned for Mount Tabor ladies a well-deserved reputation. Even the liquid brew was said to be better than town tea. Was this because the water used was pumped from a well near the cemetery? Tea also preceded the annual meetings of the teachers and senior scholars, the Society, the Band of Hope, and Foreign Missions. The last of these was held in September and often included a circuit welcome to the new minister.

At the Whit Monday treat, coffee brewed in large earthenware containers, and 8 oz currant buns were served either in the school if wet or the field if fine. 160 such buns, sometimes more, were ordered, along with eight dozen or more oranges. The singing of hymns in the village, generally from special Whitsuntide hymn-sheets provided by the Sunday School Union, preceded the tea interval which was followed by games in the field or school. The day usually ended with the formation of 'kissing rings' and the singing of old catches such as 'The green leaves are falling', and 'Green grow the leaves on the old oak tree'. Many a romance had its origin at such a time. In later years organised games replaced these more sentimental pastimes.

Harvest Festivals, though not exactly anniversaries, were annual events requiring considerable preparation. In Sheffield:

They were occasions for great dressings-up of the chapel and pulpit and great singings of 'We plough the fields' and 'Come, ye thankful people, come'. My father, notwithstanding his strictness in matters of the chapel, had a keen sense of humour and a favourite harvest festival story. The first time I heard him tell it there was at the table, unbeknownst, a Plymouth Brother, who got up and walked out at the end, disgusted. The story was of a local preacher who was planned to preach at a country chapel and had prepared his sermon on the Agony in the Garden. To his dismay on arrival he found the chapel decorated for Harvest Festival. He met one of the chapel leaders in the vestry and explained his dilemma – he'd come to preach on the Agony in the Garden not Harvest Home. 'That's all right,' said the leader, 'it'll do fine. Don't you see – Simon Peter drew a sword in the Garden when they came to arrest Jesus and cut off the ear of one of the servants of the High Priest. There you are then – "first the blade and then the ear"!'

A joker once pinned up a bunch of white stone turnips
very insecurely over the organist's head and in a very loud
passage the fastening relinquished its hold and the turnips
dropped all over the organ manuals.

Nonconformists eschewed anything that partook, however
remotely, of idolatry. Yet showiness crept in through, as it were,
the back door. There was to be no representation of the cross,
nor of the saints, no swinging censer and incense, no gorgeous
robes, no display. Yet at Harvest Festivals – and Flower Services
– display there was. Fruit, flowers and vegetables were heaped
in decorative patterns, ivy twisted its way up the pillars of the
galleries, bread was baked in special moulds and marrows had
texts grown into their skin. An uninstructed observer might
have imagined himself at some pagan festival.

The anniversary of the foundation of the individual chapel
was sometimes a less exciting occasion. At Cranbrook, Kent,
Congregational, it was held on a week-day, with a service in the
afternoon, tea for friends and visitors, and a public meeting in
the evening,

at which my father's voice seemed to me strange and distant
as he presented the year's statement of accounts. The cult of
the anniversary was not so assiduously observed by us as it
was by the Strict Baptists, with whom it was the occasion for
a 'get-together' from all the 'Places of Truth' round about.
They also had an annual Thanksgiving, but with no display
of fruit and flowers as with us.

The anniversary service at the little chapel at Iden Green,
Benenden, was always held on Good Friday, and parties of
us used to walk over and join in. The Iden Green chapel
shared a minister with us, although it was otherwise
independent. The Sunday service was in the afternoon, and
our minister would drive over in a hired horse and trap to
conduct it. When we had a guest preacher, one of our
members would do the driving. If it was my father's turn to
take the reins he would sometimes let me go with him. This
would be a joyful day for me. The consequent release from
Sunday School and the novelty of the place endeared Iden

Green to me. It was a square, plain Meeting House, weatherboarded and painted white without, varnished within and lighted by oil lamps.

The school room was at a higher level than the body of the chapel, into which it looked from three arched openings behind the pulpit. At service time curtains would be drawn back and the Sunday School scholars would be revealed, looking out over the preacher's head. The old chapel at Iden Green was ruined in the late war and has been replaced by a modern building on a different site. The Iden Green friends had a successful Sunday School, which used to receive commendation at the annual meetings of the Beult Sunday School union.

These meetings were held on Easter Monday and were the highlight of the Chapel year. The Beult Sunday School union comprised the Congregational chapels of Cranbrook, Iden Green, Staplehurst and Sutton Valence, and the Baptist chapels of Tenterden, Hawkhurst, Sandhurst, Curtisden Green (Goudhurst) and Bramble Street (Horsmonden). Headcorn was a doubtful adherent. It was a general Baptist church which had become Unitarian early in the last century but had later reverted to orthodoxy. None of the Methodists chapels participated. No one seemed to be able to explain why the union had been named after the Beult, that sluggish Wealden river which joins the Medway at Yalding.

The *venue* of the meetings was one of the larger chapels, and parties from the others would arrive by various forms with an address from a delegate of the National Sunday School Union, a report on the work of the schools by an appointed visitor, and a discussion. At the cold collation which followed toasts would be drunk (not in alcoholic liquor!), beginning with the Loyal Toast. Individual members of the host chapel would have prepared the cold meat for the feast (my mother sometimes would cook the veal). A guest preacher would conduct service in the afternoon. Tea would be followed by a public meeting, addressed by the Delegate, the guest preacher and other friends. After its most flourishing days, about the turn of the century, the Beult Union suffered a decline. The day was

changed after the last war from Easter Monday to the
Saturday in Easter Week.

Some chapels in the North played the chapel anniversary with
variations, as in Sheffield around 1910:

I remember very vividly being 'on the Sermons' which in
effect was really the Chapel anniversary. We had to go to
practice quite early in order to be assured of a seat on the
platform on the appointed Sunday and anyone who turned
up on the day not wearing white was rather looked upon with
disdain. Special hymns were sung by the children and the
platform went up in tiers almost to ceiling level. The chapel
itself was packed and chairs were put in the aisles. Every inch
of available space was occupied.

Recitations were also said and I well remember reciting
'The Haven'[1] as follows:

The sacred day was ending in a village by the sea,
The uttered benediction touched the people tenderly,
As they rose to face the sunset in the glowing lighted West,
And then hastened to their dwellings for God's blessed boon
    of rest.

But they looked across the waters, a storm was raging nigh,
A fierce spirit rose above them, the wild spirit of the air,
And it lashed and shook and tore them, till they thundered
    race and boomed
And alas for any vessel in that yawning gulf entombed.

And at last, across the water, a brave woman strained her
    eyes
And she saw upon the billows, a large vessel fall and rise,
Oh, it did not need a prophet to tell what the end must be,
For no ship could ride in safety near that shore on such a sea.

The pitying people hurried from their homes and thronged
    the beach,
Oh, for power to cross the waters and the perishing reach,

---

[1] Authorship unknown.

Helpless hands were wrung with sorrow, tender hearts grew
  cold with dread,
And the ship urged by the tempest to the fatal rock shore
  sped.

She has parted in the middle, oh, the half of her goes down!
God have mercy, in his Heaven, for to seek for those who
  drown!
Lo! when next the white shocked faces looked with terror on
  the sea,
Only one last clinging figure on a spar was seen to be.

Nearer the trembling watchers came the wreck tossed by
  the waves,
And the man still clung and floated, though no power on
  earth could save,
Could we send him a short message, here's a trumper,[1]
  shout away –
'Twas the preacher's hand that took it and he wondered
  what to say.

Any memory of his sermon – firstly, secondly – Ah no,
There was but one thing to utter in that awful hour of woe.
So he shouted through the trumper – 'Look to Jesus, can
  you hear?'
And aye, aye Sir rang the answer o'er the water loud and
  clear.

Then they listened, he is singing – 'Jesu Lover of my Soul,'
And the winds brought back the echo – 'While the nearer
  waters roll,'
Strange indeed it was to hear him, 'Till the storm of life be
  passed,'
Singing bravely o'er the waters, 'O receive my soul at last.'

'Other refuge have I none, Hangs my helpless soul on Thee
Leave, ah leave me not –'
The singer dropped at last into the sea,

[1] i.e. loud-hailer.

And the watchers looking homeward through their eyes by
    tears made dim,
Said, he passed to be with Jesus in the singing of that
    hymn.

During the penultimate verse of this poem the organ played
the hymn – 'Jesu, Lover of my Soul.'

Education in the broadest, as well as the religious, sense had
long been the concern of Nonconformists. But it was not
confined to educating children. Adults too, had their needs in
this age that took education seriously, not to say earnestly.
Self-help, evening classes, Mechanics Institutes were in vogue
and were encouraged by many Nonconformist ministers,
themselves often learned men.

This urge brought forth such chapel organisations as the
mutual improvement societies. The programme of such a
society at Acocks Green, Birmingham, Congregational chapel
for the autumn of 1875 is revealing:

October	5	LECTURE: 'Epitaphs,' . . . Mr E. W. Tycer.
October	12	Elocution.
October	18	LECTURE: 'Light' (*with experiments*)
(Monday)		Mr C. Clarke.
October	26	Debate: 'That the Character of Napoleon Bonaparte is worthy of our admiration.'
November	2	Elocution.
	9	Sharp Practice. (*sic*)
	16	LECTURE: (*particulars to follow*)
	23	Debate: 'Ought there to be a Redistribution of Political power?'
November	30	Elocution.
December	7	Annual Entertainment.
December	14	Debate: 'Is a Republican Form of Government more conducive to the welfare of a Nation than a Monarchical one?'

These meetings with the exception of the lectures and
entertainment are free to all. Friends are invited to attend.

Tickets for one lecture sixpence each, or for the course of three one shilling.

A chess club met on alternate Thursdays. The society produced *The Merchant of Venice* and *The Rivals*. Such activities were by no means exceptional, and it will be noted that science (the lecture on 'light') was not overlooked.

The mutual improvement society at Paddington chapel, Marylebone Road, London, had a young men's society whose object was 'the cultivation of mutual sympathy, the intellectual and spiritual improvement of young men, and for the promotion of the cause of Christ generally, to gain which objects have been successful'. Their programme was made up of Bible readings, lectures, discussions on religious subjects, and debates on secular themes. In the early days of the society classes were held for the study of logic, English, writing, arithmetic, drawing, shorthand, and French.

There is a reference to spelling-bees, which some years ago were for a time a favourite form of mild excitement. Later the committee of the society was able to state that one result was that several of the young men were engaged in evangelistic work in the neighbourhood. Another person, at one time a vice-president of the society, taught members shorthand when 'phonography', as it was then called, was by no means a common accomplishment.

The lady members of the congregation apparently for a considerable time had invaded the society's meetings, for in the Church Manual of 1880 mention is made of its new name, viz., The Mutual Improvement Society, it having been felt for some time that the old name of The Young Men's Society was misleading and inappropriate, 'inasmuch as the meetings were free to all, irrespective of age and sex'.

From small beginnings the society had grown by 1913 in numbers, in usefulness, and in the scope of its syllabus. Its programmes included essays, discussion on books, debates on various subjects, manuscript magazines, concerts, organ recitals, lectures by many of the most popular lecturers of their day, elocutionary recitals, parliamentary debates, trials by judge and jury, conversaziones, and last but not least, fruit banquets.

Paddington was a large chapel. Marlpool Congregational in Derbyshire was not, but even there week-night meetings discussed such things as 'The Coal Miners Regulation Act' and Public Health Act of 1875. The Outwell, Cambridgeshire, Wesley Guild, in October 1926-March 1927, gave a hearty welcome to all who were young in spirit and offered:

Devotional evening: The first and last Passover. The power of kindness. Lecture: Savanorola, the Preaching Politician of Florence. Debate: 'Has the British Empire reached the zenith of her power?' and another debate: 'Should all trades and professions, legal, official, and government positions be open alike to men and women?' There were talks on 'Fiddles, past and present', on 'Jane Stuart, the Royal Quaker', and on protective colouring in nature.

Libraries, too, were being formed in the days before the public library system was well established. At Little Lane and Greenfield Congregationalist chapel, Bradford, they had 200 volumes – seventeen take-out books. There was also a portable gymnasium (whatever that was) connected with Sunday School (late nineteenth-century), a Young Ladies' Gymnasium, a Ladies' Sewing Party ('busy fingers forge many coins') and a literary and social union, as well as a cycling club.

Much earlier at Dogley Lane Congregational church near Huddersfield, a library had been started for the use of the scholars and teachers. It was an established institution in 1842.

Of no less importance were lantern slides to illustrate talks. At Eythorne Baptist church near Dover:

My grandfather hired slides from the National Sunday School Union and visited all the villages with this. He also had a number of movable slides which were a source of great amusement, especially one that showed a man in bed eating rats.

Nor were games overlooked, at any rate in such chapels as the Newtown Congregational, St Helens:

20 November 1908 – Men's Institute was opened. The institute under the church, well lighted and comfortable, was furnished with two billiards tables, draughts, dominoes and other games, and papers and magazines provided, so that recreation could be available for all members. A code of rules and conduct was drawn up.

Many of the men, reclaimed by the Pleasant Saturday Night for the Christian way of life, found fellowship and an outlet for their skill at games in the institute.

Among other manifold social activities, dying was not forgotten. A good many chapels had a lugubriously-named Funeral Society for there was a great fear among many humble people of having to be buried by the Parish. At Dogley Lane Congregational chapel such a society was founded as early as 1843:

> There were at that time frequent subscriptions to be made in the school for the burials of children. This society was formed to enable every family to help itself. By means of a subscription of 1d. per month for scholars and 1½d. for teachers, a sum of £2 could be paid on death of a scholar or £3 for a teacher. Thus was commenced a work which the late Bishop Sugden described at the Jubilee Celebration (1893) as a 'co-operative effort', which 'maintained and supported a spirit of independence'. From that year to the present, an unbroken succession of annual meetings have been held on Good Friday or Easter Saturday, and have constituted a happy reunion for many, who, having removed from the neighbourhood, came back to the tea, and social and business gathering. The rate of subscriptions has never been raised.

> In 1845, a Friendly Society was formed to help the members in time of sickness. The original rules admitted persons of between sixteen and forty years of age, who were not members of any other similar society. One of the rules was: 'No member shall propose the removal of this society from Dogley Lane school room, upon pain of exclusion'. Funeral Benefits, etc., were allowed, of the usual kind.

In the mid-nineteenth century there were attempts in some chapels (not least among the Quakers) to put good works before the salvation of the soul and in extreme cases this led to a secularising of the chapel concerned. One of the best-known proponents of good works and social conscience was the Rev. George Dawson who became Minister of Mount Zion Baptist chapel, Birmingham, in 1884. Later he founded his own chapel. Fixed creeds he regarded as 'productive of mischief' and the bond between Dawson's congregation was 'a common end of purpose – to clothe the naked, to feed the hungry, and to instruct the ignorant'.[1] Such aims were noble but they led, perhaps inevitably, to a line of Nonconformist 'political' ministers; and such now hold the reins in many chapels. Significantly, as they have increased so have congregations declined.

Furthermore, their prominence has obscured the fact that most chapels have always put good works high on their list of priorities, though never as high as the salvation of the individual soul. For instance well before the time of the Rev. George Dawson, the Paddington chapel in London had clubs raising money to supply at cheap rates such items as blankets, sheets, warm shawls and coal. Its 'Infants' Friend Society' aimed 'to assist women at the time of their confinement, uniting Christian instruction with temporary relief' – which comprised 'one quart of oatmeal, one pound of loaf sugar, one pound of tea, and a New Testament'. Bed linen and garments were provided for mother and infant and two shillings given.

Nor did the metropolis have a monopoly of such organised charity. Up and down the country, chapel people, often themselves poor, sought to help the poorer still. At Wesley Hall, Great Ancoats Street, Manchester, a Christmas breakfast was given to the poor children of the district and a Father Christmas gave presents from a huge tree laden with gifts provided by the 'better-off' members of the congregation.

During the depressed days of the late 1920s at Park Road Baptist church, St Helens, clothing and food parcels were distributed:

[1] See *Victorian Cities*, by Asa Briggs (London, 1963), pp. 197–8. Dawson himself was already very political, not least on foreign policy questions.

A Christmas Cheer Fund was started, and help sought from less depressed regions of the country. In this way the hearts of many were touched and brought into the fellowship, where the need for mental and spiritual training was attacked with the same sincerity and forthrightness as were the needs for physical cheer.

In industrial areas, chapels often took the lead in helping the unemployed. At Queen's Road Baptist church, Coventry (founded in the 1660s), clothing clubs were started before the First World War and a mock pub was open on Saturday nights. A Christmas tea was given to crippled children. During later slumps in the motor industry, members of the congregation privately gave money to the minister. Then: 'Men who had often tramped for miles and sometimes had a job waiting in a week's time but not a penny until then were immediately given cocoa, bread and margarine in the manse. The minister then arranged for a hostel and paid for their keep.'

In the large towns where home missions were begun there were other activities such as midnight meetings 'for the benefit of fallen women'. At the Liverpool mission, for instance twelve 'cocoa rooms' (or 'British workman public houses') were opened in 1875. The Leeds mission had a guild for seventy young women who came straight from work. They were offered tea and sewing instruction during which suitable books were read aloud. (This same mission organised classes in theology, New Testament Greek, domestic economy and, being Yorkshire, cricket). At the Hull mission 15,000 free breakfasts were provided for poor children within the first eight months of its existence (1891).[1]

Often money was willed by members to chapel uses, as at Harrold congregational church:

By his will, proved 1887, John Goff willed to the Trustees of Harrold Independent church the sum of £1,000, the interest of which, after investment, to be used for the better support of the minister and also to help in the expenses of the Sunday School. Any residue after and above this he desired should be spent in providing coal for poor widows residing

[1] From *At the Centre: the Story of Methodism's Central Missions,* by George Sails.

in the parish. From this source coal was distributed every winter from 1887/8 to 1903. The account book for 1890 shows that forty-nine people were given 2cwt. each. The purchase cost:

5 tons at 15/3	£3	16	3
Cost of carting from Sharnbrook and distributing	£1	3	6
	£4	19	9

But it was not only – nor perhaps mainly – through organised societies that chapelgoers showed kindness and compassion: it was through multitudinous private acts – most of them unknown to the world at large, and therefore impossible to record. The following description is, however, typical. In a Yorkshire dales village in the 1820s a farmer in moderate circumstances and his wife led the little Methodist group which met at their house:

> On many a night, after these meetings, the same good man and his family would hold a council. Charles would say, 'I noticed that old Matthew seemed low-spirited, I doubt he is getting stuck fast with his bit of land'. Then turning to his son, he would say, 'Isaac lad, thou must take the old mare up to Matthew's tomorrow and do anything he wants'. Or Charles's wife would say, 'Old Mary seemed down-hearted. I'm afraid she's going short. I'll take her a basketful of something to eat in the morning'. Next day she would follow this up with, 'I've been to old Mary's, and she has scarcely a bit of coal in the place. Isaac, you must take her a good bagful tonight'.[1]

Mainstream Nonconformists enjoyed their social life together; they took their religion seriously and enthusiastically and sought to bring it to others. Doubtless some were stiff and introverted. Yet as a body and as individuals they probably had to their credit, more than most men and women, those 'little, nameless, unremembered acts Of kindness and of love' which Wordsworth regarded as the 'best portion of a good man's life'.[2]

[1] *Recollections from a Yorkshire Dale*, by C. J. F. Atkinson (London, 1934), pp. 56–7.

[2] 'Lines composed a few miles above Tintern Abbey', 1.33.

5

PREACHERS AND HEARERS

*The Religion of England is preaching
and sitting still on Sundays.*

John Evelyn (1659).

Preaching is as old as Christ himself – older, since the Hebrew prophets and scribes were preachers. In England, the Reformation revived the art which, the Mendicants apart, had fallen into desuetude, and by the sixteenth and seventeenth centuries a preacher of repute 'combined the attractions of modern journalist, publicist and lecturer'.[1] Among such preachers were Lancelot Andrewes, John Donne, Baxter, Calamy and John Bunyan. But by the mid-eighteenth century preaching had once more commonly become unimpassioned, formal; sermons were usually read.

The Wesleyan revival changed all that: Wesley, Whitefield, John Elias charged their sermons with fire, drama and emotion, and Anglicans, particularly the Evangelicals, followed suit. In nineteenth-century chapels the great names were R. W. Dale, J. H. Jowett, C. H. Spurgeon, John Clifford, Hugh Price Hughes, Charles Brown, James Martineau; and of a later vintage, well into the twentieth century, Silvester Horne, Luke Wiseman, Dinsdale Young, William Younger, Scott Lidgett, Cloudesley Shovel, Townley Lord, Russell Maltby, Leslie Weatherhead, and many others.

Nonconformist ministers were often men of great learning though the best of them retained the common touch. Just how learned they were may be gathered from E. E. Kellett in:

> A Methodist minister, for instance, after two or three years at college, had four years of probation before he could be ordained. At the end of each of these years, he had not only to pass a really searching examination on set subjects, but to

---

[1] *Oxford History of English Literature, 1600–1660*, by Douglas Bush (Oxford 1945), p. 313.

satisfy his superiors that his general reading had been of an
intellectual kind. One candidate of whom I have heard made,
indeed, somewhat exaggerated claims. He asserted that he
had read the whole of the *Decline and Fall* and had 'verified all
the references' – thus effectively securing his rejection. But
the vast majority, more modest and truthful, certainly made
good use of their time, and found or strengthened, during
these probationary years, a taste for reading which never left
them.

I have never met more persistent students than were to be
found among the Nonconformist intelligentsia. One minister
I knew was a perfect miracle of reading; he must have
rivalled Magliabecchi or Macaulay. He was a master of
ecclesiastical history from A.D. 1 to 1845; but he contrived to
read almost every book, on any topic whatever, that came out
in his time whether it was the *Origin of Species* or James Hinton's
Mystery of Pain. How he found the time for it all I cannot
imagine for he was a good pastoral visitor and prepared his
sermons carefully; nor was he like another I knew, who learnt
the Greek Testament by glancing at a verse between knocking
at a door and obtaining admission.

There are, wrote Frederick Ammann in *The Reminiscences
of a Spiritual Tramp, 1889–1944*,[1] three kinds of preacher – the
one 'you cannot listen to, the preacher you can listen to and the
preacher you cannot help listening to'. Some preachers were
racy in language and dramatic in gesture, pacing the pulpits
which in Nonconformist chapels were often large enough to hold
a string ensemble. Dr Joseph Parker, an early incumbent of the
leading Free Church pulpit, City Temple chapel in London
(opened 1874), pronounced his anathema on Abdul Hamid in
the words 'God damn the Sultan'.[2]

Many of these preachers had not hesitated to adopt political
attitudes – generally of a left-wing or Christian socialist nature.
Most were men of striking appearance often with hair in the

[1] An account by a sermon 'taster', in mimeographed copies, London
1944.
[2] A somewhat ugly man with an attractive wife, he once retorted to a man
who called out 'There goes beauty and the beast', with the words: 'How dare
you call my wife a beast?'

long, shaggy style of Lloyd George (himself a Baptist) and voices as capable of infinite mutations as a great actor. As Mr Ammann wrote: 'Some of them were little more than pulpit orators'.

Indeed E. E. Kellett records that 'Dr Parker, in the City Temple preached to overflowing audiences, not only on Sundays but on Thursdays: and these week-day services were constantly attended by actors and actresses, who wished to learn what the human voice at its best, aided by gesture at its most expressive, could accomplish. Why should people to whom such a pleasure as this was open desire to go to the theatre? Had they gone, they would only have heard the pupils; in the City Temple they heard the master.'

Kellett writes also of another minister whom he calls perhaps the greatest orator of the sixties, not excepting Gladstone and Bright. This was the Methodist minister, Dr Morley Punshon, 'who though now, by the common fate of great speakers, almost utterly forgotten, was a stupendous power in his own generation'.

As a boy I repeatedly heard Dr Punshon, both as a lecturer and as a preacher, in his later years: and certainly it is hard to imagine that Demosthenes himself could have been more effective. He tried the most daring flights, and never faltered, for tone and gesture were always right. Every word was given its due emphasis and carried its proper weight. Sudden pauses, the rapid rush of sentences and their retardation, the whisper and the crescendo, were all studied, but the art concealed the art. Unfortunately, he had his imitators, who just missed, and therefore utterly failed. When people say that the grand style of eloquence is discredited, they are thinking of these mimics. Were another Punshon to arise, with the same amazing genius, he would, I think, succeed even today, like his predecessor; but till he does arise, it is as well to keep to the present conversational and restrained style.

Every gesture, word and tone being thus carefully prepared, Punshon wore himself out and died comparatively young. I have been told that this preparation worked against him as an extempore speaker, and that as a debater he was unsuccessful.

Most Nonconformist ministers were extempore speakers –

that is, they prepared the substance of their sermons, but left the words to the inspiration of the moment. Kellett notes,

> This vastly increased the force of their appeals – when the inspiration came; a sermon read from a manuscript, or one learnt by heart, can scarcely vie with one which has a touch of spontaneity.

But when there is no real inspiration, and yet the flood of words is unimpeded, the critical hearer is sometimes offended or amused. I remember one preacher whose system, apparently, was to prepare a short discourse, and multiply it by three during the process of delivery, utilising for the purpose the abundance of synonyms which marks our language. 'If there be anything that obstructs, if there be anything that hinders, if there be anything that opposes nevertheless let us advance, let us proceed, let us go forward.' By this method he easily made a discourse of ten minutes into one of half an hour. Some of the rhetoric, again, whether prepared or not, was a little too sublime – like the elevated passages of Ossian.

Sermons in Nonconformist churches ranged from the blood-and-thunder to the modernistic (R. J. Campbell at the City Temple, the author of *New Theology*, denied the Virgin Birth, most of the miracles and was disgusted by hymns extolling 'the fountain filled with blood drawn from Emanuel's veins').[1] There was a genus of sermon known as 'Judgement sermons'. One preached at Kingswood Methodist school, Kellett recalled, 'was never forgotten by those who heard it. "We must all appear before the tribunal," cried the orator. "The greatest will not escape. Napoleon Bonaparte will be there." A solemn pause. "I myself shall be there." '

Most sermons were based on a Biblical text and had to begin with a certain amount of exegesis. Yet in essence, behind the charming voice, the grace of gesture, the meticulously chosen diction, the studied economy in the use of emphasis lay an attempt to create 'waves of spiritual influence'. As A. H. Driver wrote in his history of Carrs Lane Congregational

[1] See *Museum Piece*, by James Laver (London, 1963), p. 26.

church, Birmingham,[1] referring to the Rev. J. H. Jowett, congregations were 'led to expect a message from the Lord in somewhat the same way as the devout sacramentarian expects something to happen at the Elevation in High Mass'. This 'something' did happen with the best of the Nonconformist preachers and it was not so much emotional as spiritual, even mystical. Because of this mystical element, the religion purveyed by the great (and many of the lesser) preachers was far from the mechanical moralism, the pietistic stuffiness and sentiment which latter-day writers sometimes connect with Nonconformity. The great Congregational minister, R. W. Dale, wrote:

> There is a region lying far beyond the limits which confine the activity of the intellect – a region where infinity and transcendent glories and terrors cannot be represented under the forms of the logical understanding: it is there that those who are taught of the Spirit see divine visions and receive revelations of the Lord.[2]

It is at this point that Nonconformists meet – though not through sermons – with the Roman Catholic, Eastern Orthodox and Anglicans in the belief in the possibility of direct, personal contact with the divine spirit. The difference was that, while most Christians relied on liturgy,[3] private prayer and contemplation and the beauty of the Holy Spirit, most Nonconformists sought the same effect through extempore prayer and the sermon. And the sermon, incidentally, often contained, as well as copious Biblical references, poetry quoted from such writers as Browning ('The Grammarian's Funeral'), Tennyson ('Locksley Hall') and Wordsworth ('Peter Bell').

Needless to say, the great preachers often exhausted themselves. Theirs was no self-exhilarating performance; too much came out of the very pith of their being. So that we read of their Monday morning 'blues' and how some had recourse to such

[1] Published in Birmingham, 1948.
[2] *Essays and Addresses* (London, n.d.), p. 27.
[3] Speaking of Liturgy, one correspondent states that, 'In Wesleyan Methodist churches *in London* the Prayer Book service was followed at morning service until 1918 or perhaps later. I believe this was a legal obligation, laid down by conference.'

relaxing pursuits as golf. The Rev. Charles Brown, for instance,
felt nervous dread before any service he was to conduct. 'For
many years I could eat no breakfast on Sunday.'[1] And on
Mondays supervened something that his mystical predecessors
would have referred to as 'the dark night of the Soul'.

Yet these black times were far from universal among the
preachers. E. E. Kellett records that:

> I have seen men who could say that they did not know what
> lowness of spirits meant. John Wesley once owned to having
> been depressed for a total of fifteen minutes in fifty years; and
> I have seen men like Wesley in that respect. I never hope to
> see any human being more uniformly cheerful than some
> saintly (though perhaps bigoted) persons I came across in
> my youth. Confident in the divine favour, certain that the
> 'eternal God was their refuge, and that underneath were the
> everlasting arms,' they took good fortune and ill with more
> than the equanimity of Horatio.
>
> Even when death came, and their dearest were taken from
> them, they were calm: the parting was but for a moment, and
> the sundered would meet once more in a better world. At
> funerals they habitually sang cheerful hymns by the grave-
> side. When we, their grandchildren, think of them as
> miserable, it is because we imagine that people can be happy
> only in our way. How can creatures who never went to the
> theatre, rarely attended a concert, and then only when the
> 'good' Jenny Lind was singing, who never danced, and
> frowned on cards and billiards – how could they enjoy life?
> The fact is they enjoyed it to the full and they would have
> said of our pleasures what we say of theirs.

The great ministers have had their due meed of tribute paid
them, often in print, and now buried in dusty libraries and
mouldering typescript. Yet it can scarcely be over-emphasised
that at all times within our period it was the countless humble
Circuit ministers and local preachers – miners, sailors, gypsies,
bank clerks, teachers – who provided for the majority of
Nonconformists. It was they who – after passing certain basic

[1] 'Charles Brown of Ferme Park, 1855–1947', by W. MacDonald Wingfield
(MS.).

Bible examinations – by their rough eloquence, homely turn of phrase, humour and insight held congregations enthralled – or sometimes bored them stiff. As one correspondent brought up in a Pennine village near Rochdale notes:

Oddly enough it is the local preachers I remember best. One snowy-haired old man who, announcing the hymn 'Hold thou my hand' reached up his own hand above his head and I wouldn't have been surprised to see the hand of God appear to clasp his. Another old man was always brought by his daughter because he was blind and read from a Braille Bible which she always carried.

How powerful some of these local preachers were – at least in their effect upon small gatherings in (then) remote parts!

At Bispham Methodist chapel near Blackpool:

What wonderful times these ancestors of ours would have as they gathered in their 'Bethel' with its rough seating, heated by a large stove in the centre and illuminated in those days by candles, and later with hanging oil lamps. And in some senses, owing to the convincing manner in which the message was presented to them, what terrible times they also had.

Stories are told that the preacher on one occasion had made the devil so real to those present, and promised that he was lying in wait for them outside, that many of his hearers were afraid to leave the precincts of the House of God. And on another occasion after the Man of God had proclaimed his message with much effect and was going amongst and button-holing his hearers, that one cried out under fear, 'Dunna cum near me'.

It is easy to sneer at these 'Men of God'. Nevertheless, as an elderly correspondent from Outwell, Cambridgeshire, remarks:

Many of the preachers are today spoken of as being ignorant, but I am still thanking God for those early teachers and preachers who helped to shape my life; although they knew very little about theology, they preached chiefly from experience, not only what God had done for the old saints but what He had done and was doing for them.

Many of these teachers and preachers were good, upright, kind men. Consider William Bruce, the pipe-maker who lived at Chester-le-street:

He was converted [the *Durham Chronicle* recorded on his death in 1871], in the year 1810 and joined the Methodist Society. About a year after that period he began to preach that Gospel which had proved the instrument of his salvation. He possessed a vigorous mind, a discriminating and well-balanced judgement, a clear and acute understanding, and a richly-stored memory. He was a man of frank and genial disposition, artless simplicity, and thorough integrity. The basis of his elevated character was his habitual and un-affected Godliness. This was felt in the family, in social intercourse, and in all the engagements of his business life. Full of warm and generous impulses, he could not gaze upon the wretchedness and moral darkness around him without feeling and making some effort to dissipate the horror of its gloom, and make the world pulsate with the throbs of a new and happy life. He saw in the Gospel a boon and a blessing for the world. Like the sun, it was to shed its radiance upon all; like a bright and beautiful rainbow, it was to span the whole arch of heaven, and he felt his call to be a co-worker with God in bringing to fulfilment the vast design of mercy in leading back from the verge of ruin to the plains of heaven trophies of redeeming love.

Gifted with a good voice and an active imagination, his sermons were full of Divine truth, delivered with animation and force. One Sabbath morning he preached with such power and Holy Unction at Old Pensher that the congregation left their own service in the after part of the day and followed him to Coxgreen, that they might listen to him again. He 'Walked with God', and this was the secret of his remarkable power in prayer.[1]

Nor were all the locals ignorant of book learning, as the Paddington chapel monthly for June, 1913, records in an encomium of Thomas Nicholson:

[1] An off-print of this encomium was widely circulated in Durham and comes to me with note: 'a lovely record'.

His favourite studies were Systematic Theology and New Testament Greek. He gained high marks also in Apologetics and Philosophy. Dr Fairbairn, in one of his examination reports, paid him the tribute of a special reference in respect of a 'fine gift of analysis, accuracy of thought, and precision of phrase'.

Some locals were undoubtedly oddities. At Zion Congregational chapel, Flockton, Yorkshire, was a certain Robert Milthorpe, 'who was a most eccentric person':

He lettered his own tombstone, with, of course, the exception of the date of his death. This he did on a stone step, which he afterwards laid, with the lettering downwards, outside the door of his house. A friend of his promised to fill in the date of his demise, and the stone was subsequently raised over his last resting place. He also executed a similar piece of work albeit of a more novel character, to the memory of his son, J. G. V. Milthorpe, which bears the date 1849. This stone was formerly used as a land roller, but he begged it from his master – a farmer – for the purpose named. This curious monument is now erected.

Eccentric some were but seldom lacking in dramatic gift. At Eighton Banks, Grimstead, Co. Durham, United Methodist church, one minister, Casson by name, is recalled:

Casson, on his removal to a new sphere of labour, found that much was to be desired in the attendance of worshippers at his church. On visiting a house in the village, Casson requested the good lady of the house to lend him a clothes line. His request being granted, he proceeded, to the astonishment of the woman, to fasten the line to a hook in the roof, and placing the rope round his neck stood on a chair. The woman rushed out of the house shouting that a man was going to hang himself. The neighbours quickly crowded the kitchen, when Casson dismounted the chair, quietly fastened the door and commenced to talk to his hastily gathered and excited audience on their need of salvation. Casson never again lacked a congregation at his chapel.

The stories of the strange ways of preachers are legion. From Hampstead:

One godly man, a Mr R's, whose peculiar facial characteristics and actions in the pulpit always closely reminded us of the wicked hero of a certain ancient and popular street show, for he invariably ended his more fervid and soul-stirring sentences by throwing his long arms crosswise over the pulpit and bending his head over them.

A very diminutive man, a certain Mr H., when he came to preach had, in consequence of his diminished stature, a very elaborate structure of hassocks erected in the pulpit for his special benefit. On one occasion he was particularly vehement in his denunciation of those who had not received and would not receive grace, and, in his efforts to impress his words upon his hearers, the foundation of his elevation gave way and the little man disappeared from the view of his audience, to his intense discomfiture.

One local preacher in the Northwich, Cheshire, area would start his prayer in his pew. Then, still on his knees, would shuffle down the aisle to the communion rail. No one laughed for they were aware that he was caught up in his prayer and that this was a solemn moment with the Holy Spirit present.

One local preacher in the Sheffield area always spoke extempore and, as he was in his eighties, often would forget what he had intended to say and, knowing many of the congregation personally, he would drift off into eulogies about them. Addressing the organist he would declaim about him to the congregation telling how long he had been organist and finish 'Eh, 'Arry lad, it's good ter see thee ageean – God'll pay thee thi wages, lad!'

One local preacher called Sampson in the Chesterfield area preached on the evils of drink. 'You all know Satterthwaite,' he said. 'Oh aye,' the congregation intoned. 'Well, you might not know it but he's been sent to Matlock for t'cure. He were swimming about in t' bath when attendant threw a lighted match into t'water. But Sam were that riddled with whisky that water went up in a sheet of flame.' There was a pause. Then a member of the congregation said: 'I don't believe it.' To which Sampson replied 'Oh well, let it pass then.'

Some Nonconformist preachers had gifts they were ready to display beyond, as it were, the call of duty:

> Two ministers came to us who had been missionaries in West Africa and charming they were and most entertaining in every way. Their wide experience of whites and blacks, their stories of the manner in which the simple negroes responded to their presentation of the Gospel, their struggles against the influence of the witch doctors made rapturous listening to our youngish ears. The Rev. Mr Greensmith was one of these, with his charming wife, a full cut above the average minister. In addition he was a remarkable conjuror too, pennies and pepper pots disappearing like magic before your very eyes and reappearing remarkably in someone else's pocket. Furthermore he was a great slow bowler and the cricket club did very well when he was in residence.

And there was the odd minister or pastor who was regarded as difficult. In one church history it is told how a Mr C commenced his ministry on 7 July 1946 and in January 1947, after a very short and stormy career, this pastorate was terminated.

> I do not wish to dwell on this very painful episode, but if I am to give a true and faithful account of our history, I cannot neglect to record this section of it. Trouble arose in various forms, but seemed to stem from the pastor's desire to be the supreme authority in the Church.
>
> This, of course, had to be opposed, for we, as a Baptist community recognise no authority but the Body of Believers themselves. Inevitably conflicting loyalties fought for supremacy and in the heat of the battle many things were said and done by all parties which were afterwards regretted. Some members left the Church with Mr C to form a new worshipping body, but this was a complete failure. Others who left the Church for a time, rejoined us after further reflection.

As might be expected, some of the local preachers were no

milk-and-water characters. From Melton Mowbray in the 1880s
we hear of one:

> An exceptionally powerful man was returning from preach-
> ing. Going up a hill, the pony walking, he sat in a low gig. Two
> men stopped the pony and were on either side of the gig. They
> asked him if he'd any money so he rattled his pocket and they
> said: 'We are having it'. He said he thought not, so they
> leaned over the gig to get it and he took each by the scruff of
> the neck and bumped their heads together till they cried for
> mercy. So he gave them a lecture on the error of their ways
> and let them go. It was said he could take a raw potato in his
> hand and squeeze it till it was a pulp and came out between
> his fingers. The men would know when he got hold of them.

> Another local preacher was driving home late on Sunday
> evening and singing. A policeman stopped him and asked
> how many there were and he said four. The policeman turned
> his light to see and called him a liar. He said 'No, you cannot
> see, the Father, Son, Holy Ghost and poor old me'.

In earlier days 'Methodies' were regarded as an easy target
for 'young bloods'. In *Recollections from a Yorkshire Dale*,[1] we read
of farmer Charles – a wrestler in his youth – and his wife,
Susannah, who held services in their farmstead. After a time,
some young labourers thought it a good jape to plague them by
making noises round the house at meeting times, hustling and
insulting the believers as they came or went. They were asked
to behave themselves but replied to the effect that 'You soft-
headed psalm-singers can't make *us* quiet'.

After a particularly disorderly evening farmer Charles got
together all his papers and books, saddled his horse and rode to
Otley where he surprised the Superintendent Minister by
resigning his membership of the Methodist church. The Minister
remonstrated, but Charles insisted and refused all explanation.
At length the Minister reluctantly agreed to accept his resignation.

Charles then rode home, sought out the mischief-making
youths and told them he intended to teach them better

[1] By C. J. F. Atkinson, pp. 56–7.

behaviour. They jeered at him and said 'What can a softy Methody like thee do about it?'

To which Charles replied, 'I'm not a Methodist now', and proceeded to give them the mauling of their lives until they begged for mercy. Shortly afterwards he returned to the Superintendent and told him he wished to take up membership again. For twenty years more he led the little cause in peace.

The preachers feared God and preached his word but some might have come out of Dickens's novels. At Fakenham, Norfolk,

> A dear old chap who had walked five miles and was wearing trousers with flies was preaching on Jonah and kept repeating: 'The whale wriggled his tail and out came Jonah' and all the time he had his hands in his trouser pockets which made the front quite open – my friend sitting next to me in the choir pushed into me and said: 'If he don't mind, Jonah will come out.' Imagine keeping a straight face then!

They were all entirely themselves, without pretension. *The History of the Providence Baptist Chapel, Lumb, Lancs.*, by Annie Buckley, records that in 1854 the Rev. Samuel Jones, on 'one blazing afternoon became so roused that in the glow of his enthusiasm he threw off his coat, flung it behind him in the pulpit and proceeded to deliver a sermon long remembered by all who heard it. Absentees from the Sunday service invariably received a visit in the early part of the week and were forcibly reminded of the error of their ways.'

Some ministers, as well as local preachers, had lurid pre-conversion histories which they were far from ashamed to retail. The Rev. James Flanagan, a Primitive Methodist minister, did great work in the East End of London at Old Kent Road. In his younger days he was a drunkard and layabout. Often he was thrown out of pubs in Nottingham. He was a wife-beater and everything that was bad. He had a remarkable conversion and became an impulsive and whole-hearted Christian. He tells the story about himself, that as he lay in the gutter sodden in drink, people passed him by and said, 'Poor old Flanagan', but he was not worth lifting up. After his conversion he began his work of saving his pals themselves.

Another recollection of a Birmingham correspondent has its amusing aspect:

> The preacher was late in turning up and everybody was milling round. The organ was playing a voluntary. After some time I happened to cast my eye into the far corner of the room nearest the back door and there sat a poor old man. He had a dirty white beard as if he was a heavy smoker. He had on a black frock coat turning green. It was a very wet Sunday and I really thought he had come in out of the weather. I walked over to him, held out my hand to him and said: 'Good evening, Sir, but I don't know you.' He said: 'No but you will know me before the night is out, I'm the preacher.' He was sent as a substitute and he was an old Ranter. Didn't he lay into the Devil, I tell you it was a fair fight. He had a head cold, like many old men do have. And as he was flinging his arms about the streamers were running from his nose before he could use his handkerchief, he dashed the dew drops away with his fingers – or rather cut off their retreat. The congregation were spell-bound and all the choristers were sitting well forward in their seats.

Entertaining, too, were some chance juxtapositions. During the First World War, the following notice appeared in the press:

Mount Pleasant Free Church.
Morning 10.45. Subject: 'A Peep into Hell'.
The choir will sing the Anthem: O Taste and See.

The distances local preachers covered, often on foot, were legendary. At Station Road Primitive Methodist chapel, Doncaster, one was late to arrive:

> One of our local men started the service but after about twenty minutes William arrived hot and panting (it was a summer day). He had missed the trap and had walked the seven miles from Doncaster.
>
> The horse and trap started off from Doncaster, Christ Church at 12.30 and carried generally about six preachers. Two alighted at Hatfield but one of them had to walk to the next village, namely Woodhouse. Then the remainder would

STROUD CIRCUIT.

WESLEYAN METHODIST PREACHERS' PLAN,

From March the 7th, to July the 4th, 1858.

Morning Lessons.

> " Ye shall go and pray unto me, and I will hearken unto you." Jer. xxix. 12.

> " Lo ! I am with you always, even unto the end of the world." Matt. xxviii. 20.

PLACES & HOURS.	MARCH. 7	14	21	28	APRIL. 4	11	18	25	MAY. 2	9	16	23	30	JUNE. 6	13	20	27	JULY. 4	NAMES and RESIDENCES.
STROUD 10½	2	3	1½	2	3½	1	2	3	1	3	1	4	1	2½	1	2	1	2	1 J. BROWN., Stroud
.... 6½	3	2	3	1½	2	1	2	3	2	1	3	1	2	3	3	1	2½	1	2 J. WILLIS .. Brimscombe
Tuesday 7	1	2	1	2	1	2	1	3	7	1	2	1	2	1	1	2	1	2	3 J. KNOWLES., Cirencester
Friday Prayer M. 7	1	1	1	1	1	1	1	1	1	1	1	1	1	1	1	1	1		4 T. BLANCH., Bisley
CIRENCESTER...... 11	3	16	3½	1	2	3	1	4	3	1	2	3½	1	2	1	2	2½	3	5 W. HALL ... Cirencester
Tuesday 6	3	16	3½	3	1	3½	1½	4	3	1	2½	3	9	2	1	2½	3	16	6 J. WHITING., Bisley
.... 7	3	3	3	3	3	3	3	3	3	17	3	3	3	3	3	3	3	3	7 J. PRATT ... Stroud
Friday, Prayer M. 7	3	3	3	3	3	3	3	3	3	3	3	3	3	3	3	3	3	3	8 G. KING... Stroud
LITTLEWORTH 10½	16	9	2½	11	12	22	3½	8	4	1½	7	10	2	15	14	3½	7	16	9 R. CUMLEY .. Throop
.... 2½	16	9	2½	14	12	22	3½	8	1	15	10	2	15	11	3½	9	16	7	10 J. CHESNEY.. Chalford
Tuesday 7	1	2	1	2	1	2	1	2	2	1	7	2	1	2	1	2	1	2	11 H. MORTIMER... Littleworth
BRIMSCOMBE 10½	21	1?	9½	7	10	2	4½	11	15	16	10	16	2½	10	14	1	4	9	12 T. LEWIS .... Oakridge
Wednesday 6	12	1	2½	15	18	14	3½	15	1½	16	7	8	2½	10	3	11	12	2	13 C.M.SAVORY,.. Cirencester
.... 7	2	1	2	1	2	1	2	1	2	1	1	2	F	1	2	1	2	1	14 T. WEBB.... Chalford
CHALFORD 2½	4	1?	11	8½	21	4	9	2	15	14	11	17	7½	2	16	1½	9	F	15 R. GRANT ... Stroud
Thursday 7	F	2	1	2½	8½	14	2	10	9	15	6	11	17	7	12	16	1½	9	16 C. CARSON ...Stroud
.... 7	P	2	1	2	P	2	1	2	2	P	1	2	F	P	1	2	P	2	
RANDWICK 10½	14	15	4½	18	1	16	8	2½	1	3	19	17	15	4	4½	9	1	16	ON TRIAL
.... 6	1	15	4½	24	1	16	8	2½	1	9	24	3½	10	1	7	4	8½	2	17 G. RANDELL .. Cirencester
Thursday 7	2	1	5½	4	2	1	P	1	P	1	F	1	1	P	1	7	1	2	EXHORTERS
BISLEY 10½	8	2	1	3½	19	15	16	1	17	2	8	1	21	3½	10	13	8	14	18 J. H. C. .. Randwick
.... 6	8	4	7	4½	9	15	16	12	1	4	8	9	1	4½	7	12	4	3	19 J. S. ... ...Littleworth
Wednesday 7	1	2	2		2	1	2	1	2	1	1	2	1	2	1	2		2	20 Prayer Leaders., Stroud
OAKRIDGE 2	15	19	14	16½	4	8	7	1½	17	2	13	1½	11	3½	9	4½	8		21 Prayer Leaders., Cirencester
Wednesday 6	15	2½	10½	16½	21	8	9	12	1½	21	21	16	12	19	3½	9	4½	8	
.... 7	3½		3		2		3		2		3½			3½			3½		FROM OTHER CIRCUITS.
TARLTON 2½	6	14	17	3½	16	19	21	13	1	21	12	4	7	13	16½	19	17	10	22 FORD ... Horsley
Wednesday 7	3		3	3	3		3	3		3		3		3	3		3	3	23 WHITE ... Stonehouse
TUNLEY 2½	8		2½	10	4½	21	12	9	19	1½	21	4	16	11	12	7½	10	13	24 FORD ... Stonehouse
.... 6		19		20		1		14		13	20			16		20			
THRUPP 2½	19		9			17		14		17	16		10		17	2	3		
.... 7		2				1				20					20				
DAGLINGWORTH ... 2	17	16	21		13	3	17		3½	3	13	1	3½		13	17	2		
Wednesday 7		3			3		3		3		3		3			3	3		

A LIST OF THE MINISTERS

Stationed in the Stroud Circuit, from the year 1797, when it was separated from Gloucester, and became the head of a Circuit.

1797. James Rogers, William Moulton.
1798. James Rogers, William Moulton.
1799. James Rogers, William Palmer.
1800. John Pritchard, John Bagnal.
1801. John Pritchard, Thomas Gee.
1802. Jeremiah Brettell, William Williams.
1803. Jeremiah Brettell, Hugh Ramson.
1804. Benjamin Rhodes, Samuel Woolmer, John Rogers.
1805. Benjamin Rhodes, Samuel Woolmer.
1806. Robert Hopkins, Edmund Shaw; Ben. Rhodes Sup.
1807. Joseph Cole, Edmund Shaw; Benjamin Rhodes Sup.
1808. Joseph Cole, William Blagborne; Ben. Rhodes Sup.
1809. James M' Byron, Jonas Jagger; Ben. Rhodes Sup.
1810. James M' Byron, Jonas Jagger; Ben. Rhodes Sup.
1811. John Ogilvie, Charles Greenley.
1812. John Smith, Charles Greenley, George Moorhouse.
1813. John Smith, Michael Cousin, John Appleyard.
1814. F. Collier, M. Cousin, R. Moody; J. Sqarebridge Sup
1815. Francis Collier, Richard Moody, Thomas Hayes.
1816. William Shelmerdine, Richard Wintle, T. Eastwood.
1817. William Shelmerdine, Rich. Wintle, Philip Rawlins.
1818. William Shelmerdine, Rich. Wintle, Philip Rawlins.
1819. John Dean, William Woodall, Seth Morris.
1820. John Dean, William Woodall, Seth Morris.
1821. James Blackett, William Sleep, William Mowatt.
1822. James Blackett, William Sleep, William Mowatt.
1823. James Blackett, W. Sleep, William Harrison junior.
1824. Samuel Woolmer, H. Parsons, W. Harrison junior.
1825. Sam. Woolmer, Humphrey Parsons Daniel Hateley.
1826. Charles Hawthorne, Tho. Fletcher; D. Osborne Sup

NOTICES.

1. The Quarterly Meetings will be held at Stroud, on Wednesday, March the 31st, and Wednesday, July the 1st, 1858, at Three o'clock. The Local Preachers to meet precisely at Two.

2. The Quarterly Fast Days will be Friday, March 26th, and Friday, June 25th.

3. Every Preacher is expected conscientiously to attend to his own appointments, or get them supplied by an accredited substitute.

4. Both Parents are expected to be present at the baptism of a child.

5. The Stroud Annual Missionary Meeting will be held on Monday, May the 10th. One of the Deputation may be expected to preach at three o'clock in the afternoon.

6. A Tea Meeting will be held at Brimscombe on Wednesday, March the 3rd. And a Tea Meeting also will be held at Tarlton, on Wednesday, May 26th, in aid of the Funds of the Chapel.

7. The Wesleyan Magazines, the New Sunday School Hymn Book, 4d. each, embossed gilt edge, 9d. The Conference List of Lessons, Reward Books, &c., may be had of the Superintendent.

8. The Annual Meeting of the Trustees, and chapel Stewards of the Circuit, will be held in the School-room, Stroud, on Monday, April 19th, to commence at six o'clock. The Steward of each Chapel is desired to bring or send his book and accounts properly balanced.

REFERENCE.
S. Sacrament of the Lord's supper.
P. Prayer Meeting. L. Lovefeast.
c. Address to Sunday-school Children
T. Tickets Renewing.
M. Quarterly Collection.
SS. Sun-school Anniversary.
E. Education Fund Collection.
M. Missionary Sermons.

LIST OF MINISTERS continued.

1827. Charles Hawthorne, Thomas Fletcher.
1828. Jonathan Williams, William Baker.
1829. Jonat'an Williams, Willian Baker.
1830. James Whitworth, Thomas Steele.
1831. James Whitworth, Thomas Steele.
1832. James Whitworth, John Gordon.
1833. Paul Orchard, John Gordon.
1834. Paul Orchard, John Gordon.
1835. Paul Orchard, James Bartholomew.
1836. Robert Wheeler, James Bartholomew.
1837. Robert Wheeler, William Jackson junior.
1838. Robert Wheeler, William Jackson junior.
1839. Joseph Marsh, William Jackson junior.
1839. Joseph Marsh, Thomas Bolas.
1840. John Stevens, Samuel Lawrence.
1841. John Stevens, John Fletcher.
1842. John Stevens, John Fletcher; Thomas Fletcher Sup.
1843. John Wevill, John S. Jones; Thomas Fletcher Sup.
1844. J. Wevill, J. S. Jones, John Lyth; T. Fletcher Sup.
1845. J. Wevill, Timothy Moxon, J. Lyth; T. Fletcher Sup.
1846. J. Nicklin, T. R. Moxon, J. Lyth; T. Fletcher Sup.
1847. J. Evans, W. Worker, J. H. Rigg; T. Fletcher Sup.
1848. John Evans, William Worker, James H. Rigg.
1849. T. Webb, G. B. Mellor, J. Bramley; W. Mowatt, Sup.
1850. Thomas Webb, G. B. Mellor, John Brown, 3rd.
1851. Thomas Webb, G. B. Mellor, Thomas James.
1852. John Connon, T. James, John L. Bull.
1853. John Connon, Thomas James, J. L. Bull.
1854. John Connon, Samuel Wesley, W. P. Johns.
1855. John Brown, 2nd, S. Wesley, W. P. Johns.
1856. John Brown, 2nd, S. Wesley, Joseph Willis.
1857. John Brown, 2nd, J. Willis, John Knowles, 2nd.

PRICE TWOPENCE.

C. H. Savory, Printer, Stationer, &c., "Journal" Office, near the Post Office, Cirencester.

THE PLAN: All Methodist Circuits, i.e. groups of towns and villages organised under a Superintendent and with usually one or two other ministers, issued a regular plan to show who was to conduct the services in each chapel in the circuit. Many of these scheduled were 'local' (i.e. lay) preachers. The above from Stroud has some of the complications associated with Bradshaw's railway timetable.

continue the journey to Stainforth where another one would alight. Then on to Fishlake where the driver-preacher would leave the horse to the attention of a local farmer to feed and water it, while the remaining preacher had to walk to the village of Sykehouse, a distance of four miles, take the service there, and then start off back to Fishlake for the return journey. You can imagine the time the party arrived back home especially when the weather was unfavourable. Such arduous journeying was not always rewarding. One local preacher in the Doncaster Priory Place circuit was planned to preach during the First World War some twenty-seven miles from his home. On his return home he curtly wrote to the Superintendent Minister: 'I have just got home having cycled fifty-four miles to preach to three people. Please do not plan me there again.'

The Sunday I most looked forward to was when we children used to hurry to Chapel because the fishermen were going to preach. Two brothers West would preach. From Bacton, Norfolk they would come dressed in the ganzies[1] that was the typical navy blue sweater like all the fishermen wore.

I must not forget to tell you there came a day when one of the brothers West was drowned at sea. After that the other brother preached alone but it was never the same. They sang with such feeling.

Some correspondents are by no means blinded by nostalgia in their memories, as a lady from Oldbury, Worcs., makes clear:

We thought the local preachers were awful and too fond of their own voices. There are always the exceptions of course. These worthy men have improved over the years. We were beside ourselves one occasion when the local preacher said 'and Jesus turned the local water into wynd'! Another treated us to an accordion solo and another apologised for removing his teeth.

Many of them were very hard working men, I am sure most sincere but how they went on, taking up a lot of the Lord's time! It was a treat to have a student from a neighbouring theological college or the resident ministers – some better than

[1] As jerseys came from Jersey, so ganzies originated in Guernsey.

others. We had a selection of these because of the change[1] every so many years.

At the time we started, the junior minister was young and to us girls very romantic as he had lost his fiancée by death some weeks before the wedding day. There was another – a very small nice man – but we felt sure he had to help wash the baby's napkins as the women of the Women's Own meeting told us he came with the end of his fingers crinkled as though they had recently been in hot water! Another nice man, a bachelor, hot-footed it to our home on Sundays to partake of the cold joint.

The strangest things happened in the pulpit as the son of one preacher remembers:

When he [his father] was planned to preach in some of the country chapels not too far away, he would take me with him. On one occasion of this kind I have a very vivid recollection. He sat down, meditating, with his eyes closed for the first four verses then fell on his knees and prayed. I was sitting in the front and he disappeared from my sight. It was a terrible shock to me. I thought he had dropped down dead! My thought was that I was alone, nobody knew where I was and I did not know the way home and so I was lost for ever.

Oh, the joy when he stood up to continue the service! I remember how I clung to his hand more tightly than ever on our way home.

Incidentally, this correspondent and others reveal much about the life of the children of a minister. In the 1900s,

My mother was never able to speak in public but she attended every meeting at Chapel. We had a little maid at home who looked after the children when they were too young to go.

This was the regular pattern of one of the Sundays. We went to Sunday School an hour before the morning service. We sat through the service – about one hour and a half – no

[2] Methodist ministers in particular moved from one Circuit to another every three years, though at the request of their congregations the period could be extended to five.

children's address in those days. We went to dinner. Our
Sunday dinner we had on the Saturday so that there would be
no unnecessary work on the Sabbath. Then to Sunday School
in the afternoon. An hour and a half or two hours relaxation
when we read Sunday books – *Pilgrim's Progress* (I can see
clearly the terrifying illustrations even now), tracts such as
'Children leading adults to Christ', 'Buy your own Cherries' –
all with improving morals. Then we sallied forth to join the
mission band, my father leading the way, generally walking
backwards, his hair flowing in the breeze, we following,
singing lustily:

> Turn to the Lord and seek salvation,
> Sound the praise of his dear name,
> Glory, honour and salvation,
> Christ the Lord will come to reign.
> Let not conscience make you linger
> Now of father fondly dream, etc.

At each street corner we all gathered round my father,
people standing at most open doors, many smoking. My father
would give a little homily and invite them all to the service
at our chapel. Occasionally one or two would join us.

Evening service was followed by a long noisy prayer
meeting. Returning home, we and some of our day school
friends, many of them not Methodists, would gather round
the harmonium and sing our favourite hymns. Supper after
they had gone and so to bed.

I can imagine some readers saying, 'What a dreadful day!'
but it was not. To us it was a very happy day.

There were many characters whom we were delighted to
see in the pulpit. There was an old local preacher who could
not read or write. He began his sermon in the orthodox dress,
but getting warm he would take off his coat, roll up his sleeves
and really get to work. He didn't like people knowing that he
could not read and he opened the pulpit Bible and acted
exactly as if he could read. He could recite the passages of
scripture, 'line out' the hymns perfectly well. Once, if not
more times, some naughty person had got in before the service
and turned the Bible upside down, but he read it just as well

as usual. (The choir were behind and could see the open Bible and it was from them that we learnt what had happened.)

Sunday for the children of strict Nonconformist parents was not always a day of rejoicing, for example from Sheffield:

> Sunday was a dull day for us. No lay music was permitted either on the piano or the gramophone. Nothing but religious music in the form of hymns or cantatas. Mother was always a sluggard in getting up on Sunday morning, so father would be up and about early making sure everybody would be ready in time for Chapel. 'Time for Chapel' he would call every few minutes when it was getting near to 10.15 a.m. One Sunday morning mother actually remained in bed until it was far too late to go. 'Maggie!' he shouted, 'you'll miss Chapel!' A faint response came from mother's bedroom, 'Damn the chapel!' Upon this father rushed upstairs and said: 'What did you say, Maggie?' She said, 'I said damn the chapel.' This was not to be tolerated and all the power of the Almighty was orally brought to bear on mother, who obstinately refused to recant. The outcome was that father the next night removed all his clothes out of their double room and slept in the spare room for a week by himself as a condign punishment for mother!
>
> Mother had tried all the usual experiments with cooking for Sunday. Roasting the joint on Saturday and having it cold on Sunday – most unpopular with father, who liked it hot with Yorkshire pud, his portion having currants in it, so that he could have sugar on it instead of gravy, and leaving the joint to cook slowly during the time the whole family was out at chapel. On two attempts this had resulted in the most charcoal biscuit of a joint, annoying father more than mother's lost Chapel. Hence Mother's preference to stay at home on Sunday morning.

The Chapel ethos, a Leeds correspondent observes, was an extension of that of his home. Although his mother did not go to the length of cooking the Sunday dinner on Saturday, as some Nonconformists did, there were many things he was not allowed to do on Sundays. He had to chop enough wood on Saturday night to light both the Sunday and Monday fires: no chip-chopping on Sundays. He could play no games. His reading was censored. He might go for a walk between afternoon school and tea but he must not pick flowers. They sang hymns round the piano between tea and the evening service!

After the service we usually had two or three friends in and I was allowed to play some pieces, but only those which my mother supposed to be 'Sunday' pieces. Her standard was simple. Anything gay and bright was not Sunday. Years later, when in her eyes I could do no wrong, she would ask me, after some livelier movement from a Beethoven sonata, if I was sure that was a Sunday piece: the slow movements went un-questioned. A baritone singer was allowed to sing about Nazareth or Jerusalem. We all joined in 'The Lost Chord' whose final climax I played with as much *sforza* as I thought my mother would tolerate. This was really too enjoyable to be proper and if the chord had not been lost from a church organ she would almost certainly have stopped us.

One man, a local preacher for fifty years, remembers a service he conducted at the Methodist chapel in Sheringham, Norfolk, when most of the congregation were old salts of the sea in sweaters. His text was 'Wake them that sleepeth'.

It was a rather hot day and towards the end of my robust discourse I shouted 'Awake! them that sleepeth' and caught my hand on the big Bible in front of me. It fell on the head of a poor old fisherman who was fast asleep. He gasped and jumped up and the whole congregation laughed.

The same preacher recalls two other occasions. Once he was playing the organ at a big Methodist revival meeting in a village. The preacher was a big man with huge hands and he was prone to 'Spoonerisms'. He put up his hands and said: 'Pause, Brethren' and some boys in the front giggled. I think they were thinking of 'paws'. However this ruffled him and he shouted out 'I want you to come to the Shoving Leopard'.

Again, a certain shortsighted preacher at Wroxham was fumbling for his glasses to read out the next hymn. Eventually he found that he had left them in the hymn-book at the back and he involuntarily said in a loud whisper: 'Well, I be damned.' The service did not seem a success after that. He was never asked again.

Some local preachers emerged from the poorest – often cruel – circumstances. In the history of Mount Tabor Wesleyan church, Halifax, 1820–1970, is the story of Jonathan Saville, who was born near Bradford of poor parents. His mother died when he was only three years of age, and his father, being unable to support him, sent him to the local poor house. He was then given into the charge of the manager of some neighbouring coal mines, where he was compelled to do laborious and exhausting work. He gradually sank beneath the hardship, and his master found it necessary to remove him from the drudgery of the coal pit to his own house where he was employed at the spinning wheel. He was still treated cruelly and on one occasion was so wickedly belaboured that his leg was broken. No medical aid was called in and he had still to continue his work.

Happier times came when his employer returned him to the workhouse. Here, through the kindness of the master, he regained considerable strength and was able to learn the rudiments of reading and writing. His industry in a few years enabled him to take up a position with a Mr Swaine of Cross Hills, Halifax. About that time he was converted and applied himself to the work of God. He became prayer leader, class leader, and local preacher. He traversed the whole district of Halifax for the purpose of establishing and holding prayer meetings and exhorting his hearers to diligence and faithful service.

The same chapel history refers to the type of preaching then prevalent. There was, for example, the celebrated preacher, Isaac Marsden, who on one of his visits to Mount Tabor, took a piece of chalk and drew a line on the floor of the chapel inviting his hearers to step over into eternal life or remain for ever in outer darkness.

Another eccentric local preacher was Thomas Greenwood from Luddenden Dean. His popular name was 'Tommy o' th' Heys'. He was a farmer and to save the time taken in changing clothes, he would often conduct the service in his clogs and working garments. The simplicity of the times is illustrated by several stories concerning this worthy. A circuit minister preaching at the Dean was entertained by 'Tommy o' th' Heys'. The frugal meal consisted solely of a large bowl of porridge. Unused to fare of this kind the good man hesitated to partake of it. Whereupon Thomas said, 'Fotch 'im a thaum [thumb] o' butter, lass!' The hostess left the table and returned with a piece of butter on her thumb. This she put in the porridge, Thomas remarking as she did so, 'Oss na! tha's t' fat o' t' land i' t' front o' thi.' ('Fall to now! you have the fat of the land before you.')

It is also said of him that, after acting as treasurer of Ludden-den Dean Sunday School for a year, at the auditing of books he produced an old teapot from which he poured money, remark-ing as he did so, 'I've put all in theer 'as I've drawn, an' I've ta'en all aat 'as I've paid.'

The feeding of these travelling preachers was a problem in days when food was a scarce commodity, as we learn from Oswestry, Shropshire:

About 1904 when I was eight years old my father, who was a local preacher, took me with him to Hindford, about six miles from Oswestry, where he was to conduct afternoon and evening services – in those days it was nothing for preachers to *walk* up to twenty and more miles to take services.

After the first service we had started to walk home to Oswestry for tea, when an old woman who had been at the service said to my father: 'Where are you going, Mr Francis?' 'Back home for tea,' replied my father. 'Has no one asked you to tea then?' – 'No,' said my father, 'you see there are two of us!' 'Well, well,' said the woman, 'you can't walk all the way back and return for the service tonight. I've never taken a preacher, but I could give you a cup of tea.'

We went in her little stone cottage; I remember the walls were about a yard thick and in the window was a lovely red geranium in full bloom. She got a few sticks and soon had a fire going, but what a bare room, no pictures on the wall, no carpet or mats, just a table and a few chairs – yes I remember no table cloth. She was a widow of about seventy and of course there were no widows' pensions in those days.

The kettle boiled, the tea was made and we three drew up the table. A pot of tea, part of a loaf of bread (no butter nor

5.1 BAND OF HOPE procession, Coventry.

TANOA

THAKOMBAU

RATU TIMOTHY

TWO PRINCESSES

FROM CANNIBALISM TO CHRISTIANITY: FOUR GENERATIONS.

5.2 CANNIBALISM TO CHRISTIANITY:
An illustration from *The Methodist Recorder*,
Christmas 1899.

6.1 SALVATION ARMY: 'Early Day Witness', picture from City of Refuge, Paris.

6.2 SAILORS' REST: Liverpool Wesleyan mission, late nineteenth century.

margarine). She went to the cupboard and brought a small jar with about an inch of damson jam in the bottom. 'I expect your son will like that, it's a bit of home made,' she said. My father 'gave thanks' and we began our meal. To my dying day I will remember with gratitude this wonderful meal, for she gave all she had. It was a most uplifting communion in the real sense and I shall be ever grateful to God for this experience. My father took for his text for the evening service: 'The Widow's Mite'.

About 1904 my father, who was a Primitive Methodist local preacher, took me with him to West Felton, near Oswestry, where he was to conduct the afternoon service – the chapel was in a loft over a cow stable – the sermon was about the falling of the walls of Jericho. When he was three-quarters of the way through his sermon one of the cows in the stalls below the chapel let out a mighty bellow, whereupon my father said: 'Friends, that noise was *NOTHING* compared with that which blew down the walls of Jericho,' and then gave out the closing hymn.

It should not be supposed that all the fervour and physical energy went out of Nonconformist evangelising with the end of the reign of King Edward VII. During the Second World War, the Rev. Leslie Newman travelled through a part of north Yorkshire on horseback, as John Wesley had done. He describes it in his book, *Highways and the Byways*:

I have often referred to a meeting on a village green, there were between forty and fifty such but I select the one at Slingsby for from here we journey naturally to the Wolds. When we were still some eight miles from the village I knew something was going to happen, for a passing cyclist greeted me with the words: 'I know where you are going.' 'Oh, where?' 'Slingsby, and they are expecting you!' It became clearer when entering the village, several mothers came out and called to their children, saying: 'Eh, cum here and look at the preacher.' It was abundantly clear when coming to the green, I saw that someone had brought out a number of chairs and forms and that not only was every seat occupied, but a large number of people stood around under the trees. Nothing had been forgotten. There was a piano, even a groom to take charge of Dick. We were just going to begin the meeting when the local rector walked up. He readily responded to an invitation to lead us in prayer, 'May God bless this meeting,' he said earnestly, and if ever a prayer was answered this surely was. To borrow appropriate language from Wesley's journal: 'For an hour the people listened without movement.' Incidentally Wesley himself had preached on this green.

Noting the piano, I recalled that in the hymn-book there is a tune called 'Slingsby' and I asked if they could sing it. Sing it! They could! They sang with a fervour and harmony that might have been envied by many a city choir. I shall never sing that tune again without seeing the cheerful crowd singing it in the village after which it is named. Later I discovered that the tune had been written by the son of a predecessor of the vicar present with us.

Speaking of hospitality to visiting preachers, the historian of the Methodist church, Thornhill Edge, Dewsbury, Yorkshire, himself a member of the church and a preacher, records that the problem was not always food; it was sometimes awe:

> In olden days it was a pleasure to most to make a cup of tea for a stranger, but a preacher! Well, a preacher was regarded with a kind of awe and good people feared lest they should do or say something out of place in the presence of these holy men. Please forgive this observation and, you who read this history, please remember that we preachers are just ordinary people; some may have larger appetites than others but may the victuals be plain or costly it is the spirit in which they are given that matters. And those who receive are justly proud to be welcomed to your homes be they humble or palatial. This same difficulty had been troubling the congregation of our church in the year 1890.

Narrow-minded some Nonconformists certainly were in the nineteenth and early twentieth centuries. They were, for instance, fixated on the dangers of alcohol, even in small sips taken by those attending the sacrament of the Lord's Supper. So in the *Methodist New Connexion Magazine* of March 1906, this advertisement appears:

PURE COMMUNION WINES

Their purity and freedom
from Alcohol make them
the ideal Wines for use
in our Church Services.

OVER 5,000 CHURCHES HAVE
ENDORSED BY REGULAR USE
THEIR EXCELLENCE & MERIT.

Made entirely of sound Grape
Juice and absolutely undiluted.
Send 2/6 for four samples of
various kinds to F. Wright,
Mundy & Co, Kensington, London, W.

Nevertheless, the non-alcoholic nature of the communion wine did not dim the enthusiasm, for in the same magazine is the story of David Hall, the founder of the church at Crigglestone, near Wakefield, Yorkshire. David was a Midgley man and was converted there. He was still in young manhood when a serious affliction overtook him and he drew near to the gates of death. The Rev. T. Batty and other friends, however, came together and prayed for David's restoration.

After his recovery David vividly narrated his heavenward flight; for he most solemnly declared that he had been to Heaven. On the way there he had been mysteriously furnished with a certificate of admission, but, fearing that he might lose it, he made several of his own. On arriving at the gates of Heaven, he presented a certificate of his own manufacture, but was refused admission. He then exhibited the original and was at once admitted. Immediately he was accepted, he sensibly experienced seraphic bliss, being caught up into the realm of sweetest song.

By and by, there came to him a holy one who said he would have to return for a while; but David expressed his whole-hearted desire to remain. 'Nay, nay,' said the angel, 'you must go.' Then said he, 'I'll be sure to come again?' 'Yes, yes,' said the other angelic beings about him, 'you'll be sure to come again.' From the very hour of the intercession of his friends for him, David Hall began to recover.

The fervent spirit of David Hall continued and when the chapel was opened he would secretly steal into it day by day and ascending the pulpit, he would earnestly petition his Lord that His preaching servant of the ensuing Sabbath might be filled with power. From the pulpit he would pass on to the pews, and, taking them in order, he would kneel down in the places where any usually sat for whom he felt that special prayer was needed.

Joshua Butcher is himself an outstanding instance of the many answers given to David Hall's prayer. Joshua had resisted the Gospel appeal for some time, when on one Sabbath evening, as he returned home alone across a field-path he was seized by Almighty and Invisible Hands stretched out from Heaven itself. Instantly he cried out, 'Lord, if Thou wilt spare me until tomorrow night, I will go to class and give myself up.' Joshua kept his word and was standing trembling at the door, when David as if expecting him, came and welcomed him with a hearty 'Come in, lad,' and a warm handshake.

David's sympathies were with the teaching and preaching which wooed and won by Christ's constraining love. How often have tears been seen to stream down his face at the very mention of the Lord's crucifixion! Oh, for the mighty increase of such praying brethren and such spiritual leadership in the Methodism of today![1]

The Nonconformists, incidentally, were the first to accept the fact that women, too, could and ought to play a part in evangelising. Apart from the Salvation Army lasses, there were the deaconesses. A Sheffield correspondent recalls that the deaconesses attached to the Chapel wore navy blue costumes and navy blue bonnets with long blue and white streamers hanging down the back. Not all lady evangelists, however, were well regarded:

There was the Sister M, spragged toothed and (unkindly mention) rather moustached for a female. Whenever she came to preach she *always* came home with us for Sunday dinner.

[1] This, it is historically worth repeating, in A.D. 1906.

She continued with the sermon right through dinner – no one could get a word in edgeways. She finally subsided, at father's request on a settee, snoring but at last off the sermon. We youngsters rather thought she fancied the old man.

The question of pay for ministers – or stipend[1] as it was usually called – was a delicate one and varied from one denomination to another. Many had free houses, particularly the Methodists who normally moved every three years, and often were provided with basic furniture, heating and lighting. Money, of course, has changed greatly in value, so that some of the amounts given below require considerable multiplication to give a contemporary equivalent.

The Rev. John Sowerby, ordained at Zion Congregational chapel at Flockton in 1833, got only £8 a year for two years, and for several years after various sums up to £20 a year; but being a weaver by trade he stuck to his loom, and, as it was said, while he manufactured cloth he also manufactured sermons for his flock on the Lord's day. Things improved, however, and he was able to bid adieu to the loom and bring up his family on the emoluments of his church, viz., £80 a year and cottage rent free.

In this connection, a comment of George III is not inapposite. It is reported in the history of the Independent Congregational chapel at Gloucester Street, Weymouth, that:

> One of George III's household attended the meeting-house in St Nicholas Street. The King said to him:
> 'Clarke, does your minister pray for me?'
> 'Yes, please your Majesty, always and very devotedly.'
> 'Then tell your minister I am obliged to him for he isn't paid for it.'

At Swingfield Methodist chapel near Folkestone in the 1840s: 'The Missionary (the chapel had just opened) received as salary in 1845 the sum of three guineas a quarter.' If Goldsmith's vicar was 'passing rich on £40 a year', then the financial state of these

[1] A somewhat *risqué* story, current in emancipated Nonconformist circles, relates that a minister's wife explained that she and her husband were unable to have many children 'because of my husband's small stipend'.

early Methodist preachers was a kind of miraculous poverty. In these early days there were also women pastors. Several laboured in the Swingfield area and their quarterly salary was £1 15s.

Some older chapels could afford more. At Tottlebank Baptist church, near Ulverston, formed in 1669 under the Five Mile Act of 1665, by Colonel Roger Sawrey, formerly a Parliamentarian soldier, a pastor who started in 1896 was the second highest-paid accredited minister of the six Baptist ministers in the north-west (i.e. Coniston and Hawkshead, Ulverston and Dalton-in-Furness, Barrow-in-Furness, Millom, Maryport, being the others) and received a manse rent-free and £80 per annum. (The minister of Coniston and Hawkeshead only received £60 per annum.)

At Woolton Congregational church, Liverpool, in 1891 the books show:

	£	s.	d.
To Rev. William Davies, Salary for quarter ending March 1891	50	0	0
To coals, 7 tons at 15/6	5	8	6
To clock-winder (6 months)		5	0
To W. Smith, Chapel-keeper (wages to June 30)	10	0	0
To R. Roughley & Sons, 1 washer on cistern; To Plumber, 1 hour		1	0

Visiting preachers, however, were not always so undemanding. Some time before the First World War at West End Methodist chapel, King Cross, Halifax:

> The minister spoke well, and at one point in his sermon he appealed to the young folks to be more diligent in their service but he asked, 'Where are the young people?' We did look a few in number in that large church, but many of us were distressed. We didn't deserve that. The climax came. The collection was about £10 and the Rev. F. Ballard's fee was £8.8.od. When told of the struggling little cause he accepted £6.6.od.

The redoubtable Methodist evangelist, Gipsy Smith, undertook a fourteen-day mission in the New Forest where his marquee was frequently packed. But he took a good stipend and two chapel members had to foot the bill. Gipsy Smith also visited Hockcliffe Street chapel, Leighton Buzzard. Some of the boys there expected him and possibly his family to arrive in caravans, possibly selling pegs. He drew up in a Rolls Royce.

Some chapels luckily had generous patrons. From St Thomas Street Methodist church, Claremount, Halifax, it is recorded in February 1856, that Mr Joseph Crossley[1] kindly offered the circuit one hundred guineas to keep another preacher, and 'we thankfully accept his offer'.

The Reverend Samuel Laycock was employed at one guinea a week, 'to mission the town and present a journal of his labours to the circuit committee once a fortnight'.

At this time the New Bank Society was meeting at Widow Horsfall's in Lower Garden Street, Charlestown, but Mr Crossley offered to pay for a room to be used for preaching. For five years Mr Crossley gave financial support to the circuit showing a special interest in the Charlestown (or New Bank) Society. In May 1862 a deputation met him to purchase land from Crossley's for the erection of a chapel and two days later the local committee approached the Connexional Building Committee to buy land at New Bank (and also at Brighouse) for new chapels. A third preacher, supported by Mr Crossley, was given special oversight of societies 'over the Bridge' and classes were established at Shibden and Northowram during this period. Crossleys gave £350 towards the erection of chapels at Norland, Bradshaw and Brighouse as well as New Bank.

If preachers were sometimes a trial to their congregations, so were some of their congregations to them:

One lady who had a rather large family, was a regular attendant. She used to come with a child, not more than a few weeks old. She did not feed the child on the breast, but out of a ginger beer bottle, one with a glass marble in the neck of the bottle. It was a regular thing for a trick to be played on the woman. When the child had finished its feed the woman put the bottle on the floor beside her. Someone sitting in the row

[1] Presumably of the Crossley carpet-manufacturing family.

behind her would jut his toe to the bottle and it would go careering down the aisle of the church, making a proper commotion and rattle.

A preacher was sometimes rather obviously ticked off:

One well-known character was the treasurer of the Chapel at Batley Carr, Yorkshire. At the start of a sermon he would ostentatiously place his gold hunter in front of him, and woe betide the minister who exceeded his allotted twenty minutes. Our treasurer would then 'Humph and Gerumph' and should this fail to stop the spate of words, he would shuffle his backside on the polished pew until the resulting rude noises would dry the poor parson up, by sheer volume of decibels.

There was, for instance, Old Sammy, a member of the Common Hall Street chapel at Chester in the late 1880s:

Old Sammy was *very* old, poor and wizened, quite un-educated but with a remarkable knowledge of the Bible. He had a living by pushing another old man to a neighbouring chapel in a pushcart and so often had to leave meetings early. We youngsters used to laugh at him, but we had a real respect for him, he was so honest.

One Sunday morning the second minister was preaching on the prodigal son. He was describing his plight and saying something like this: 'All his friends had forsaken him and he could only get a job looking after pigs, and he was so hungry that he ate the husks that the swine did eat.' This was too much for Sammy. He knew his Bible too well and he stood up, facing the minister and shouted: ' 'E never did fill 'is belly wi' the 'usks, 'E never did fill 'is belly wi' the 'usks,' picked up his hat from under the seat and made for the door. He opened the door, turned and looked at the minister and almost screeched ' 'E never *did* fill 'is belly wi' the 'usks' and went out and slammed the door. Consternation! Poor Minister!

Even the animal kingdom was not always kind to preachers. At Luddenden Dean chapel near the moorland about five miles from the centre of Halifax, one warm August day, the chapel doors were left open during the service. The sermon was about to start when a panic-stricken donkey being attacked by vast numbers of infuriated bees dashed into the body of the sanctuary. There was pandemonium for a time before the animal could be quietened and the insects expelled. It was the custom at that time of the year for bee keepers to bring their hives to benefit from the heather then in bloom. They used donkeys for transport and combined business with religion. The animal in question had been left to graze during the service and had suffered the penalty for too closely examining the hives. It is possibly apocryphal that the preacher's text was 'And the Lord opened the mouth of the ass and he said unto Balaam . . .'.

Even the vocally devout could be a distraction as at a remote Dorset village, early this century:

> I remember an old crippled man with a long white beard who would suddenly go down on his good knee and say 'God Bless us all,' and all the people answered 'Amen. Praise the Lord.' Then he would usually say 'Bless our dear brethren, keep them from temptation, for the Devil do creep in every corner of us if we don't look out.' How I used to shiver!

Just occasionally congregations – or parts of them – fell from grace in all too human a way. At Exeter Mint Methodist chapel the watchnight (New Year's Eve) service in 1895 was an unfortunate occasion. One reads in the Circuit Record: 'A small contingent had tarried at their cups too long and their excited behaviour marred alike the comfort of the worshippers and the freedom of the preacher.'

No wonder, perhaps, that some chapels, such as Park Road Baptist church, St Helens, decided on 'closed' Communion and members of other Baptist Fellowships had to apply to Pastor and Deacons should they wish to sit at the Lord's Table in the Meeting House:

> Jealous for the good name of the Church, members' personal behaviour was strictly watched; and anyone being known to 'misbehave' or 'act in a disorderly manner' [as the old records say] was suspended from the Lord's Table or from church meetings for given periods of time, after which he or she would be allowed to re-assemble at these services. Where

behaviour was exceptionally bad, the culprit had to confess before the Lord's Table, and signify his repentance.

In 1930, however, discussions arose once more concerning 'Open' and 'Closed' Communion – the decision being made that all who love the Lord Jesus Christ be invited to join with us round the Lord's Table.

Among most congregations there was often a self-appointed watchdog such as at the Primitive Methodist chapel at Bolehill, near Wirksworth:

> 'Aunt' Mary Land, the midwife who brought most of us into the world, took upon herself the duty of controlling the young in the congregation from her seat at the front of the gallery. Any whispering or fidgeting resulted in the agitation of the jet-beaded aigrette on her bonnet, followed by a fierce glance which quelled the culprit.

Incidentally, until well into the twentieth century, the belief that no inessential work – even cooking – should be done on the Sabbath persisted, as an elderly man from Redditch recalls:

> One Sunday I went to church with a small cut on the chin. One of the older ones said: 'You have a cut on the chin Mr Newton.' I replied, 'Yes, I did it shaving this morning!' He replied: 'Do you mean to say you shave on the Sabbath! I have never shaved on the Sabbath day in my life!' Me, being a very rude young man, replied: 'I thought cleanliness was next to Godliness!'

As a tail-piece to chapel-preaching – sometimes soaring into the empyrean with moving oratory, sometimes falling into comedy and bathos – is the subject of 'Chapel language!' Few chapel-goers ever died. One pastor at Providence Place Congregational, Cleckheaton, Yorkshire, departed thus: 'The Angel of Immortality touched him lightly on Christmas Eve 1900 and his spirit fled to receive its "well done" reward and to continue its great ministry in the Eternal City.'

There was one who had 'passed to the fuller service'; another who went 'to claim his portion of the Kingdom'. In the Dewsbury Road, Leeds, Wesleyan Methodist Magazine, 1912, we read:

In Memoriam. It is with much regret we have to record a threefold loss, in the calling from our midst by the angel of death of the friends whose names appear below, and to the sorrowing families we tender our sincere sympathy, and pray that as they pass through the dark valley they may be divinely sustained.

[Another of these deceased 'passed to her reward'.]

Another, Mr Samuel Pooley, a London City Missionary, from Paddington chapel, London, was honoured by the erection of a marble tablet recording that 'he fell asleep in Jesus on Sunday afternoon, 30th October, 1887, within an hour of closing his Bible Class here. Aged 63 years.'

Yet another chapel worker 'passed away from the Church Militant to the Church Triumphant'. Some were 'called home', others simply 'passed on'. The Peculiar People spoke of 'having crossed death's river'.

The impulsion to clothe the fact of death in soft verbal garments is far from being confined to Nonconformists but their circumlocutions have a flavour all their own – a flavour, however, that almost always reflected their deepest beliefs: 'gone to claim his portion of the Kingdom' was an exact statement of a credo far from the coy habit of some Victorians who referred to pregnancy as being 'in an interesting condition', or birth as 'a happy event', or who draped dining-room table legs in cloth. Many true believers in all Christian churches have welcomed death because, if they had obeyed the Commandments, it led to heavenly life, to Paradise.

And there were other periphrases. E. E. Kellett[1] refers to some of them:

'I shall not stand for that office,' declared another minister in the Methodist Conference when a post was offered him which he disliked. 'Then you'll have to sit down.' 'I shall not sit down either.' 'In that case,' answered the chartered libertine of the Conference, 'you'll have to be suspended.' 'Worn-out minister', 'connexional man', 'horse-hire fund', 'brother in the Lord' – all these were phrases which for various reasons, the uninitiated may need to have explained. 'On the

[1] *As I Remember*, pp. 366–7.

plan' means to be a recognised preacher in a circuit and to have your name on the prospectus of services for the ensuing quarter. I have already noticed 'sat under a preacher' for 'was a regular listener to him'.

Many other phrases are pleasantly recorded in a once-famous novel, *Isabel Carnaby*, by Ellen Thorneycroft Fowler, a daughter of that distinguished Methodist, Lord Wolverhampton; but she by no means exhausted the list. Such scriptural phrases as 'fall from grace', 'cultivate earnestly the best gifts', 'press toward the mark', 'the bond of iniquity', 'the blood of Jesus', were constantly on the lips of pious people, and were spoken with perfect simplicity. 'I have been marvellously sustained,' said a good man who had recently lost his wife; 'I had fainted, but the Lord helped me.' 'Backsliding' was the regular word for a reversion to evil ways after a period of 'walking in the light'. These might, and did, irritate the ordinary man; but there was no religious pedantry about them as they were used.

And there was a prayer for 'journeying mercies', e.g. for those about to go on their summer holidays.

Some of this language was not periphrastic or euphemistic at all, but simply harked back to the early days of Nonconformity or even to the Bible. Sheila Kaye Smith, in her novel, *The Tramping Methodist*:

> It was a characteristic of John Palehouse that he always preferred Bible phraseology to that of modern times. 'Preaching' with him was 'prophesying'; his manner of life was his 'conversation'; he had not gone before but had 'prevented' me on my journey. He spoke thus without the slightest affectation; it was part of his nature.

Whatever their language or their varied beliefs, the Nonconformists were a people *sui generis*. Although all over the world Christian sects proliferated, there were few who, once they had been liberated from the laws the establishment enacted against them, contributed so much colour and character to living as the English Nonconformists.

6

CHAPELS AND THEIR UPKEEP

Hear us, architect divine,
Great builder of thy church below!
Now upon thy servants shine,
Who seek thy praise to show.

Mrs Bulmer.

It was for long considered that upon Nonconformist chapels the 'architect divine' had scarcely shone, that indeed he had gloomed. They were, asserted Anglicans dazzled by the magnificence of Chartres, Norwich and Westminster Abbey, no more than four-square boxes, squat and boring, and often erected in inappropriate surroundings. Or they dismissed them as 'little Bethels' built – as some really were – of corrugated iron or of wood. They were considered beneath the notice of guide books and even Pevsner in his 'The Buildings of England' series is generally dismissive.

Recently there have been signs of change. Sir John Betjeman, a pioneer in this as in other fields, has shown the way to a new approach to Nonconformist buildings,[1] and this has been followed in an excellent short work with many illustrations by Kenneth Lindley, *Chapels and Meeting Houses* (1969), to which the artist, John Piper, wrote a perceptive foreword.[2] In the book I write, however, I am concerned above all with Nonconformist *people* and their memories of Chapel days, more particularly here with the humdrum business of keeping chapels heated, clean, lit – and standing. Alas, Nonconformists have not always been successful in the latter aim and almost every month chapels are

---

[1] In e.g. *First and Last Loves* (1952), and *English Churches* (1964) in collaboration with Basil Clarke.

[2] There are several other more specialised works, pre-eminent among which is George W. Dolbey's *The Architectural Expression of Methodism* (London, 1964).

pulled down or turned over to other uses, from furniture repositories to bingo halls.

The oldest surviving Nonconformist chapel is the Congregational (formerly Independent) at Horningsham, Wiltshire. Dating from 1566, it has a thatched roof, large windows and a pulpit on a pedestal. During the seventeenth century quite large numbers of Baptist chapels – particularly in Kent and the southeast – were built. The oldest Methodist chapel is the one in Horsefair, Bristol, erected in 1739 though not then in Methodist use. We have to go to distant Newbiggin in Teeside to find the oldest Methodist chapel (1760) in continual use for Methodist worship.

Wesley never, until towards the end of his long life, countenanced the erection of chapels as more than meeting places; he always encouraged his followers to worship at the local Anglican church. So that perhaps the finest eighteenth-century chapels were those of the Unitarians, originally Presbyterians, who did not despise decorative treatment. The Baptists, too, built well but usually in apparently unlikely places, their choice of site often being dictated by nearness to streams or ponds where they could practise total immersion for adult baptism. Most other Nonconformists were 'sprinklers' of babies.

Some eighteenth-century chapels were in what has been called the 'farmhouse style', but others were more elaborate and in much the same mode as the plainer Anglican churches. Wesley's chapel in City Road, London, is essentially akin to St James's, Piccadilly, though lacking the genius of its architect, Wren, and of Grinling Gibbons who designed the altarpiece. Conversely, as Sir John Betjeman has noticed, Wren's City churches were often primarily preaching-houses in style.

In general, however, chapels then and afterwards sprang from concepts different from those of Anglicanism. They were part of revolutionary movements where preaching and singing (though not at first with the Strict Baptists) and congregation participation were of the essence, and sacerdotal ritual came nowhere. This is why in them the pulpit dominated, high and centrally placed with (in early days) the communion table behind it, though later it was placed in front of, and at the foot of, the pulpit. For a long time steeples were avoided as reminiscent of Anglican idolatry though they crept in when in the mid-nineteenth century even Nonconformists were affected by the Gothic revival. Many chapels had galleries, supported by iron columns, round three sides and meeting the organ on the fourth.

The variety of nineteenth-century chapel building was spectacular – neo-classical, Gothic, angular Perpendicular, even *art nouveau*. By this time, when Nonconformist merchants had grown rich, architects were employed, where earlier, in medieval fashion, small builders, carpenters, glaziers and decorators, often in voluntary labour, followed the rough plans of ministers, deacons and chapel stewards; and the later celebrated church architect, William Butterfield, was employed to design High-bury Chapel, Bristol, which he did (1842–3) in the Perpendicular style.

The nineteenth century had a mania for chapel (and also church) building. It rampaged through all levels of society as fiercely, if not as lethally, as did the Spanish 'flu' in 1918–19. It arose from a variety of impulses – not least the belief in God and the need to bring Him closer to the deprived millions, flotsam of the industrial revolution. Thus in such places as Bow (east London) and Plaistow Marsh, where new docks had been built, and where there was a population of 60,000 with scarcely any provision for public worship, chapels began to be built in the 1860s. Bow Wesleyan chapel was opened in 1865.

Few Nonconformists ever really looked at the outside of the chapels they attended all their lives: it was the inside that counted and that became most deeply fixed in their minds because of the hours they spent in them as children. Not all such memories are beautiful. James Laver[1] recalls from his early chapel days that

> the interior was painted in two shades of chocolate – milk and bitter – with a frieze of what looked like flat-irons. The upright box-pews were of varnished pitch-pine and in me they evoke nothing of the Betjeman nostalgia. Naked butterfly gas-jets flared in round, glass globes. When in winter one entered the chapel for evening service one was almost knocked down by the smell of gas. . . . Fainting was quite a common occurrence.

[1] In *Museum Piece*, p. 28.

Most correspondents agree that the typical chapel smell was a mixture of pine, varnish and wax polish. The walls were distempered, the pew cushions red, and in front of the sloping pulpit desk hung a square of velvet edged with gold braid, perhaps with I.H.S. (In His Service) embroidered on it. The sign of the cross was rare in Nonconformity since it carried a whiff of idolatry about it. Because of the taboo on religious imagery, decorations, such as they were, partook of meaningless arabesques (in the Mohammedan fashion), though walls and even organ pipes often bore stencilled texts, also ornate, shouting such messages as 'God is Love' or 'Repent ye: for the Kingdom of heaven is at hand'. A clock usually faced the pulpit and the pulpit desk had a space beneath it for a glass of water. Pews carried at each end a small brass frame with a card on which was written the renter's name.

There were many local variations. Of Holmer Green chapel, Frank Winter writes in his history:

> The interior was simple but not unattractive with its curved ceiling of plaster and decorous windows, two of which still remain though somewhat in eclipse at the present time. Above the wooden dado were hat and coat pegs which would be heavily laden at harvest festivals and other anniversaries with corn or flowers according to season.
>
> We know nothing at all of the original pulpit but the design of the late Victorian rostrum which replaced it, a capacious affair with *art nouveau* balusters and crimson curtains, was not at all bad in its way. Above it – real Victorian stuff this – was a circular window of coloured glass, and on a summer evening the younger members of the congregation would find it agreeably diverting to watch their elders being transformed one by one in lurid tints of amber, red and blue as the sun worked its way round and the sermon wore on.
>
> The building was lit, as might be supposed, by oil lamps suspended from the ceiling or hooked on to the walls and heated by a stove that used to get alarmingly red-hot at the top. Water whether needed for drinking or any other purpose had to be collected from the roof as in the case of all other buildings in the village until the 1920s or after and hauled up with rope and bucket when required.

7.1 CENTRAL HALL: East Ham, London.
7.2 CONFERENCE TRAIN arriving at Bradford 1937.

8.1 METHODIST SACRAMENT: Barnet area in the 1950s.

8.2 MODERN METHODIST BUILDING (1963): at Deeds Grove, High Wycombe, Buc

The building of some chapels was decidedly unorthodox. The Cranbrook Baptist chapel, opened in 1803, was of wood, prepared and framed in London and carted to Cranbrook in waggons – possibly the first example of prefabrication. And Baptists always had the problem of providing adequate means for total immersion of adults: at Sutton Valence a malting vat was used; at another Kent chapel wells were dug in the vestry floor (15in deep and 3ft diameter). Baptists walked many miles to be immersed, then dripping but rejoicing walked home in their soaking garments.

Wesleyan Methodist chapels were on the whole more restrained and rather cosier than others. St Mark's, Sheffield, was a very dignified stone building in pseudo-Gothic style, standing on the brow of a steep hill. It upgraded itself about the turn of the century from a little edifice in the valley, an engine shed-type plain affair dating back to the 1830s. The new chapel was built mainly from contributions from various sides of the (correspondent's) family, plus the inevitable overdraft at the bank and the interior was a considerable concession from Puritan styles, sporting stained glass windows, mostly depicting late members of the family being helped through the clouds by the outstretched hands of the saints. There are no 'Praise ye the Lord' texts painted in glorious technicolour on the wall behind the pulpit – just a small circular glass window illuminating Alpha and Omega, the beginning and the end, and with varnished pitch-pine pews and pulpit and a handsome Conacher organ it was and still is a tastefully decorated place of worship for a Methodist chapel.

Chapel windows – round-headed or pointed or oblong – were either plain, pale green or sometimes with coloured glass in some sort of nebulous pattern of flourishes. Occasionally there were pictorial windows but seldom of such distinction as that by Burne-Jones of the Good Shepherd in the 1860–2 Congregational chapel, King Street, Maidstone. 'The Shepherd,' writes John Newman,[1] 'is a romantic figure with his heavy brown locks and his piebald breeches, and a big red sun gives him a halo. Vivid emerald greens, blues and purples.'

[1] *West Kent and the Weald* (The Buildings of England), by John Newman (London, 1969).

12

And, Mr Newman adds, 'How it comes to be here, goodness knows.'

Schoolrooms were sometimes underneath the chapel itself and sometimes attached. At Dogley Lane Congregational, Huddersfield:

> There was a door from the road into the schoolroom, and a door and aisle were made through the centre of the south pews of the church, opposite the pulpit, connecting the school and chapel directly. The schoolroom was one storey high, for the second storey was set apart for a second schoolroom, at the level of the gallery in the chapel. At this date the 'Top School' was not separated from the rest of the gallery by any partition. Opposite the two side doors of the Bottom School were staircases leading to the Top School with folding doors halfway up separating the two. A large fireplace on the ground floor served to heat the Bottom School. The President's desk stood at the head (East End) of the room. The school was furnished with a number of desks which could be folded up and placed away at the side of the room and along the wall sides; single desks were hinged to the wall, and could hang flat against it when not in use.
>
> The lighting of the church was by means of a large central chandelier, bearing two rings of candles, twenty-four and eighteen in number respectively above and below the gallery and a smaller number of candles set in five brackets over the front of the gallery. None of the new woodwork was stained or polished until 1960.

A grim Baptist chapel in Kirkstall, Leeds, is described by one correspondent:

> Between the vestry and the organ was a raised platform fronted by railings and a reading desk. Immediately opposite the vestry door and behind the platform a flight of steps led down into the boiler house and a small room used for less formal meetings. The railings, desk and floor of the platform could be removed to uncover the large tank in which baptisms took place. The newly-baptised made their exits down the steps, with a degree of haste and dignity dependent on how they had taken their total immersion in completely cold water.

The Society of Friends (Quakers) meeting houses – they refused to call them chapels or themselves Dissenters – were always *ad hoc* and undedicated so that they were used for secular, as well as sacred, purposes. All basically they required was a stand for elders on one side of one wall though some were more elaborate as one Quaker Elder recalls of his Yorkshire home-town meeting house:

> The Meeting House in the middle of the town was of grey brick, much blackened by industrial smoke, and its architecture was such that it was sometimes mistaken for a railway station. This was because it was fronted by a long, narrow, paved and roofed concourse entered from the street through ornamental iron gates opened by sliding them parallel to the street, on rollers, behind an ornamental iron railing, just like the iron gates admitting to the platforms at the local railway station.

The room where they worshipped had a very high ceiling, the four walls being blank and of an off-white colour and the only daylight came from tiny windows at the top of two of the walls. Usually some ninety to a hundred Friends and Attenders would be present and some felt that they had assembled at the bottom of a deep whitewashed well.

There was a double minister's gallery at the front and the lower front seat of this was occupied by the Elders, usually three or four grey-bearded men and three or four women, facing the main body of Friends and Attenders seated on long wooden forms. (Friends have, of course, long since recognised that this lecture-hall arrangement of seating is quite unsuitable for their type of worship; today they sit in a square, rectangle or circle, with Elders and Overseers inconspicuously among the rest.)

As you entered the room from the door at the back you would see that all women and girls were seated on the left of the central gangway and all men and boys on the right. (The Elders had the same pattern, of course.) Boys were taught that they should follow the example of the men and keep their hats on until they were seated (all boys wore hats in those days). This was to indicate, they were told, that the Meeting House was not to be regarded as in any way more sacred than any other building. One elderly man Friend went to the extreme of wearing his tall silk hat throughout the worship, except that he removed it when anyone knelt (as was then customary) to offer vocal prayer and when all others present stood up (a very disturbing practice, long since abandoned).

I recall that shortly after my parents' admission to membership in 1890 (my sister and myself being admitted at the same time as minors) my father was 'eldered' for daring to sit by my mother in Meeting. He persisted however in his reprehensible conduct, and was eventually able to persuade the Elders that the separation of the sexes in Meeting was merely a practice surviving from the seventeenth century (when Friends were accustomed to being roughly disturbed by the military).

More extraordinary still was an old Hampstead Meeting House (Nonconformist not Quaker) between 1840 and 1860:

It was a weird, old place, somewhat barnlike and situated in a back, out-of-the-way thoroughfare. Inside, the pitch of the roof came down so low in the middle that the occupants of the gallery on the south side were obscured from the vision of those on the north.

When you entered from the street, the first thing that struck you was the stove-pipe. It was quite impossible to ignore that, for, whichever way you looked, it dominated the vision. It wriggled serpent-like in all directions and clung tenaciously to certain iron supports which descended from the ceiling, till it eventually, after many struggles, found an exit in the roof, far away from its connection with the ancient stove which it served.

The stove itself was a source of tribulation and vexation to the person who, in an unguarded moment, had consented to minister to its wants, and indeed, was an infliction upon the whole of the sorely-tried congregation during the winter season, when its services were brought into use. This stove had an unholy and obstinate habit of either burning so fiercely and getting so red-hot that those in its immediate vicinity stood a risk of immolation at its shrine, or it absolutely refused to burn at all and half-suffocated the congregation with its fumes, causing such an epidemic of coughing as seriously to interfere with the decent order of service. The lighting, too, was another source of trouble. Oil lamps were used, and these required an enormous amount of attention. They used to flare up suddenly and blacken the glasses, or they occasionally went out, equally without warning, emitting a villainous smell that half-asphyxiated those in the vicinity.

On these occasions the venerable occupant of the pulpit would interrupt his discourse to invite the attention of 'Brother T' or 'Brother J' and to ask them to remedy the defect. These two worthies, respected cordwainers in the town, acted as honorary pew-openers and chapel-wardens, the dignity of the office being considered a sufficient reward for the services given. One of these gentlemen was tall and spare, with a grey well-thatched cranium and sad expression of countenance. The other, on the contrary, was short and somewhat obese in point of figure, with a jovial, not to say jolly, look and a shining bald pate. (I used to think of him as Robin Hood's Friar Tuck.)

Although these two were so different in appearance, they had one thing in common – both wore the loudest creaking shoes I ever remember to have heard; and this was particularly noticeable as they were constantly moving about, either to conduct the congregation to their pews – and they were most punctilious in the performance of this function – or carrying out other duties of their respective offices.

The pews, which were well filled at all the services, were of divers shapes and sizes. Ours was a square family one, with a table in the middle, and there were other similar ones. There were also small ones, made to fit the inequalities of the walls, which would only hold two, and very snug and comfortable these were; and there were long uncomfortable ones, running right across the body of the chapel, for the general public.

I recollect on one occasion, when our own pew was overcrowded, I had to turn out and was put into one of these long pews. Very straight-backed they were, and on the seat a particularly shiny, slippery cushion which when you seated yourself, began to slip from under you, and, there being no intermediary support for your legs, which, by reason of your youth, were not long enough to reach the floor, you – notwithstanding the frantic efforts you made to retain your position –

speedily found yourself ignominiously unseated, to your own extreme discomfiture and the surprised glances of other occupants of the pew.

There was one pew the occupant of which, to prevent the breezes which particularly favoured the locality 'from visiting him too roughly' had a brass rail placed at the back, upon which was hung, by a series of rings, a crimson curtain, which was occasionally drawn when aforesaid vagrant draughts were more than usually aggressive. This unfortunate curtain was, however, a source of trouble, for although, from the position of the pew, which was against the north wall, the curtain offered no restriction to the view of the pulpit and the greater part of the chapel to the lady occupying the pew behind, yet the innovation was greatly resented by that individual, so that she invariably, and with much indignation, pushed back the offending curtain as often as it was drawn. Need I say with what intense interest I watched these manoeuvres, to the neglect of more serious matters?

It was the Rev. Samuel Chadwick who later observed that 'pews were rented, privileged and unsociable' so that when the great mission halls were set up there were no pew-holders – and hence no pew rents.

This raises the question of how chapels were built, who paid for them, and where did the money for their upkeep come from. Some of the large chapels – the so-called Central Halls – came into being through the generosity of men such as the wealthy miller, Joseph Rank, but often money was given by rich men anonymously. As E. E. Kellett notes:

> Many Methodists among them, and not Methodists only, followed literally John Wesley's precept, 'Get all you can, save all you can, give all you can.' Cynics called the giving habit by the opprobrious name of 'fire insurance' – a composition to save from hell – but, whatever its motive, it was almost universal.

Often, too, in the country places sheer enthusiasm on the part of poor people erected a chapel: such was the west Yorkshire Baptist collier, Dan Taylor, who personally quarried the stone and almost by himself built the Heptonstall chapel. Indeed most of the funds for chapels were raised by the least wealthy among the populace. This basic poverty sometimes explains why chapels are to be found in the outskirts and backstreets of towns and villages: there a site was cheaper.

There was even a do-it-yourself guide to chapel construction for amateurs, published in 1850 by J. F. Jobson. It was entitled: 'Chapel and School architecture as appropriate to the buildings of Nonconformists . . . with practical directions for the erection of Chapels and School Houses'.

In some cases, of course, no chapel was ever built:

My grandfather came as a farmer to farm at Greenhow, north Yorkshire, in 1863. He was a Methodist preacher and had eleven children. There was no Methodist chapel nearer than four miles. The Church of England was in Ingleby village two miles from his farm. So he opened his farm kitchen for services and invited all the people on other farms in the area to come Sunday afternoon and evening. His family started a Sunday School and all the farmers' children came. When he retired my father took over the farm and continued the services. When he retired my brother took over the farm. For eighty years this continued [i.e. into the 1940s].

Some chapels were decidedly *ad hoc*, adapted from cottages, barns, kitchens or even disused hostelries. Near Thurstone, Lancashire, the topmost floor of a three-storey house became a Methodist chapel: 'the pulpit was made apparently of an old gig, the book-board being fixed to the splash-board, and the seat behind remaining'. Near Nottingham, a dwelling-house was adopted by making a large hole in the ceiling of the ground-floor 'and the preacher stood on something sufficiently high to see all the people upstairs and down. The men usually occupied the upper floor and the women the lower.'

Sometimes in early days a preaching house was built to appear as two cottages, for protective as well as prudential reasons.[1]

It was, however, a great day when at last a chapel could be

[1] *The Architectural Expression of Methodism*, by W. G. Dolbey (London, 1964), pp. 25–6.

started upon. The Methodists of Billinge, between St Helens and Wigan, began in the 1860s:

> It can be well imagined with what joy the pioneers of the Cottage Room meetings viewed the arrival of the first loads of local stone quarried from the Delph at Crank; and bought from a Yorkshire business man who owned the quarry, and was dubbed 'Yorkshire Charley' by the locals.
>
> With what zeal they helped with the building operations after a day in the pit at the coal face; one, J. Turner, farmer of Winstanley, making *his* contribution – 'Free Cartage'.
>
> Stories are told of how members of the Society were called upon to contribute £1 each towards the cost of the chapel (almost as much as a week's wage). Ingenious were the methods used in the raising.
>
> And so, with the end of 1868 the Billinge brethren saw the completion of their task, the realisation of a dream; a 'Sermon in Stone' – their chapel. Truly the seeds of Methodism had taken root.

Their difficulties should not be underestimated. The Park Road Baptists of St Helens:

> At a meeting called in April, 1868, the brethren who had volunteered to do the excavating for the new chapel were requested to meet the following day. At this time there was a coal strike and many families suffered from severe hardship. I have in my possession an account book, showing money received and spent on providing dinners of hot-pot etc., for the men while working on these excavations.
>
> At this time many people found it impossible to keep up their pledged subscriptions towards the upkeep of the church and Mr Greening [the builder] offered to take as his wages whatever came in for weekly offerings on condition that the struggling families were excused their commitments.

Money was generally scarce yet services were crowded and the work inhibited only by the smallness of the premises. At Bradfield Methodist, Essex, during, as the centenary leaflet puts it, 'the "Hungry Forties" and Dickens's *Hard Times*,' there was great pressure for a larger chapel but the debt on Circuit property in 1847 was over £3,000 (probably nearer £20,000 in 1972 terms). Nevertheless a local builder, James Cutting, proffered free skilled labour and unskilled labour was provided by the congregation, some of whom carted gravel to the site. But £300 had to be raised – and part of it was. There were, however, borrowings of £100 at four per cent and £80 of the debt remained until 1886. The chapel was opened in 1850.

Often in early days much of the physical work of building was done by the congregation, even if it were only carrying bricks. Sometimes the pulling down of the old had to precede the building of the new – though the Leeds Methodists ingeniously got round the problem. The Leeds Guide of 1809 by John Ryley says:

In the late 1760s a small band of Methodists took a cottage in a street named Appletree Garth, Quarry Hill, Leeds, as a meeting place, but this was demolished many years ago, along with the surrounding district. Within a short time the cottage proved unsuitable and it was decided to build a chapel on the site, but in order not to interfere with their Sunday Observances, the main structure was built over and around the cottage.

The shell of the building being complete the builders commenced on a Monday morning to demolish the cottage, throwing the rubble of the cottage through the windows of the other structure, with the result that by the following Sunday the new chapel was more or less complete, or should I say, suitable for occupation, and was taken into use in 1771.

The locals round about viewed this chapel and its occupants with suspicion and apprehension, calling the chapel a *Boggard House*, 'Boggard' being the term used by Leeds folk to denote things 'uncanny or mysterious'. Indeed the term 'Boggard' was used in many places in Yorkshire to denote 'A spectre, ghost, or phantom'.

Nothing now remains of this chapel, but on one or two occasions coffins have been found during excavations.

Pulling down was often viewed with mixed feelings, as at Lumb-in-Rossendale:

> On Sunday, 13 February 1881 the services were held for the last time in the old building. To most of the crowd which gathered that day it was a strange experience. Many had spent their lives in Lumb and all that meant most to them was intimately bound up with that building. The square pews, the straight-backed seats, the flagged floor, the high pulpit had become part of their lives. For these it was a hard task to pull down that old chapel, but they did it. On that last Sunday, despite the driving snow, a huge congregation gathered and crowded the chapel to the doors. The organ, which had stood below the pulpit had been removed, and in its place were the violins, 'cellos, double-basses, clarinets of the early days, to play the old 'Layrock' tunes once again. At both services a summary of the history of the chapel was read by the minister. At the morning service the Rev. H. Abraham, taking as his text 'Call to remembrance the former days', reviewed the past and incidentally drew a comparison between the material conditions of the people in 1829 and 1880 from the subscription lists of the respective building funds of those years. 'The highest contributions in 1829 consisted of £20, £15, £11 and two gifts of £10, whilst already there had been received for the new chapel £200, £84, two sums of £50, two of £30, two of £25, three of £20 and eleven of £10, making a total of £664, or ten times the amount of all the large sums given fifty years ago.'

Early next morning the work of pulling down the old building began. On that first day so many came to help that by evening nothing but the bare framework remained. A few days later the whole of the woodwork was sold by auction and many of the old pews, the pulpit, and parts of the gallery front are still in existence in various forms.

Meanwhile the committee had been at work on the new chapel. The plans had been prepared by Thomas Horsfield and Son of Manchester, for a building to accommodate 800 people. Contracts had already been made for the various branches of the work:

£

	£
Masons – John and Henry Maden (Lumb)	1024
Joiner – James Whittaker (Lumb)	825
Plasterer – Tillotson Black (Todmorden)	144
Plumber, Gas etc. – Robert Whittles (Stacksteads)	100
Painter – Joseph Whitehead (Newchurch)	95
Heating Apparatus – Henry Wormwell (Accrington)	84
Slater – John Rushton (Bacup)	80
	2352

From this it was estimated that £3,000 would be needed to cover all the expenses and to build the boundary walls.

Men gave what they had, whether pennies, material or land. At Harrold, Bedfordshire:

Wm Ray (or Wray) offered a piece of garden ground which he then owned, on which to build a chapel. A Mr Clark, a farmer in the parish, gave the stone for building and together with the pence of the poor people, and aided by a few others who were favourable to the object, the chapel was erected on the ground given by Mr Ray. This neat little [Congregational] chapel was officially opened for worship on 25 September 1808, on which occasion the Rev. John Sitcliffe of Olney, the Rev. Samuel Hillyard of Bedford and the Rev. Wm Freeman of Cotton End, all preached. From then onwards the students from Olney and various ministers conducted Divine Worship on Sundays and on other special occasions.

Occasionally congregations had to find temporary premises – with sometimes curious results. From St Thomas Street Methodist church, Claremount, Halifax, we hear that:

They had to leave the old chapel before the new one was ready: an upper room in the Liberal Club was rented temporarily. The club was licensed for the sale of liquor, and this gave rise to the following verse:

Spirits above and spirits below,
Spirits of love and spirits of woe,

The spirits above are spirits divine,
The spirits below are spirits of wine.

Pew rents were mentioned above. Yes, says one Methodist correspondent:

> Pew rents were the thing. The more expensive pews were situated at the rear of the chapel and some of these had doors and comfortable cushions. 'Class Money' also helped to swell coffers. Most chapels had to have an annual bazaar in order to keep out of debt. Sewing meetings, therefore had to be held during the greater part of the year. A certain Lancashire chapel always had a three-day bazaar opening on New Year's Day. After the opening ceremony the members would kiss one another.

The system of paying rents for pews began at different times in different chapels. At Harrold Congregational, from about 1815 onwards worshippers were asked to choose their seating and paid a quarterly subscription according to their means. The system became known as the Pew Rents. A plan of the seating of the church made about 1900 shows every seat allocated, and the income to the church seemed to be on a stable basis.

On the other hand, Moorends Wesleyan chapel, between Doncaster and Barnsley was, a correspondent writes, maintained solely by the proceeds of the Harvest Festival. These paid for heating, lighting, insurance and repairs, the cleaning being done free of charge. (Moorends had a new chapel built between the two World Wars.)

This was exceptional. For most chapels pew rents provided their staple income. At Bethesda, Ipswich, the main income of the church came from pew rents, which yielded between £20 and £35 a quarter. There were usually five or six pew rent collectors elected by the members. Collections, as known now, were taken only once or sometimes twice a quarter and, judging from the results, they were not very popular! The amount collected seldom exceeded £7 and was sometimes as low as £3.

The treasurer's duties were confined to the strict working of the church. Pastor Poock was responsible for collecting the money required for special expenses. It is recorded that he made a habit of calling on members for a modest penny a week. He must have been diligent for there are credit entries of amounts of several pounds. Later the entries refer to payments by cards, and totals are towards the £50 mark.

The £360 building debt due to Pastor Nunn and his fellow shareholders was repaid by six annual instalments between 1848 and 1853. Within four years a major expenditure involving around £500, caused by the building of galleries in the chapel and other repairs, made it necessary for the church to borrow £150 from the Baptist Building Society. It was repaid by annual payments of £15. The balance appears to have been met by an all-out giving campaign. A page caption on the treasurer's book read: 'Donations promised at the Tea Meeting held 19 February 1857.' Mr and Mrs Poock head the list with a contribution of £5. Over 150 individual gifts are shown, some for a few shillings only, with one as low as 6d. 'Cordially', friends of Zoar chapel contributed 37s.

Chapels had various charges on their incomes. At Bethesda, Ipswich, there are references to a visiting preacher's fees. They had diverse methods of transport, as the following suggest – 'A cab from the station . . . 1s. 6d. . . . also keep of a horse and ostler's fees,' usually 2s. 6d. and 1s. 6d. respectively.

Repairs to 'the singer's bass fiddle' were chargeable to the church, as, of course, was the chimney sweep's attention to the vestry at 6d. or 1s. a time.

A little more surprising are the entries which occurred annually during a period a century back [in the 1860s] as '£5 for the Singers'. Whether that was for 'services rendered' or to reimburse the orchestra for replacement of musical instruments the reader must decide.

There it was, in all the unabashed candour of the age – 'Paid to Mr. Moyes for killing rats in chapel . . . one pound.' Unedified and uninspired, the chapel history observes, the fingers turned the pages as if to shield the mind from all the implications in an attack by vermin upon the very foundations of this bastion of strong Calvinism!

The only direct indication of the spiritual progress of the

Opening Ceremony.

FIRST DAY.

The EXHIBITION and BAZAAR will be OPENED
on WEDNESDAY, MARCH 20th, at 3.30 p.m., by

MRS. VACHELL, of Astwood Bank.

Chairman - - - H. J. HART, Esq., of Birmingham.

HYMN.

" Thou God of glory, truth, and love,
Lord over all beneath, above !
Our thoughts and hearts to Thee we raise,
And with our lips proclaim Thy praise.

Creation rose at Thy command,
The seas, the floods, the solid land ;
And at Thy wisdom's high behest,
In beauteous robes Thy works were drest.

Thy goodness doth to men impart
The fount of every useful art,
The skilful hand, the inventive thought,
By which new forms of grace are wrought.

Behold, O Lord, before Thee stand
Our works of thought, of heart, and hand ;
We humbly bring them to Thy throne,
And render back with joy Thine own."

Edward Boaden.

Scripture read by .. Rev. J. C. STANFIELD
Prayer .. .. Rev. E. TODD
Words of Welcome .. .. Rev. A. H. HULSE
Statement by Secretary Mr. A. H. JOHNSON
Chairman's Remarks .. .. Mr. H. J. HART
Opening Address .. .. Mrs. VACHELL

Vote of thanks proposed and seconded by
Messrs. J. J. TAYLOR and J. HUGHES.

" We all live in the hope of pleasing somebody, and the pleasure
of pleasing ought to be the greatest."
Dr. Samuel Johnson.

church comes from the constantly recurring entry of 'Baptising fee 3s.' It seems to have been paid to the lady caretaker.

Collections at services may never have become popular but they were necessary and sometimes rewarding. At Swingfield, near Folkstone, Methodist church in 1910 the following collections were made:

			£	s.	d.
January	2	Widows' and Orphans' Fund of the London Missionary Society	5	19	3
January	23	Earl Street Mission	8	1	6
February	20	London Congregational Union	13	7	6
March	13	Church Anniversary Services	51	18	2
April	17	The Sunday School	19	2	3
May	8	London Missionary Society	19	19	4
June	12	Hospital Sunday Fund	22	2	1
July	10	Western General Dispensary and Queen Charlotte's Hospital	7	11	0
October	9	Deaconess Mission (Harvest)	11	4	1
November	6	London Congregational Union (Sacramental Offering)	17	3	8
November	13	Capland Street Sunday School	7	7	7
December	18	Our own Poor	9	8	1

Some of these accounts contain curious entries. For instance, at a branch of St Helens Methodist church, which had twenty-eight members (of whom nine were on trial), the preacher's 'meat bill' for one quarter in 1851 came to £2 19s. 6d., far the largest item of expenditure save for his salary of £4.

One favourite way of raising funds was a bazaar. At Mursley, near Bletchley, Baptist chapel a committee was formed and a building fund instituted in 1882 with the purpose of obtaining a piece of ground and building a much larger chapel. Collecting cards were distributed and many functions were arranged for raising funds. One of these was the holding of a bazaar and sale of work in the Centenary Hall, Winslow. This meant a good deal of hard work and transport problems since there were no

(*opposite*) RAISING MONEY: Bazaars were popular, and, as in the case of the United Methodists of Redditch (Worcs.) in 1912, lasted several days and a large 'handbook and souvenir' was printed on twenty or more glossy pages.

buses or even motor cars at that time. However, it was a great
success and realised the sum of £50, a considerable sum of money
in those days.

Some members of chapels, like one lady from Sheffield,
looked on these functions with a jaundiced eye and expressed
herself caustically:

> Bazaars involved months of preparation by the ladies'
> sewing meeting – flannel nighties, tea cosies, pen wipers – the
> lot – every abomination sewable. On the last night (Satur-
> day) the big panjandrum (grandpa) would announce from
> the platform that whatever the takings were he would double
> them. This caused immediate panic and confusion and
> everything floggable was flogged for whatever could be got.
> And on the Monday morning following, notwithstanding
> all this religious claptrap, he and his sons would be down at
> work exploring ways and means of duffing the income tax!

Quite large sums were raised. The Halifax Methodists did
well:

> That year a Bazaar was suggested and worked for. This
> was held at Easter 1901 and resulted in a profit of about £150,
> considered very good indeed. This gave the friends their first
> substantial surplus.
>
> However, in 1910 a great United £1,000 Bazaar was held
> at King Cross School, of which one-third (some £360 it
> proved to be) came to West End. The first tangible step to the
> building of the School Chapel.

The irrepressible Frisky Youngs thus addressed his fellow
members of the Primitive Methodist chapel, Hintringham,
Norfolk:

> Christian Friends. Feeling we are overburdened with the
> present debt on the above place of worship and in want of
> things necessary for that place we intend, if we can realise a
> few articles opening a BAZAAR for the purpose of raising
> funds to ease us, we therefore cast ourselves upon the charity
> of FRIENDS, and if we can succeed the BAZAAR will be
> opened some time in MAY 1869, further notice will be given
> as to the day of the month.

As was his wont, Mr Youngs then burst into verse:

Therefore we would thankfully receive
Whatever you may feel disposed to give –
Pins, needles, bodkins, cotton, thread and tape
Of every colour, strength, length, and shape
With stuff for making pinafores and frocks,
Hats, bonnets, shawls and little childrens socks
All kinds of stockings, men's and women's too,
Grey, white, black, speckled, brown, red, or blue,
With handkerchiefs of every kind and size,
Ribbons and buttons, stays, hooks-and-eyes.
All kinds of ornaments and various toys,
Such as will please the little girls and boys.
And try for once to see if we'll refuse
Clogs, pattens, boots, or men's or women's shoes,
Writing paper, pens, envelopes, or ink
Or useful books that teach the mind to think.
Buns, pies, tarts, biscuits, butter, bread and cheese
With sugar, spices, chocolate and teas.
Or if knitting you should feel inclined
Then hoods, purses, ruffles, lace or window blind.
But if you think that you can better spare
A set of China, or some earthenware,
Then plates and dishes, cups and mugs,
Ewers, basins, pint and half-pint jugs,
Knives, forks, and scissors if you please to give
With steel and spoons we thankfully receive.
And now my friends I think you see by this
No kind of article will come amiss.
I hope no one will be disposed to say
I've nothing for you – call some other day.
Shall the oppressed continue so?
Methinks you all with one consent say no:
We'll give our mite – will join with you in prayer
Jehovah reigns! Cheer up and don't despair.

(Printed by T. J. Miller. JNO. Steam printer, Fakenham)

Bazaars, sales of work, pew rents, collections – all these were very well and highly necessary. They kept the chapels going. But, as in all joint enterprises, behind them were a number of humble men and women willing to work regularly at the small ordinary tasks of cleaning, sweeping, tending the boilers, lighting the lamps, opening the doors, and seeing to it that there was bread and wine for the Sacrament:

> I had rather be a door-keeper in the house of my God
> Than to dwell in the tents of ungodliness.

So it was at the Methodist chapel on the High Road at Bushey Heath, Hertfordshire:

> I remember that when we were children over fifty years ago my parents always spent Good Friday scrubbing the aisles and making the chapel especially clean for Easter. This building is now demolished and we have a new Swiss-like chapel not far away which is much more compact and easier to run. My father was the society steward and treasurer and it was his job to count the collection and take care of it and neighbours at our cottage were always coming to our door to change shillings into pennies for the gas meter and we always had an abundant supply.
>
> Another thing I remember was that on Communion day my father had to remember to take a plate of bread cubes to Chapel and some wine and I believe it was sometimes home-made ginger wine. When no caretakers were available he used to cycle to Chapel before 8 a.m. and light the two combustor stoves which was not an easy job; then he would come home to breakfast and go up again to make sure the chapel was warming before changing into his Sunday best suit.

Not often did they win public praise or even thanks – until, sometimes, when they were dead. At Mount Tabor Wesleyan church, Halifax, it was recorded:

> By the death of Mr Lister Mann in December 1918 the chapel lost one of its most beloved characters. Genial and homely, he performed the work of door-keeper and sexton for nearly twenty-five years in a markedly able manner. His

cheery laugh and quaint mannerisms will long be kindly remembered by those who knew him.

None of these humble assiduous workers 'in Thy courts' – some of the chapel-keepers had living quarters in the basement – expected acclaim however modest; indeed it would have embarrassed them. 'They also serve who only stand and wait', scrub, polish, wind the clock and fill the preacher's glass with water.

7

BRETHREN, QUAKERS, PECULIARS

Ten thousand thousand are their tongues,
But all their joys are one.

Isaac Watts.

In the foregoing account of the life in and out of Chapel during the last century or so, many Christian or near-Christian sects have not been mentioned. This is because a number of them have little that can be termed social life and some have no real corporate life either. The Christian Scientists, for example, though they sing hymns, meet essentially to hear about and discuss their special system of therapy: but it is alone that each member does his mental exercises. Another sect of American origin, though existing in Europe, the Pentecostalists (the Assemblies of God, Elim Foursquare Gospel, the Apostolic Church – which latter is of Welsh origin) have an elaborate hierarchy of church officers and hold revivalist campaigns when converts speak in 'unknown tongues' (*glossolalia*). But they are a semi-closed community.

A completely closed community is that section of the Plymouth Brethren known as Exclusive. The Brethren began not in Plymouth but in Dublin as a breakaway in the late 1820s not from Nonconformity but from the established Church of Ireland. The difference between Open (or 'neutral') Brethren and Exclusive Brethren is partly theological and partly doctrinal. The Open Brethren, for example, will 'break bread' with other than Brethren; the Exclusives will not. As the years went by the rift between them became wider. All, however, remain literal Biblicists and deny all official ministries, whether in the Episcopalian, Presbyterian or Congregationalist style, believing them to be a denial of the spiritual priesthood of all believers.

The Exclusives remain strict in their admission rules. Candidates for communal bread-breaking are examined by a tribunal known as a 'care meeting'. Excommunication for

conduct unbecoming to a 'saint' is practised.[1] They frown upon
marriage outside the Exclusives. A correspondent, a former
member of the Exclusives, writes:

> The result was that social contacts were largely restricted
> to those belonging to the fellowship itself, and any such
> contacts have been rigorously condemned and the London
> or Taylor party has become increasingly cut off from any-
> thing but formal contact.

Because of this discipline, which became more severe as the
years went by, the Exclusive Brethren found their social life in
their own circle. Thus the entertainment of one another in their
own homes became an important part of their life and the
Christian virtue of hospitality was strongly encouraged, but
only within the circle.

This had its effect on young people growing up in the system.
They found themselves cut off at school from the ordinary
activities of their playmates, and they were discouraged from
going to parties and other social events. They were also forbidden to go to popular places of amusement and to mix in the
general social round.

Their pleasures were confined to activities which could be
shared with others in the same fellowship and this resulted in
the annual holiday being an important item in the calendar.
The Brethren tended to congregate, with their families, in a few
quiet seaside resorts where the young people enjoyed games and
entertainment organised by their leaders, while older ones
occupied themselves in discussing affairs current among the
Brethren at the time, or doctrinal points arising from Bible
studies.

Regular fellowship meetings involving Bible study and
ministry of the Word formed an important part of the social life
of the Brethren. They were organised on the basis of groups of
local assemblies coming together in a district and a prominent
brother took the lead in the conversational Bible studies and
addresses. Young and old gathered for these meetings and

[1] Their organisation is examined by Bryan Wilson in *Religious Sects: a
sociological study* (London, 1970). They were subject to splintering because
they had no central authority.

family ties were strengthened by the fact that there was no segregation of young and old into separate groups, Sunday Schools etc.

The importance of the family has always been stressed among the Brethren, and this has been a source of strength throughout their history. The practice of 'household baptism' meant that the children of Brethren were baptised as infants, this being the formal recognition by the parents of the fact that their children had been born into a home which was morally separated from the world. It was considered that the ordinance of baptism signified that the whole family were on Christian ground, separated from the world by the acceptance of the death of Christ, of which baptism was the formal sign. The children were to be brought up in the nurture and admonition of the Lord, and, as they accepted Christ as their Saviour for themselves, they showed themselves true to their baptism.

The result of the close integration of the children in the Christian home, and in family activities with other Christian families in the same communion, was that it was rare for children to go outside of the circle for their companionships and this was particularly so in the case of marriages. Indeed any marriage with one not in the fellowship was regarded as a transgression resulting in exclusion from the fellowship for the one involved.

As children came to some maturity it was anticipated that they would seek their place at the Lord's Table in full communion. This act of assent to the doctrinal and practical requirements of the communion was an important step for the young believer. He was then free to take his place in the adult life of the fellowship, surrounded as this life was by the disciplines and sanctions already mentioned.

There was no segregation of age groups. This was not so evident at the end of the nineteenth century when it was normal for each meeting to have its Sunday School. As matters developed in the first half of the twentieth century, Sunday Schools became a thing of the past and there never had been any other form of group segregation in the Brethren assemblies.

The family found its social life in the local meeting and through this local meeting with meetings in the district.

Inevitably however there were class distinctions even among the Brethren, and this found its expression in those with a similarity of background and outlook joining together socially, particularly at holiday time.

The acceptance of a discipline which shut them off from other Christians resulted in an inward-looking form of Christian life, concentrated more upon Church order and doctrine than upon evangelism. The result was a lack of evangelistic gift, and the Brethren tended to be maintained by generation after generation of children, rather than by the reception of converts from outside the circle.[1]

The social life of the Brethren was satisfying and had a strong influence upon young people. Those who left the fellowship often found themselves very much at sea in a world which was strange to them, cut off from all their social links, as well as their sources of spiritual information, instruction and fellowship. There was thus a strong built-in tendency to stay together, and discipline which involved exclusion was a potent weapon in the hands of leaders who acquired authority by reason of their ability to handle the Word of God.

The Brethren had no appointed elders or other officials. They relied entirely upon what they spoke of as 'evidence of gift' as a quality of leadership. In spite of this however their leaders have in fact exercised an authority which was almost papal in its character, with disastrous results in recent years.

> In my early days, [a correspondent writes] I was completely satisfied with the situation in which I found myself, apart from the somewhat difficult position which arose at school. In later years the growth of an unspiritual and autocratic authority has changed the whole position for many who have been compelled to leave the fellowship.

This is very far indeed from the fun, the evangelising, the hymn-singing, concert-giving, and bazaars of the Congregationalists, Baptists and Methodists. It approaches the insulation from wider society of the old order Amish, originally sixteenth-century Dutch and Swiss Anabaptists, who founded totally

---

[1] Other Nonconformists in the eighteenth century were not dissimilar in this respect.

segregated societies in Pennsylvania, Ohio, Delaware and Michigan. With them propinquity is all. Like the Exclusive Brethren, they do not seek to evangelise. They are possibly the nearest realisation of the Coleridgean dream of 'pantisocracy'.

Then there is, as another correspondent writes, 'that race apart from other men', the Society of Friends or Quakers. Founded by George Fox in the sixteenth century – though descendants of the Seekers sect – the Quakers did not take their spiritual lead from 'a book called the Bible', but from 'God within ourselves'. They were self-contained. Quietists and mystics, certainly, but also later pacifists, active in good causes, people who went into war zones with food, medicines, ambulances and troops' comforts. They, too, however, were not notable for hymn-singing (though they did not abjure it), conversion, great anniversary celebrations, or concerts. And they changed over the years; they, too, had their pressure groups,[1] susceptible to new ideas and new fashions in thought.

Some members of the Society today have been outraged by what they regard as the undermining of Quakerism. They believe that Fox's 'the light within' has been translated into the wholly subjective 'inner light' which is identified with the individual conscience – the dictates of which have dominated every tyrant in history. Some Quakers are as contemptuous of the Scriptures as they are ignorant of them. Others have adopted theosophy and spiritualism which, one writer claims, 'have reduced whole meetings here and there to agnostic level of confused and pretentious mystagogy'. Some have flirted with political expediencies such as aiding campaigns of violence in Africa and elsewhere. These, the correspondent observes, 'have whored after strange gods'.

What, however, Quakerism was really like in the years and the context with which this book is concerned, is well delineated by an elderly member of the Society:

As a Friend (eighty-four years of age, at present an Elder of Kingston and Wandsworth Monthly Meeting) I can recall my first attendance at a Quaker Meeting for Worship in the year 1889, being taken to it by my parents in my home town

[1] In fact, they had pioneered them in the eighteenth century.

in Yorkshire. From that time I was in regular attendance at the same Meeting until I came to London in the year 1903.

Though the fact never dawned upon me until many years later, I now realise that Friends were seated in Meeting almost entirely in accordance with the social standing of their respective families. In the front row was the family of an alderman of the town and in successive rows behind came the families of a prosperous broker, a well-known auctioneer, a multiple-shop grocer, a civil engineer, a single-shop grocer, a draper, a plumber, a watch and clock repairer and then various skilled and unskilled workers. Such a seating pattern was, I think, quite undeliberate. It came about merely because the lecture hall arrangement, with forms one behind another, lent itself to an undesigned and largely unconscious expression of the prevailing social climate. It may well have been peculiar to this particular Meeting of Friends.

One family, I recall, included five sons and five daughters, the father sitting adjacent to the gangway on the men's side, with his five sons arranged in age and size order, and the mother adjacent to the gangway on the women's side, with her daughters also in age and size and order, in each case, for obvious reasons, the youngest sitting next to the parent.

But what was the worship like? The silences, my correspondent recalls, were much shorter than is customary with Friends today. Quite often a Recorded Minister would speak for fifteen to twenty minutes (the 'recording' of Friends having a gift in the ministry was discontinued in 1924). In general the vocal ministry was of the type usual in the Friends' evangelical period, consisting of reading or quoting and commenting upon Bible passages almost always with reference to the need for individuals to accept a personal salvation based on the death of Jesus on the Cross (the substitionary atonement). Only very rarely did the Quakers hear any reference to Friends' distinctive testimonies as, for example, the peace witness, the objection to the use of oaths and their testimony concerning the non-necessity of the outward sacraments. A few older Friends held to the Quietist tradition of the eighteenth century, but they were much less vocal. Thus it came about that my correspondent never heard of George Fox and the early Friends until in his middle teens.

The attitude to the Bible of most Friends in the Meeting at this period was broadly fundamentalist. Every word in it (presumably in the Authorised Version) was to be revered as having some vital significance in relation to its central theme, the divine plan for the salvation of the human race. No criticism of the text was permissible and Bible study could be allowed only in so far as it was consistent with a recognition of that central theme.

As one of the Elders said to my correspondent by way of insisting on the infallibility of the printed word, 'Have we not in the Gospel of John a statement by Jesus himself that "thy word is truth"?' The modernist movement among Friends, involving a theological outlook consistent with scientific discovery and modern Biblical scholarship, had not yet arrived. Incidentally, as showing the contrast with the present day, no Friend of that Meeting, then or previously, ever had a university education.

In this northern town and its neighbourhood were some flourishing Adult Schools and Friends' active association with the movement had brought many manual workers into the Meeting as members and attenders and to them the evangelical approach was very congenial:

I recall especially one young man, a market gardener, I think, who would often break the silence with his rendering of a Sankey hymn, his favourite being one with a refrain:

Happy day! Happy day!
When Jesus washed my sins away!

Then there was an elderly labourer who often offered prayer in a broad Yorkshire accent and who invariably remembered to thank God that none of us was in a lunatic asylum! He was, of course, merely echoing the insistent dread of the worker of ending one's days in an asylum or workhouse.

That evangelical atmosphere, with its occasional crudities, seems uncongenial to Quakers today; yet it represented a vital spiritual experience which Friends in the quietist tradition were beginning to lack.

The Sunday morning Meeting for Worship lasted for an hour and a quarter and the children of all ages were expected to sit stock-still throughout. On one Sunday every month, however, the children had their own Meeting under the supervision of an adult Friend, when Bible stories were recounted and talked about. Each child was expected to memorise and bring to the Meeting some edifying Bible text and to quote it at the beginning when called upon to do so:

> I recall an occasion when a small boy whose text was 'if a woman has long hair it is a glory to her' received a mild rebuke from the woman Friend in charge.

On Sunday evening Friends then sometimes conducted what was called a Mission Meeting attended by some forty to fifty people, about half of those present being Friends. This followed the conventional, Evangelical, Nonconformist pattern of hymn, vocal prayer, reading from the Bible, hymn, sermon or talk and closing hymn, the hymns being from Ira D. Sankey's *Sacred Songs and Solos* and accompanied on a harmonium:

> There was a time when some older Friends of the quietist tradition insisted on holding a quiet Meeting for Worship at the same time as the Mission Meeting and, on one occasion a young Evangelical Friend was to be seen at one door in the Meeting House lobby inviting everybody into the Mission Meeting, while at the same time his aged father was to be seen at another door inviting everybody into the quiet Quaker Meeting for Worship.
>
> In the lobby was a considerable library in a locked glass case. Any Friend or Attender wishing to borrow a book had first to find the librarian who had the key, but, as the books were almost entirely restricted to reports and documents of London Yearly Meeting and the journals of Friends prior to 1850, they were not much in demand. The Evangelicals probably regarded them as relics of an earlier unenlightened age.
>
> Once a month, immediately after the morning Meeting

for Worship, Friends held their Preparative (business) Meeting and for this the time-honoured custom prevailed of the men and women meeting separately, the women staying where they were and the men adjourning to another room. It happened occasionally that the men's clerk had a message concerning the business to be conveyed to the women's clerk or *vice versa* and as a small boy my first service to the Society was to convey such a note from the men to the women. A small girl would similarly be entrusted with a note in the opposite direction.

This absurd practice of meeting separately was finally abolished, I think, about the turn of the century. I never learnt what was the business transacted by the women, apart perhaps from arranging to provide the lunch and the tea for the Monthly Meeting when that was to be held locally.

Life in those days was much less strenuous than it is today and so there were many Friends of leisure or in a position to leave their jobs for a few hours in the daytime. Hence the Monthly Meeting, where Friends from several local (Preparative) Meetings assembled to transact business for a wider district, customarily met on a weekday morning and afternoon. Monthly Meeting was the great social occasion for Friends, when they had lunch and tea together. Otherwise their lives had little in the way of social diversion since, for almost all of them, theatres and concerts were taboo. Hence one can readily believe the story of the Quaker boy, about to leave secondary school at seventeen, whose father, trying to persuade him to enter the family business, offered as one of the inducements that he should always have time off to attend Monthly and Quarterly Meetings.

For a few Friends even the reading of fiction was to be discouraged because, they said, the authors were departing from fact and so were telling lies. Other Friends objected to books like Kingsley's *The Heroes* on the ground that no Christian should sink so low as to be willing to read about heathen gods.

Nearly all Friends were strict sabbatarians and would consider it sinful behaviour to travel by train or tramcar on a Sunday. With other Christians in the town they were much opposed to a proposal that the town's tramway service should be allowed to function on that day. Eventually a compromise was reached and the trams were allowed to run after 2 p.m. I well remember my mother calling me to look out of our front window on a Sunday morning: 'Look, across the way there is a man carrying a brown paper parcel on the Sabbath.'

Until many years after the turn of the century I had never seen a Friend smoking and when eventually, at the General Meeting of a Friends' School, I did see one I was profoundly shocked because I had been taught from earliest childhood not only that smoking was injurious to health and liable to become an addiction but that, regarded aesthetically, it was a nasty, slovenly, dirty habit.

At that time, the attitude of most Friends to politics, economics and the social order was simple. The outstanding villain was beverage alcohol. What made them sure of this was the familiar sight, in the dirty, smoke-ridden town with its horrible slums, of streets rolling with drunken men and women, especially every Saturday night. They regarded this drunkenness as the cause rather than the effect of the prevailing poverty and considered that if only the working man would become a sober, industrious citizen the poverty and the slums would automatically disappear. Thus it came about that many Friends wore a strip of blue ribbon on their jacket or dress to indicate to everyone they met that they were staunch abstainers from alcoholic beverages.

The word 'Socialism' was beginning to be heard in the land, but most of the Friends of that era would have nothing to do with an economic cult associated, they considered, especially on the continent, with atheism. Many years had to pass before Friends could begin to recognise that an economic order which bestowed rewards and power upon ownership rather than upon service to the community might well be not altogether in accordance with the spirit of Christ.

A somewhat younger Quaker tells me that there were Sunday Schools for children. Indeed in Bourneville – the Cadburys' model village – there was a model Sunday School and other

Friends came to see how this school was run. No one was compelled to go to a meeting on a Sunday; they believed in extreme freedom: 'Though my father was an elder in the Society, I chose for myself whether I wanted to join or not.'

At one time people were asked to leave the Society if they went bankrupt, as was Elizabeth Fry's husband when he went bankrupt. Also they were disowned if they married out of the Society.

There were, in this correspondent's time, generally no music and no hymns as George Fox regarded this as a form of hypocrisy – people would go to church and sing praises to God and then go and commit a multitude of sins. But 'Bourneville was only a small village and so as a concession to the Anglicans they had a hymn and a reading and the rest of the service was held in silence.'

The Friends believed that there was something of God in every man and therefore they were pacifists; their normal behaviour was to speak the truth and be honest. Because of this some Friends refused to take the Oath in a court of law as they claimed they always told the truth. They became very good businessmen. Many doctors and teachers were Friends but there are very few working class.

In the nineteenth century, drink, smoking, music and dancing were associated with the devil. Many Quakers had a social fund – starting activities and sports clubs. Some even had a hockey club.

Quakers were to be found all over the world. There are Friends in Philadelphia; this group was started by Penn. They exist also in Japan and East Africa. At one time President Nixon was a member of a meeting. There are four yearly meetings in London. Once a month in London there used to be a meeting to help the Friends who were in prison.

Quakers even had conversion in what they call the evangelical period from the beginning of the nineteenth century to the twentieth century. Quaker missionaries began in the nineteenth century and went first to America. Missionaries also went to Madagascar, India and the Middle East.

The Friends were pioneers against the slave trade, for co-educational schools and in the treating of lunatics. They still

have schools to teach people to read. There are about six or
seven boarding schools, e.g. Ackworth and Bootham, both in
Yorkshire.

The Quakers for long, and even today, can claim that they
all knew each other and were 'almost without exception' (as
one correspondent states) related to each other. 'We did not
take our spiritual life from a book called the Bible. We all
experienced the power of God within ourselves.' Originally
in the seventeenth century they were largely yeomen and petty
gentry, self-sufficient. Later they became urbanised and traders
and some grew very rich. Libertarian in politics – John Bright
was of their number – they were as ingrowing as the Exclusive
Brethren, though not quite as socially constrictive. Quakers in
1860 were adjured to 'Be careful in your own conduct, and to
encourage in your families that simplicity in deportment and
attire, that avoidance of flattery and insincerity in language...';
but they were only *asked* to avoid gaming, 'unnecessary frequenting of taverns, excess in drinking'. What was *necessary* frequenting
of taverns, what excess in drinking? This was almost early
Wesleyan in its permissiveness or, at any rate, moderation.
Curiously enough, a separatist group of Quakers (the 'Crewdson
separation') commonly met in Manchester pubs and taverns in
the early nineteenth century, not of course for meditation but for
fervent wide-ranging discussion of spiritual as well as secular
matters.

The Quakers held summer schools; they founded institutes;
they organised investigations into the causes of poverty. They
formed Young Friends' groups which no doubt had their fun but
were basically very earnest, so that by 1960 a Quaker thinker
and historian, Richenda C. Scott, could write: 'The religion of
authority, based on a Holy Book, has passed from us.'[1] So, too, it
appears had the mystical faith of the early Quakers in the 'light
within'. Instead, arose 'a bold, humanitarian faith'. Like the
latter-day mainstream Nonconformists they propounded not
'the peace which passeth all understanding' but welfare and
politics. It is hard to believe that George Fox and his 'Friends'
would approve, but the Quakers have latterly, like the Swedes,

[1] The Journal of the Friends' Historical Society, vol. 49, no. 2, Spring
1960.

made a passionate fetish of 'change' for change's sake. God and the inward light were relegated to the boiler-room.

It is probably true that the creed was at best onanistic: God in me; me and God as 'two movements in mutual interplay, mutual struggle, and reciprocal communion'.[1] To the outgoing Nonconformist, concerned with saving other men's souls as well as his own, this would sound merely selfish. Little wonder that the great warm-hearted gatherings of Nonconformists did not exist with the Quakers, nor that fellowship (save in the narrowest sense) was not one of their objectives.

Of all the Protestant sects of England, the Peculiar People was by its nature social and was in a constant fervour of conversion-revivalism. It was, in the eighteenth-century sense, pervaded by 'enthusiasm'. Confined almost exclusively to Essex its origins were curious and curiously complex.

A Church of England parson, a Mr Atkin of the Isle of Man, had 'the Spirit of the Lord' come upon him in 1834. 'Being an earnest man' he believed that 'in Jesus Christ there was perfect salvation which brings perfect satisfaction'.[2] He prayed and 'laid aside the Parson's Gown and left the Established Church with all its forms and ceremonies'. He preached in Liverpool 'the glorious gospel of Holiness and the New Birth'. 'Separating himself from all sects and religious bodies', he began open-air preaching in London. Taking his stand outside a hotel, he annoyed the proprietor who engaged men to harass him. At the same place a few days later, he learned that the proprietor and his wife had suddenly died: 'this gave him more boldness to preach, feeling assured that God was his upholder.'

His preaching – 'where many souls were born again and received the gift of the Holy Ghost' – attracted the attention of a Methodist local preacher, William Bridges, a hat-block maker of 8 Grand Lane, near Aldgate, E.1. Atkin preached on the text 'Enoch walked with God' and Bridges was a changed man, now 'believing that Christ had borne away all my sins

---

[1] *The Person and Place of Jesus Christ*, by P. T. Forsythe, p. 336.

[2] Sources for what follows are mainly two leaflets: 'The Centenary of the Peculiar People, 1838–1938', London, n.d. (a short leaflet) and 'The Origin of the Peculiar People', a leaflet dated 1882.

in His own body on Calvary'. He received 'life and joy to my
soul'.

While rejoicing in this wonderful change, Bridges visited his
sister in Rochford, Essex. The year was 1838. There he preached
and there he met another fervent Wesleyan, James Banyard.

Banyard, described as an ugly man with a voice of thunder,
was born in 1800, the son of a ploughman. Like many other
convertees he had been a 'bad' man – poacher, friend of smug-
glers, public-house haunter and composer-singer of rough,
jocular songs, one of which, 'The siren wrecked on the West
Rock', is said to have been long remembered in Rochford. In his
unregenerate days he excelled in conjuring tricks and mimicry,
'pulling out his lips like a horse's mouth till he had deformed himself'. He had scoffed at religion and thrown dried peas on the
chapel steps with the intention of tripping up the devout.

Banyard had been a jobbing labourer. After his conversion to
Wesleyanism he learned the trade of cobbler. Now Bridges
invited him to London, promising him to supply him with books
and information about teetotalism, then a new cause far from
generally accepted by the Wesleyans.

During his sojourn with Bridges in Aldgate Banyard heard
that his friend had found 'something better than teetotalism' and
that he had been 'baptised with the Holy Spirit. Bless God,
there is no fear in love, no doubts in believers, no sin in Christians.' So affected was Banyard that he beseeched Bridges to
show him, too, the light. After prayer in Bridges's bedchamber,
he was 'baptised with the Holy Spirit and with power'. He
departed for Rochford – and Bridges from our story though he
founded a chapel in Bath Street, Clerkenwell, and 'many found
their way to God through his ministry'.

In Rochford Banyard preached his new-found faith and the
Wesleyans rose up against him, some saying that he had returned
crazy from London. When he preached in Rochford square,
dead cats, pails of filth and rotten eggs were thrown at him and a
former boon companion mocked him by putting on a white
gown and declared that *he* would preach for a year and a day,
nonstop. He was banned from preaching in the chapel and began
prayer meetings in his own house. Many came to hear him until
his landlord objected. So that a house was hired in Union Lane,

14

Rochford, which seated about twenty-five and cost two shillings a week rental.

Here in due course Banyard and his followers formed themselves into a Church with prayer meetings each morning at five o'clock, on Tuesdays and Thursdays at 7 p.m. and on Sundays at 6 a.m., 10.30 a.m., 2.30 p.m. and 6.30 p.m.

At all meetings Brothers and Sisters may offer their thanksgiving praises and requests to God the Father and His people, except Sunday afternoons and evenings when the Leader will preach from the Word of God.

We will accept no money for preaching, make no laws, have no book of rules, but the Word of God alone. For unless one knows his sins are forgiven and that his name is in the Lamb's Book of Life, we will not accept him as a member of the Church of God. Preachers are not to burden the Church of God, but to subsist by their manual labour.

So were formed the Banyardites, New Lights, Ranters, later to be called, by themselves, 'The Peculiar People', from the sentence in Titus (ch. 2, 14) and the first epistle general of Peter (1, 2–9): 'Ye are a chosen generation, a royal priesthood, an holy nation, a peculiar people . . . which had not obtained mercy, but now have obtained mercy.' The word 'peculiar' meant a separate, distinctive group; but 'peculiar' in the common sense they also were.

They were devoted to physical healing by the laying-on of hands, basing their belief on such references in the New Testament as those in St James (ch. 5, 13–16) and St Matthew's Gospel where Christ touched the leper and he was cleansed, touched Peter's mother and the fever left her, touched the eyes of a blind man and he received sight.

This caused great offence, particularly among doctors whom the Peculiar People refused to employ. At Prittlewell in Essex, where a chapel was started in North Street, the Church of England curate preached against their delusion and they suffered persecution. But 'not long after this the curate was taken ill and died in a few days'. Such swift vengeance was regarded as only proper.

The Peculiar People, however, claimed many successes for their form of healing – of, for instance, lock-jaw, agues, cripples. When, however, they refused to have doctors attend their members, particularly children, who subsequently died, they were frequently prosecuted. Some of their members, however, lived to advanced ages; such a one was William Heddle of Southend who died in 1948 at the age of 101 years. With some humour they said that they had no objection to taking pills – when they were well.

Despite their rejection of anything but the Word of God, the Peculiar People in 1852 made four 'bishops'. They chose James Banyard, naturally, Samuel Harrod, David Handley and James Thorogood. 'The last three laid their hands upon James Banyard and designated him their bishop. He then in turn ordained the other three.' It was not dissimilar and no less illegal than John Wesley's creation of Methodist bishops in the North American colonies.

Banyard's propagation of the Gospel as he saw it was much assisted by his marriage to a Miss Tamara Knapping; her money helped the building of the Peculiar People chapel in 1850 in North Street, Rochford, and other chapels in the county. Banyard died in 1862. By 1937, however, there were thirty Peculiar People chapels in Essex, one in Kent at Gillingham and one in Bath Street, London. Yet less than twenty years later on 31 March 1956 they were dissolved as a denomination and their remnants assimilated into the Union of Evangelical Churches. They had lasted just 118 years.

The Peculiar People were Nonconformist Protestants – with a difference. For a long time they had no Sunday Schools, though by the 1930s they had twenty-eight. They rejected organisation, but they had Elders who, in the Methodist manner, came on a preaching 'Plan' in 1867. Indeed they were greatly influenced by mainstream Nonconformity, holding Harvest Thanksgivings, first in 'booths in meadows at Southend, Daws Heath and Chelmsford', later in Congregational chapels. Tea meetings took place on Good Friday and Christmas; the Lord's Supper was celebrated from 1865; and, like the Baptists, they held 'Baptisms of Water to Converted Members' (i.e. adult baptism) from 1870. In latter years they even had 'ministers' who, despite the sect's early protestations were at one time apparently paid. Latterly they had a Young People's, Women's and Mission Fellowships. Not all Peculiars were breakaways from the Non-conformists. Some, as at Stanway, Essex, had been Anglicans. As a result of a chance visit to the Peculiars' chapel at Witham, a Miss Tracey opened her cottage for meetings and neighbours and friends were invited. That was in 1880. Then a larger room was made available and afterwards William Johnson, a seed-grower, provided a barn with straw strewn over the floor. Eventually in 1886 a chapel was built in Stanway in what was later called Chapel Road. John Miller was recognised as an elder by the 'presbytery' of the Peculiar People and served for forty-five years.

When the therapeutic laying-on of hands failed and members died there was the problem of burying them. Until the purchase in 1882 of a burial ground at Daws Heath, near Thundersley, funerals were by grace and favour of the Established Church. It was rumoured that when one of the Peculiars died the rest spent the night dancing and singing round the corpse. Certainly, at a Daws Heath funeral they sang joyful hymns at the graveside, happy that one of their number had 'crossed death's river' into the better life.

The Peculiar People believed that conversion changed their very nature, that Jesus was within them and that salvation and the forgiveness of their sins were guaranteed them here and now. Their meetings, a correspondent from Essex tells me, resembled 'Negro spiritual revival meetings, chanting, singing, hand-clapping, tambourine banging'.

They expected the Holy Spirit to descend upon them during every service. Often they were moved to walk or even run up and down the aisles, giving their testimonies. As they scampered, they repeated verses from the Bible. This was known as 'getting a blessing'. As in Quaker meetings whoever felt impelled to speak spoke, and sins were loudly confessed after the Bible reading. Even during the reading there would be such ejaculations from the congregation as 'beautiful, Amen, Thank God, Mercy!'

Since the Peculiars were opposed to any form of 'idolatry', their chapels were bare with neither altar nor pulpit. One such chapel is described in Israel Zangwill's[1] novel *Jinny the Carrier* (1919):

> The painfully crude walls, a little dingier with the passing of the years, the broad table-desk at the head of the hall at which Deacon Mawhood and the Elders throned it in Sunday black, the rows of spruce wooden chairs sexually divided by a gangway and exhibiting in its left section a desert of elderly females with a few oases of hobbledehoy girls.

Until well into the twentieth century the Peculiar People wore black clothes equivalent to the 'best' of an upper farm worker or small shopkeepers in the mid-nineteenth century, and at some chapels the 'sisters' wore black skull caps, or 'Queen Victoria' bonnets, with street-sweeping skirts. The men were always clean-shaven, and wore bowler hats reminiscent of undertakers. They sang hymns (unaccompanied in early days and mainly by Charles Wesley), and in 1860 produced their own hymn-book compiled by S. Harrod, D. Handley and W. Lewin. There was no organ so, when starting a hymn, if they found the note too high or too low for them to sing, they stopped and made a fresh start. The hymns themselves were from a variety of sources – Watts, Wesley, Doddridge and others – and included versified psalms, with Hebrew letters (e.g. Aleph, Beth, Gimel, etc.). But their services retained an informal, extempore perfervid quality to the end.

Once a year they joined together in Chelmsford Corn Exchange for a thanksgiving tea when, one writer recalls,

> the streets of our county town were besieged by hundreds of these people, the 'sisters' easily recognised by their neat clothing and little black bonnets and the 'brothers' by their bowler hats and clean shaven faces.

One Colchester correspondent writes:

> I remember these people holding services in a pair of old dilapidated thatched cottages in the parish of Wakes Colne

---

[1] Zangwill (1864–1926) was a popular novelist and dramatist of London Jewish life. How he came to be so knowledgeable about the Peculiars is not clear, though curiously enough their first hymn book was printed in 1860 at the 'Operative Jewish Converts' Institution, Palestine Place, Bethnal Green.

about nine miles north-west of Colchester well over sixty years ago and as I only knew of two families within a mile of this chapel their Sunday crowds must have come from a wide area. As there were no restaurants within miles of this place, I have no doubt they followed the example of a small Baptist chapel in the next parish by bringing food for the day and having tea parties between services.

On a quiet summer evening their singing could be heard at my home three-quarters of a mile distant. They eventually had a new chapel built nearby and this was still going strong when I left the district twenty years ago [i.e. about 1950]. It was a well-known fact that these people would rather die than seek the aid of a doctor, but as this chapel had no burial ground a doctor's certificate had to be obtained before other priests would accept them for burial.

The Peculiars, who had come from a distance, did, indeed, eat their midday meal in the chapel, during which large jugs of water were available on the Elders' table. Often they brought hunks of bread and meat in red handkerchiefs.

The Peculiar People remained peculiar in the eyes of many people from beginning to end. An elderly Brightlingsea, Essex, man writes:

It is sixty years since my pal and myself looked in at their service, if you could call it a service. As we were passing a man stood at the door and asked us to come in. When we got in what a din! They were dancing, singing and clapping their hands in a ring. Then they would stop. The head would say something and then they would start all over again.

We stopped for a while. They would break for refreshments and then they would start all over again – dancing, singing and clapping their hands. When we got outside we thought: 'so much for the Peculiars.' This was at Upchurch, Kent.

Yet many did find satisfaction in the Peculiars' beliefs and practices:

I have never been so happy – Church twice on Sunday, weekly service and also prayer meeting, five miles bike ride, but so happy, money of no account, awful hard up and I read the Bible as never before.

Alas, my correspondent in Billericay, Essex, lapsed and says he has been in the wilderness ever since.

Members of the sect were by no means innocents abroad, though they were fiercely evangelistic. Reginald A. Beckett in *Romantic Essex* (1901) records:

> I went with a carrier once who struck me as having more than these men usually possess of shrewd insight into common everyday things. Some remark he made led me to quote a text of Scripture. He looked round at me like a war-horse that hears the trumpet and preached there and then a discourse on my text that for sheer practical wisdom and terseness of expression was in its way a masterpiece. I found afterwards that this man was a leading member of the Peculiar People, which perhaps explains the marked acerbity of language which occurred when his cart nearly collided with the trap of the village doctor.

Essex has for centuries been a breeding-ground for Nonconformity. Some of the most moving scenes in Foxe's *Book of Martyrs* and Bloomfield's *History of the Martyrs* took place in the county; simple peasants for participating in 'seditious' conventicles or practices were fined, jailed, transported to the 'plantations' and even nailed to stakes and burned alive, clapping their hands with joy.

Of such the Peculiars were descendants, a special working-class emanation of that flat, marshy county which essentially until latter times was agricultural and seafaring. It was a county left high and dry and still remote by the tide of industrialism flowing most strongly in northern and western England. Here is a paradox. Why should such a county – far from the stresses and strains of the industrialism sometimes thought to have precipitated religious enthusiasm – have bred one of the most extreme forms of it? The high eighteenth-century maxim of *surtout point de zèle* was well and truly extinguished in the Essex of the Peculiar People. So, in turn, were they once the old agricultural life was over.

8

CLASS DISTINCTION AND THE FUTURE

Quick now, here, now, always –
A condition of complete simplicity
(Costing not less than everything)
And all shall be well and
All manner of things shall be well. . . .

Four Quartets, 'Little Gidding',
by T. S. Eliot.

At the end of this 'total recall' of what Nonconformity meant to the ordinary individual within or near the lifetime of some of us, certain awkward questions have not so far been met. One is the fact that class distinction between the various Nonconformist groups did exist. It is true that, for example, most of the early Wesleyan Methodists in the days of John Wesley himself belonged to one class only, namely those, whether peers of the realm or bakers' roundsmen, who took religion seriously. That there were, in fact, few peers indicates only that most such did not as a rule take religion seriously, or at all, except in the sense that the Church of England was an arm of the state and as such must be defended and protected. Exactly in the same way another Oxford Movement – the High Church group – attracted a wide spectrum of people drawn together by belief not by a class.

Since Wesley himself was an 'A.M.' of Oxford and a fellow of Lincoln College, some of his earliest followers came from similar backgrounds and differed little from the later Evangelicals who remained, as Wesley had wished to do, in the Church of England; and those Evangelicals in the beginning, though not later, were usually the hereditary upper classes and the well-to-do.

The Methodist break-away movements – Primitives, New Connexion, Bible Christians – seldom had such backgrounds, early or late. They were and remained essentially working-class with a sprinkling of tradesmen. So that in some eyes the Wesleyans retained the edge, socially speaking, over all the other Methodists; thus even as late as the years just before the First World War, the fact was recalled by a Sheffield lady:

The name of the chapel is St Mark's Methodist, evolving from St Mark's United Methodist when they combined with the Wesleyans. The Wesleyans looked down upon us ordinary Methodist mortals and the feeling on the other side was that the Wesleyans were a bunch of snobs.

A Leeds man, writing of the Edwardian period, says:

There were six places of worship in Kirkstall in those days and they were distinguished from one another, in my mind, less by their doctrinal than by their social differences. The Church of England was easily top of the social league table. It was attended by such gentlefolk as still lived in the village: the Butlers, for instance, who owned Kirkstall Forge and walked every Sunday past the end of our house on their way to church from their big house in St Anne's Lane because they would not use their carriage and horses on Sunday: and their friend, Miss Hargreaves, a well-to-do spinster who built the alms-houses, still standing in Kirkstall Lane. The Vicar, Canon Egerton-Leigh, belonged to the same class.

The Wesleyan Methodists came after the Church. They were largely well-to-do middle class and many of them may well have voted Tory when to vote Tory was not only political betrayal but religious heresy. This was the time [1902–3] when the stricter Nonconformists were refusing to pay the fraction of their rates destined for the maintenance of church schools. Our Baptist minister, a 'passive resister', allowed the local authority to take and sell his books rather than pay voluntarily. The Wesleyans were suspect: they hovered on the edge of the Church: but there was no doubt about their social status.

The Congregationalists were the intellectuals. The Men's Adult School met in their schoolroom at eight o'clock every Sunday morning and was attended by working men whose thirst for education was such that they were prepared, after a week's early rising to go to work, to get up early even on Sundays to

get a share in it. They were the descendants of the old Independents who, with the Unitarians, are said by E. P.
Thomson to have had in the early nineteenth century 'a small
but influential artisan following nurtured in a strenuous
intellectual tradition'. My day-school teacher was a Congregationalist, which may account for the pencil and paper
games at his son's Christmas parties. There was less romping
and more modest intellectual exercise than at other houses.
And the Congregationalists were not given to uninhibited
religious enthusiasm.

The United Methodists, meeting in Zion chapel, were
remarkable to me chiefly for their pagan pleasures. They had
the parties and the dramatic and musical entertainment of
the kind which would never have been tolerated in the Baptist
chapel.

The Primitive Methodists and the Baptists were certainly
at the bottom of the table. Here were none of the paganisms
of Zion, the intellectual pretensions of the Congregationalists
or the social pretensions of the Wesleyans and the Church of
England. Here religion was serious, austere, intolerant and
deadly earnest. They were concerned with the saving of souls
and whilst a Christmas party or an anniversary tea might be
allowed, not without some headshaking on the part of some of
the deacons, these were but means to that end. These were the
places of the religious revival meetings with their impassioned
overflow of powerful feeling; and they were the religious
resting places for the over-burdened, tired and often
desperate working classes.

These distinctions were more visible in cities than in villages
and in any case, as far as the Methodists were concerned, must
have disappeared after the union of three of the Methodist
churches, including the Wesleyan, in 1932.

But it is doubtful whether these class feelings were ever widely
true. In many places there was never more than one Methodist
chapel of whatever variety; and for instance, in the Yorkshire
Dales little distinction was made between Methodism and even
the Church of England for some of the remoter villages had a
chapel only, so that people went there *faute de mieux*, but still on

special occasions travelled to the nearest Church of England church.

Nevertheless, in less remote places, between any brand of Methodism and the Church of England a social gulf existed, as one lady writes:

> I came back to England from Paris in 1906 when I was seventeen; my father was a Methodist minister in Abingdon, Berkshire. He had been to Cambridge and my mother was the daughter and granddaughter of colonial officials, born and brought up as Evangelical Anglicans. In Paris it did not occur to me that people would not want to mix with me because I was a Nonconformist.
>
> In Abingdon I soon learned that the educated Anglicans of Abingdon would not mix with us, except the headmaster of the grammar school which was my youngest brother's school. In the Abingdon train once I heard two girls, Anglican daughters of a retired officer, saying that the sisters of the school headmaster had spoilt their social position in the town by seeing too much of me. I popped aside from the paper and said: 'I'd better remind you I'm here, I'm Irene Whelpton.' They naturally looked embarrassed.
>
> The vicar did not call on father and the Anglicans never mixed with any Nonconformists. They, the Wesleyans, came to chapel or the schoolroom several times a week and that was (beside their life work, mostly trades people), all that they knew about.
>
> Father knew the other Nonconformist minister who had a 'fraternal'. I was a student at Oxford, commuting several times a week. I soon was a theological student, mostly at Mansfield Congregational. I mixed with other home students – but remember the shock of one who shared Greek lessons when calling on us she realized I was not the vicar's daughter but the Minister's daughter. 'Coaches' in Oxford made no difference of course.

Often there were specific, even political, reasons for antipathy between Anglicans and others. Relationships, for instance, between Nonconformists and Anglicans in Henley-on-Thames (in 1847) were very strained, particularly over education, accord-

ing to one correspondent. Children of Nonconformist families
were threatened with expulsion from the Grammar school for
not attending the parish church services on Sundays. James
Rowland wrote: 'She is leaving us to go with her husband to the
parish church, in which the Gospel, we have reason to fear, is
not at present preached.'

Doubtless the Balfour Education Act of 1902 like Forster's
1870 Act – objected to because it ordered that Church of England
schools be paid for by the rates – caused further animositities. The
cry of 'The Church on the rates' swept the country; and an
amendment to the Bill placing religious instruction at ele-
mentary schools under the authority of the whole body of the
managers of a school merely antagonised the Anglican parsons
in turn.[1]

Much, as always, depended on the individuals concerned:

At the age of eighty-four [in 1971] I am still thinking of the
time when as a child I was sent with 3d. on a Monday morning
to a supposed Church of England school for lessons. It was
instilled into me that the property really belonged to the
Primitive Methodists. The vicar had borrowed the key from
the caretaker, then kept it. A suit at Staindrop [Co. Durham]
police court was lost because the big-wigs wouldn't allow anyone to speak, except a grocer who trembled like an aspen leaf
while they smiled like cherubs. The schoolmaster who arrived
from Ousten Ferry was told of the sordid affair, but what could
he do? The vicar sank into oblivion.

This setback, however, didn't stop further activities. En-
livened by a visit from William Clowes and Hugh Bourne, the
Primitives acquired a meeting place down a yard. A stove was
bought and rough forms. Eventually three oil lamps were
suspended from the ceiling to replace candles. This drew forth
wrath from a dear old woman who had walked from Summer-
house. She exclaimed as she opened the chapel door, 'Oh,
'ave mercy, that light's enough to knock a body down.'

The new vicar proved to be very sympathetic towards the
roaring ranters. He subscribed generously to their carol
singing. He treated them with respect. He visited Mr Shornton

[1] This was a factor in the rout of the Conservative Government in 1905.
See *Arthur James Balfour* by Kenneth Young (London, 1963), pp. 202–5.

regularly and listened to him making arrangements for three cottages to be pulled down for the erection of a new Primitive Methodist chapel. It now stands in a prominent position in the village of Ingleton, a monument to a noble band who years ago would not be subdued.

As successive disabling Acts against Nonconformists were removed, matters improved, yet there were always awkward people. At Mursley, near Bletchley, Baptist chapel the Rev. George Parker commenced his ministry on 29 September 1885. On 6 November he buried Thomas Collyer in Mursley Churchyard being the first Dissenting Officiant to do so under the new Burial Act, but at the rector's insistence had to stand outside the churchyard wall for the service.

There was a considerable row when, at the turn of the century, Canon – later Bishop – Hensley Henson accepted an invitation to conduct a Congregational anniversary service in Birmingham. At the local vicar's insistence, Bishop Gore, though reluctantly, issued a formal inhibition, which Hensley Henson ignored without further consequences. In later years Nonconformists and Anglicans often cooperated in, for example, united missionary campaigns; until at the present day there is a move for union between the Church of England and Methodists.

With regard to class consciousness within an individual chapel it cannot honestly be said that the Nonconformists – at any rate in the larger, richer chapels – were much less susceptible than anyone else. At the famous Carrs Lane, Birmingham, Congregational chapel in the mid-1850s, female servants, unlike other unmarried females, did not have 'Miss' placed before their names in the members' list. Week-night meetings were designated for 'Christian Tradesmen', 'Female servants' and 'Artisans'. All may have been equal in the eyes of God but not in those of deacons, class leaders and stewards.

Nor of course in many respects *were* they equal. Some could not read or write, few could contribute much to collections and none owned pews although some chapels always reserved some pews for the poor – who were thus *seen* to be poor. Moreover the very poorest who were in rags would not go to Chapel at all. 'The working classes,' wrote J. L. and B. Hammond in *Age of*

Chartists, 'were plunged in such deep barbarism that they were in a clan apart from the average Nonconformist.'

Only perhaps in such missions as those to seamen or to railway-men was there something nearer equality – and later in the great missions whence sprang the Central Halls in industrial towns. A report from the Sunderland mission claimed that:

> The composition of the congregation is striking. Now and again medicine is represented; merchants come to worship and see what is being done for the artisan; members of the Mercantile Marine find their way there; tradesmen and toilers in the shipyards sit side by side, for every seat is free; the man in fustian is quite at home with a merchant's clerk on his right hand, and a well-dressed shop assistant at his left; . . . the woman who makes the shawl answer the purpose of millinery is always welcome.[1]

In the larger denominations, Congregationalist, Baptists, Wesleyans, there had always been well-to-do people and many who were not originally well-off became so, in part as a consequence of the well-ordered way of life – no drinking, no gambling – and the belief in hard work. On the other hand, while converts from the lower classes were being made, there was an outflow of some of the very affluent who either abandoned religion altogether or preferred socially to appear on Sundays in the Church of England. They wanted to be part of the establishment and to mix socially with princes and princelings of the Church rather than with Superintendent Ministers and revivalist laymen. This did not – and does not – apply to all: the Chamberlain family remained Unitarians, the Frys, Rowntrees and Cadburys Quakers, the present Speaker of the House of Commons, Mr Selwyn Lloyd, a Methodist.

Nor was the departure from Nonconformity confined to the affluent laity. A number of ministers switched their allegiance to the Church of England just as a number of Anglican parsons – chief among them Newman – became Roman Catholics. Within the Nonconformist churches such changes were less common (or less commonly recorded) but it was not unknown for Methodist

---

[1] *At the Centre: the Story of Methodism's Central Missions*, p. 17.

laymen to become Unitarians, Jehovah's Witnesses, Spiritualists or Christian Scientists.

On the other hand, the Nonconformists often benefited in membership as a result of schisms in the Church of England. Thus, a considerable number of Evangelical or Low Church Anglicans joined the Wesleyans or Congregationalists as a result of the High Church or Anglo-Catholic movement. This they regarded as a reaction towards idolatry and away from the principles of the Reformation. Incense, candles, florid robes and all the trappings of priesthood (rather than ministry) nauseated them; and in the 1890s and Edwardian times papers were full of the acrid controversies between evangelical laymen and allegedly Romanising vicars and bishops. Accusations of Popery were tossed about – though ironically enough the Pope has no fiercer enemies than the Anglo-Catholics.

In general, however, such animosities are today almost dead, along with huffy feelings between Wesleyans and Primitives, and 'race-card' categorising of Nonconformists on the social scale. They have ended, in part, because former Christians have voted with their feet and departed from chapels and churches, in part because of the rising – if somewhat stage-managed – tide of ecumenicism. The former manifestation was probably unavoidable because of a whole concatenation of political, economic and materialist or humanist causes, though it is probably not irreversible. We may confidently ignore the 'Jesusfreaks' and the transient (and scarcely new) interest in Eastern religions.

Nevertheless, the buoyancy created so abundantly by faith is a permanent necessity, indeed an attribute, of man; and in the West (including, if we may, Russia and many parts of Africa and Australasia) the faith in God the Father, the Son and the Holy Ghost remains as something more than merely residual. As Pastor Richard Wurmbrand has reminded us,[1] where the Christian faith is most severely persecuted, as in Russia, there it is most tenaciously clung to by men and women to whom its profession, even in some hole-and-corner chapel or in a forest clearing, may well bring at the least a bar to material advance-

[1] *In God's Underground.*

ment, at the worst Siberia or 'psychiatric' treatment. Indeed almost within living memory in England persecution for the faith was not unknown. E. E. Kellett wrote:

> Those who dwell on its [Nonconformist] narrowness and darkness can never have seen, as I have often seen, humble privates of the Salvation Army, after being beaten, stoned, or otherwise maltreated, then punished by magistrates for their sufferings. The faces of these martyrs, as I can personally bear witness might be scarred with wounds, but they shone with joy. If this is misery and gloom, then it might be well for the present generation if it could be similarly gloomy and miserable.

Christianity is still a unique solace, through its gospel of love, of redemption, and through the ministrations of the Holy Ghost by means of prayer and contemplation: 'Come, Holy Ghost, our souls inspire, And lighten with celestial fire,' an anonymous hymn dating from the ninth or tenth century A.D., expresses the reality at the heart of the Christian religion – a reality that countless millions have known personally.

Ecumenicism is a different matter. No one supposes that the varied socio-religious life of the different Nonconformist sects, which has been the subject of this book, will recur; it was created by historical circumstances themselves non-recurrent.

Ecumenicism, however, is a deliberate attempt to squash all Christian believers into one mould – another example of that amalgamating passion which has already reduced large businesses to a mouse-like anonymity. It may also be seen as part of that 'one worldism' which is death to the individual and which leads, in political terms, to world dictatorship; or of that social democracy, the most insidious of dictatorships, under which the Swedes now live.[1]

A man, to remain a human individual, must be able to worship God in the manner and style best suited to himself, his background, his predilections and prejudices. Any attempt to water down the distinctive tenets of a dozen varieties of Christianity to make them palatable to all will result only in producing pap, a not very nourishing diet. Nor is the Roman Catholic

[1] See *The New Totalitarians*, by Roland Huntford (London, 1971).

attitude helpful as expressed in the old joke of the priest observing to the Methodist minister with an unprejudiced air: 'You must worship Christ in your way; I in His.'

The differences between Congregationalists, Baptists, Quakers, Wesleyans and their many splinters, sometimes became contumelious but they were seldom trivial: they fitted exactly the variousness of men and, it should be emphasised, the freedom to be different was a guarantee of the liberty of the individual. To say freely 'I disagree' is the first freedom. Nonconformity, in fact, was an immensely important liberation movement. And those who strive for a blanket uniformity in religion – or in any other field – are the enemies of liberty. For their objective differs little from that of all authoritarian movements.

History does not repeat itself; it is merely, A. J. Balfour said, historians who repeat each other. Yet it would scarcely be exaggerating to say that Christians are today as beleaguered as they were in the early centuries A.D., or in the dark ages which followed, or during the slumbers of the Church in England before their awakening by Wesley. Christians in England, well within the memories of those now living – among them those who have written to me – were free to flourish unchecked.

But throughout the later nineteenth and twentieth centuries, faith has been subtly and not so subtly eroded, not so much by the enormous success of science (and the great scientists are seldom rigidly atheistic) but by propaganda from many sources – not least Russian Communism, but spreading deviously through many who would deny any such politico-philosophical connection. It is obvious why authoritarian states such as Russia seek to stifle Christianity; the rage of others against it is not so easy to explain, nor is it my concern here. What I am sure of is that, like the eastern Roman Emperor, Julian the Apostate, who sought to set the clock back to paganism, the neo-pagans of the twentieth century will fail.

Inevitably, there has been emphasis in the foregoing on that eternally recurrent question '*Où sont les neiges d'antan?*' That there has been a great melting of these particular snows – for reasons suggested in the Introit – can scarcely be denied. But it is proper to state that still, in their dozens, if no longer their hundreds, old and, yes, young flock to the chapels in great cities for the anniversaries, carol services, missionary meetings, garden parties, knife-and-fork teas. Many of my correspondents point out that their Sunday School anniversaries still have tiered platforms for the children who still sing solos. The old anthems – 'The Heavens are telling' from Haydn's 'The Creation' – or Handel's 'Arm, arm, ye brave' are sung with an orchestra accompanying; so, too, are the old hymns – Havergal's 'Take my life and let it be Consecrated, Lord, to thee', Watts's 'Sweet is the work, my God my King', and George Herbert's 'Let all the world in every corner sing'.

Some chapels, it is true, have 'gone modern', not only in what is preached but where. A few chapels have stylish interiors, which will probably look as eccentric in twenty years as do now the more extravagant Gaumont cinemas of the 1930s. In such chapels the pulpit has been replaced by the apron-stage layout more apt for discussion than for teaching, let alone praying. Chapels, of course, have usually been more fit for congregational participation than for silent devotion, to which the town or country Anglican church is more appropriate. A newer trend still is for some Methodist chapels to have an altar with a cross upon it which would have outraged many of the nineteenth-century Primitives.

The most significant change, perhaps, is the diminished status of the preacher, minister or layman, symbolised by the modernist antipathy to the physical pulpit itself. The days of the great autocratic preachers seem to be over. The causes are several: the levelling process of the times combined with a fashionable anti-authoritarianism; the fact that, with entertainment in every home, sermon-going is less attractive; and that doubtless as a consequence, there are few great preachers about. The persuasive little chat – originated by wireless parsons to fit the nature of the medium – has replaced the dramatic oratory of the past.

None of these changes is, in my opinion, necessarily permanent. Many people today suffer a lack of anything that can reasonably be called a social life. They also suffer, consciously or not, from an ignorance of God. As men and women increasingly find tasteless the stone proffered them in lieu of the bread of the Spirit, as the world becomes bleaker and life and the

universe the more inexplicable the more they are 'explained',
as the former variety of ways of worshipping and knowing God
is flattened into uniformity, so a new nonconformity may arise
however different in style.

But if it is to light the fire in the heart that the Wesleys and
their successors lit, it will have to be God-centred, prayerful and
high-principled; it will need to recognise that, as men differ, so
must their approach to God; that doctrinal differences do matter since in His house are many mansions; and that persecution,
whatever form it may take, will bring each group into that
fellowship which warmed the early Christians as it did the early
Baptists, the Methodists, the once-stoned Salvationists and as
it does today in the Christian sects of Russia.

ACKNOWLEDGEMENTS

The author wishes to thank the following and regrets any inadvertent omission:

J. Abbot
M. Ainsley
D. M. Amery
A. F. Ammann
H. M. Anderson
C. Angell
D. Appleton
Gladys Armitage
J. Armitage
D. D. Ashley
R. W. Bailey
H. M. Baker
Jesse Barber
A. A. Bardo
S. P. Barham
D. Barker
Doreen Baxter
Frank Beckwith, M.A.
George Berrington
J. Betts
Mary E. Booth
H. F. Bottomley
W. H. Braithwaite
L. Brindley Marten
Winifred Brook

Frank P. Brooks
Nellie Burnett
J. W. Butcher
Sister Florence Chislett
W. P. Clark
C. C. Coates
W. D. Coleman
G. E. Colthorpe
T. Cooper
Elsie A. Darwen
Lena Davies
G. W. Dent
W. M. Dodd
J. W. Drew
Luther C. Dudley
Ben Durrant
Frank Ella
Edith Ellis
D. M. Emery
Jeffrey Evans
E. Eyres
Barbara Fletcher
P. Forward
E. Francis
M. E. Freeth

Mary German
Rev. David Gibson
M. Gibson
E. Goldthorpe
F. S. Gough
Bob Grass
H. G. Griffin
Alfred A. Grimwade
Muriel Hall
Rosalind Hall
Norman Harrison
R. Harrison
E. E. Heagh
Rowland Heddle
Rev. G. Henton Davies, D.D.
K. M. Hill
Rev. H. R. Hindley
Dr P. Holding
Henry Holmes
Rodney Hood
N. E. Hooley
Rosalind Hunt
Janet M. Huntley
James Hyde
Cecil Ind
G. Jackson
A. James
Rev. G. W. Kirby
A. Kitching
U. M. Lascelles
Kenneth B. Lennox
Daisy A. F. Lewis
Rev. G. E. H. Long
N. Mainprize
Douglas Malpas

Brian Marshall
S. M. Martin
Norah Mills
Norman Molyneux
R. Montagnon
J. M. Morgan
Thomas Morgan
L. Murgatroyd
D. Musgrave
Gertie Nelson
Raymond Newton
C. S. Nicholson
S. L. Ogbourn
W. H. Osbourne
Margaret Peacock
H. Pickering
Sydney Pickering
L. Porritt
E. M. Punshon
Marion Purseglove
M. W. Richards
L. Robertson
Georgina R. Sage
A. E. Sandford
A. R. Sharman
E. A. Sharpe
W. Sharpe
E. E. Shelley
E. L. Shirly Smith
M. H. Short
M. Siddall
Agnes M. Simpson
Dorothy Smith
F. G. Smith
Irene C. Soltau

M. Spicer
J. Stansfield
Hilda Stevens
Hilda Stone
J. B. Stork
Carrie Stott
Malcolm C. Surman
G. Sutcliffe
Joyce Taylor
D. B. Tewson
F. Thomason
E. Thorpe
A. Towett
R. W. Verner
C. S. Walden
Dorothy Walker

F. Wanless
J. T. Warren
W. J. Webster
Dr B. R. White
Philip C. Whiteman
E. P. Whitethread
M. M. Whiting
Rev. Leonard Wide
W. M. Wigfield, M.A.
Minnie Wilkinson
H. Wilmer
Dennis Winney
Frank T. Winter, F.R.I.B.A.
Simon Wood
Joy Youngman

INDEX